Writing and Reading in Early Childhood

a functional approach

Roy Moxley

DEPARTMENT OF CURRICULUM AND INSTRUCTION
WEST VIRGINIA UNIVERSITY
MORGANTOWN, WEST VIRGINIA

ILLUSTRATED BY
Lydia Moon

EDUCATIONAL TECHNOLOGY PUBLICATIONS
ENGLEWOOD CLIFFS, NEW JERSEY 07632

Library of Congress Cataloging in Publication Data

Moxley, Roy.
    Writing and reading in early childhood.

    Bibliography: p.
    Includes index.
    1. Language arts (Preschool) 2. Language arts
(Primary) I. Title.
LB1140.5.L3M68   372.6   81-9686
ISBN 0-87778-180-X   AACR2

Printed in the United States of America.

Library of Congress Catalog Card Number:
81-9686.

International Standard Book Number:
0-87778-180-X.

First Printing: January, 1982.

Writing and Reading in Early Childhood

a functional approach

Acknowledgments

The source of many of the ideas expressed in this book can be traced to my graduate work in the late '60's at the University of Michigan Reading Improvement Service (since renamed the Reading and Learning Skills Center). This Service and Center is located in a house on 1610 Washtenaw in Ann Arbor. The graduate students worked closely together there under the supervision of Donald E.P. Smith, who was largely responsible for designing this effective learning environment and providing a seemingly inexhaustible source of provocative ideas. He was my advisor and the director of the Reading Improvement Service when I came there. Since then, Dale Brethower and presently Rowena Wilhelm, who were there when I arrived, have taken on that task. My first experiences in education, in kindergarten, and my last, working on my dissertation, were my most satisfying. In each case, I think there were similarities in that I was encouraged to do things, supported for even small signs of progress, and given the freedom to pursue individual projects over time. The Reading Improvement Service has been my model of an ideal learning environment for graduate students. Other members and associates of the R.I.S. with whom I interacted to varying degrees included Martha Abbott, Karen Brethower, Kay Burr, Ray Cabot, Reuben Chapman, Ruth Cohen, Elvi Fitzgerald, Audrey Gomon, Frank Greene, Marcia Heiman, Glen Knudsvig, Jan Laird, Jeanne Leeds, Ann Muffoletto, Geri Markel, Rosemary Nagel, Dick Olds, Dave Patten, Carl Semmelroth, Chan Smith, and Tim Walter.

A more recent source for the refinement of these ideas are my colleagues and students at West Virginia University. Pamela Meadowcroft and Julie Vargas are the two colleagues with whom I have had extensive discussion and interaction in this area. I would also like to thank Bobbie Gibson, Pamela Meadowcroft, Jeri Ribovich, and Rowena Wilhelm for their comments and suggestions on earlier drafts. In addition, students in my classes on Language Skills in Early Childhood have been furnishing me with data for several years now from their field projects, and my debt to them, of course, is enormous. A few of these students have been cited in the text, but that by no means exhausts those who have contributed to this work.

And finally I would like to acknowledge the support of West Virginia University in granting me a sabbatical leave in order to complete this book and the Claude Worthington Benedum Foundation in providing financial aid through the West Virginia University Foundation for the preparation of illustrations.

Preface

This book is for teachers, students, parents, and others who want children to learn to write and read more easily and more effectively. This may occur in learning environments at home, preschool, nursery school, kindergarten, or the early elementary grades. The general approach presented here is one of assuring that children produce consequences when they write and read and that they respond to those consequences. Unfortunately, attention to consequences has been neglected in the teaching of writing and reading. Phrases like "suffer the consequences," "face the consequences," and "truth or consequences" suggest that our culture has often found consequences to be aversive and avoided. This attitude is changed when consequences prove rewarding and attractive. In arranging for and augmenting the natural consequences of writing and reading, teachers and parents can assure that children encounter attractive consequences in their learning. This makes it much easier for children to learn to write and read and to progress to highly developed levels of these skills. The practical application of this view extends the appropriate consideration for the development of writing and reading to a very early age, and it extends the areas of consideration for writing and reading throughout the educational curriculum.

This book covers the traditional content areas indicated by the common usage of "reading and writing." In this customary usage, "reading" is placed before "writing." However, the emphasis in this book places writing before reading. Research evidence shows children with an interest in writing before they have an interest in reading; logically, something must be written down before it can be read; and the process of writing entails reading what is being written. To call attention to these and other reasons, e.g., to give priority to overt responses over covert responses, writing is placed before reading.

Roy Moxley
March, 1981
Morgantown, WV

Table of Contents

To Lou Ann, Mary, Judy, Tom, Kathy, Jim, Jane, john, their parents, and their children

Writing and Reading in Early Childhood

a functional approach

Chapter I

A Functional Approach to Writing and Reading

Why should writing and reading be so much more difficult to learn than speaking and listening? We learn a spoken language quite easily when we are young. We talk about immediate experiences. We respond to the models that adults have provided us. And the responses we make in conversation are soon followed by consequences that show us how well we are doing. We learn much from these consequences. In a conversation, participants can see for themselves the effects of what they say and can check for themselves the meaning of what they have heard in a continuous reciprocal exchange. This on-going feedback from a highly interactive, mutually causal exchange allows us to easily learn many new things. We have problems when we are cut off from feedback. We would have problems if we were to ride a bicycle blindfolded or carry on a telephone conversation without any response from the other end of the line. We could alleviate these problems by doing things to regain feedback, by peeking under the blindfold or exhorting responses from those to whom we are talking. Problems in writing and reading are also problems in getting feedback. When the consequences are insufficient for writing and reading to develop easily in the child, then it is the task of the teacher or parent to arrange for effective consequences. This can be done by providing occasions and making arrangements for consequences to occur. We can further supplement or augment existing consequences to make them even more conspicuous.

EXPLANATIONS FOR WRITING AND READING

Explanations for writing and reading can look to the present,

3

the past, and the future for causes. Different variations of these causal explanations have been given at different times, and sometimes a mixture of them is given. Nevertheless, a brief exposition of the critical features of each of these explanations can still serve to highlight some of the critical issues in writing and reading instruction for young children. While there is no necessary conflict in a balanced integration of these views, the advocacy of one is often seen to be isolated and in conflict with another, as when the personal subjective expressions of the present are seen to be in conflict with the formal rule structures of the past. This conflict can be mediated by increasing sensitivity to the functional consequences of the future with a balanced integration of all three sources of explanation. Unfortunately, functional views of learning are often so little understood that they are simply ignored. See Figures 1, 2, and 3.

The focus on the present typically gives explanations in terms of inward causes that appear when they are ready to do so. The child will simply learn to read when the child is ready. This view often characterizes informal, incidental learning approaches to writing and reading as well as some applications of language development theories based on innate maturation. Given "normal" conditions, the child will respond when it is appropriate for the child to do so. Botanical growth metaphors are often used. A child will read, like a plant will blossom, when it is time for the child to do so. One somewhat extreme variation of this view proposes that reading is now becoming a biologically innate skill. It argues that just as children are now born with innate genes for speaking and listening, children of the future will be born with innate genes for writing and reading.

Educational applications that focus on the present are sympathetic to the subjective viewpoint of the child and whatever the child expresses. The child does what is natural for the child to do. Beginning interests in writing and reading are looked for and accepted when they naturally occur. The role of the teacher is to provide a nourishing environment that encourages a wide variety of writing and reading responses when the child is ready to initiate them. However, structured planning and feedback beyond what

"I feel emotions inside me that want to be expressed in words."

"Now, how shall I say this?"

"I know there's something there."

Figure 1. Attending to inner feelings that are immediately present.

"Follow my directions."
"Copy this down."

"Eyes on your paper."

"Point pen to your shoulder."

"Feet flat on the floor."

"Write at a 60° slant."

"Don't misspell."

"Be neat."

"Hurry."

Figure 2. Attending to past structures and rules.

Display
"YOU DID IT"

Comment
"WHAT'S THAT WORD?"

Discuss
"CHANGE THE ENDING"
"I LIKE THAT IDEA"

Revise

Present
CLAP! CLAP!
CLAP! CLAP!
CLAP! CLAP!

Send To Someone

Receive Reply

More Consequences
"I LOVED IT"

Figure 3. Attending to future consequences after the initial responses.

happens to be immediately given to the child's expressions are often neglected. Details of the learning conditions in such classroom approaches to writing and reading are typically obscure.

An exclusive focus on this viewpoint tends to minimize the role of the environment and of learning. It also relieves individuals of responsibility for arranging the environment in a specific fashion for individual children. Following the plant metaphor again, the role of the teacher or parent is likened to that of the good gardener whose basic job is to provide a nourishing environment in which the plants or children are to grow. Under these conditions, plants and children will become what they become because of what they have in them. Some will grow well, some not so well. Some will be selected for further cultivation, some will not. Some will learn to write and read, some will not. There is little that can be done beyond providing for nourishing surroundings, according to someone's personal interpretation of what that means.

In views that look to the past for explanations of writing and reading, attention is directed to past structures and the rules for following those structures. This perspective often characterizes traditional formal approaches to writing and reading as well as some applications of reading theories based on a cognitive psychology. A previous structure causes a subsequent structure. This may mean the child is copying or following something inside of him or her as well as outside. As with some maturational views, innate internal structures may be seen to cause behavior. A structural point of view may then provide antecedent cause-and-effect chains of explanation from inner causal structures to outer behavior. Some structural explanations give more attention to what is happening inside, other structural explanations are directed more to what happens outside, and some are directed more to linking the two together.

In school applications of structural approaches, writing and reading are typically seen to develop in causal chain relationships where antecedent structures must first be formed, link by link. For writing, this means linking the elementary parts according to the rules for forming and joining the strokes of handwriting, the letters of spelling, or the parts of speech. The emphasis is on providing instructions for following the rules for joining the parts properly to each other. There is little attention to consequences beyond checking to see whether the parts were correctly joined together. Similarly, reading is largely seen as a problem of "decoding" the structure of print into the structure of speech. Oral reading reveals reading proficiency, and sounding out is to be learned by matching units of sound to units of print and then linking the sound units together according to the rules. Comprehension tests consist of recall and matching performances in a one-to-one correspondence like the other rule-following procedures. Children need to learn each of the necessary antecedent skills before they can continue. A reading problem means there was a faulty link in the past. Remedial reading then consists in going back to "repair" the faulty links in the chain.

An exclusive focus on this viewpoint can lead to the imposition of exaggerated structural restrictions on writing and reading. Writing and reading are oversimplified in the direction of standardized, isolated components that can be combined into complex structures. The focus is on the topography or form of the behavior in terms of standardized parts. For example, identifying letters is simply matching the sound to a letter; comprehension is saying the word aloud; reading is oral reading in an unfamiliar text; handwriting should start at the top and move down for each manuscript stroke; spelling is memorizing and recalling letter combinations with the assistance of memorized rules and their exceptions; and writing is imitating the correct forms of grammar and punctuation. The procedure is to begin with isolated structural elements, or building blocks, trying to build up more complex structures from mastery of the elements: e.g., requiring the mastery of strokes that begin at the top and move to the bottom, then combining these stroke elements into letters before moving on to producing words and themes; requiring mastery of matching sounds to isolated letters (or isolated words) before reading for meaning in a context. Textbooks provide a survey or list of the procedures for teaching standard handwriting or reading. What we have then is a listing of structures for the teacher to duplicate and a listing of structures for the child to duplicate.

Since the emphasis is on restricted standardized responses, there is little encouragement of response variations or elaborations. Writing, especially creative writing, is neglected as well as extended consequences that could follow from writing and reading.

At best, a dependency on rules and structures oversimplifies a complex situation. Sometimes this oversimplification may make successful performances easier when we are isolated from effective feedback that would show our progress. But then the question is raised, Why should schools require artificially isolated conditions for dependency on rules? Furthermore, the rules may not have been well formed. They may be an inaccurate guide for success in complex events. However, this inaccuracy may never be revealed if attention is solely directed to whether or not the rules are being followed. Even if the rules were accurate at one time, conditions may change and make the rules inappropriate. This inappropriateness may still go unnoticed as long as attention is focused on following the rules. For example, when children used copperplate pens, it made sense to recommend downstroking. Upstroking with copperplate pens dipped in ink from inkwells increases the likelihood that the pen point will catch on the paper and splatter the ink. Ballpoint pens have long since replaced copperplate pens in schools, but the downstroking rule in manuscript handwriting continues to be recommended in handwriting books and to be followed in the schools.

Views that look to the future for explanations of writing and reading focus on the consequences and functions of behavior. In a functional response class, a wide variety of behavior may produce a consequence. The form of the behavior becomes secondary to the consequences it produces. For example, if the goal is to produce a word to obtain a response from others, it becomes secondary whether the word is handwritten, typed, or dictated. Furthermore, improvements in language come from developing the consequences rather than standardizing a particular form. The natural consequences of even dictated writing may include oral and dictated written comments by the teacher and fellow students. These comments can be solicited and encouraged through a conspicuous display of what the student writes.

Consequences can be made even more conspicuous by accumulating collections of such writing and recording the student's progress on a chart indicating features of interest, such as the number and kind of words or sentences used by the student. By increasing the frequency of feedback and valued consequences of responding to texts, the writing and reading skills of the student can be increased in any direction desired.

Individual applications of functional approaches to language are not new, although their systematic application is. Consequences were emphasized by Charles Peirce, William James, and John Dewey in their philosophy of pragmatism. Dewey also joined this view to the progressive education movement and active responding in naturalistic settings. Language experience approaches, activities programs, and language arts approaches are related movements in this direction. They have been characterized by (1) encouraging a variety of language-related responses in a whole-to-part differentiation of language skills for responding to texts, words, and letters; (2) expanded occasions for a naturalistic setting and integration of language skills that relate personal experience, oral and written language, and their production and reception; and (3) an emphasis on the purposes and functional consequences of writing and reading. In Dewey's time, the use of charting to augment consequences and to provide an instrument of measurement, assessment, and evaluation had yet to be systematically practiced in functional approaches to education. When American industry found that charting progress over time could be used to make worker performances and consequences more conspicuous, the rate charts of Henry Gantt were used for counting the rivets driven in ships of the First World War. By 1924, charts were being recommended in education for reading: "Each pupil should keep an account of the number of lines and pages he [or she] reads each day. By knowing the average number of words per line and dividing by the total number of minutes used in reading, a pupil may get his [or her] score in number of words read per minute. If these scores are kept on individual class charts, the children will be stimulated to beat their records and raise their class score" (1). Since then, operant psychology has used charting extensively for the functional analysis of behavior, and increasing applications for recording behavior and its consequences have been used in the classroom.

While even language experience approaches in the classroom may be presented as a set of structural procedures for a limited part of writing and reading with limited consequences, these structural limitations are not inherent with a functional approach. One of the particular advantages of record-keeping and charting over time is the development of sensitivity to extended consequences and the broad range of conditions which contribute to changes in performance. In short, charting supplies the measurement methodology for references to individual progress. This was lacking in the early days of progressive education and efforts to develop functional approaches to learning about language.

CONSIDERATIONS FOR A FUNCTIONAL APPLICATION

A full functional account includes the variety of behaviors in a response class, the extended antecedent conditions, and the extended consequences. These relationships are constantly being transformed. Behaviors are selected by consequences, and after the consequences occur, the remaining effects become part of the antecedent conditions for subsequent responses. A thorough-going functional approach explains how undifferentiated initial responses are refined into useful structures. It encourages a variety of initiating responses in natural settings in order that they may be progressively selected and shaped by consequences, and it encourages attention to the fine details of planning and sequencing in a cyclical process. Approaches to writing and reading which disregard any part of this process are not fully functional.

The Importance of Responding

The priority of active, overt responding has been emphasized by many views of learning and development. It was a prime principle of Dewey's Pedagogical Creed: "I believe that the active side precedes the passive in the development of the child-nature; that expression comes before conscious impression; that the muscular development precedes the sensory; that movements come before conscious sensation; I believe that consciousness is essentially motor or impulsive; that conscious states tend to project themselves in action" (2). This precedence of active, expressive responding over passive receptivity or mere exposure to stimuli continues as a strong theme today. In a biological, developmental sense, motor development is followed by perceptual development. The embryological development of the motor system occurs before the perceptual system (3). Infants show generalized bodily movement, crying and kicking, before they look at things. "In the beginning was the response," says Piaget (4), and an operant psychologist says likewise: "In the Beginning, There was the Response" (5).

Conspicuous responses and consequences become less so. The importance of overt responding is particularly relevant for reading. The various relationships between reading and active, overt responding are often neglected, and that is a mistake. This results from looking at the skills we have attained, forgetting how they were once acquired.

For example, we can imagine those times when books were rare and an important text was read aloud and discussed by the community. Some of this discussion may have led to recalling past experiences, some of it may have led to novel responses that were reinforced by members of the community. In the absence of others, the individual reader may have had a dialogue with himself or herself in response to a text. When the reader does this covertly, we say the reader is thinking about what has been read. And the reader may use the same strategies of recall, problem solving, and creative thinking that the community used in their discussions. This suggests that we can develop skills of covert thinking in response to a text by developing skills of overt discussion in response to a text.

Another relationship between reading and overt responding is that we read what we have constructed in writing. We make changes, additions, and continued writing responses on the basis of reading what we have written. We often take for granted the extent to which behavior controls perception and how what we perceive is dependent upon what we have done beforehand. And writing is often ignored as a means for improving reading.

As skills are acquired, there is a transition from varied, elaborate, conscious behavior to more simple, automatic, unconscious behavior. In the beginning, we need to do many things to see what happens. By much doing, we discover what the consequences and relationships are. Later on, we can guess or imagine what they would be. We can perform mental short cuts, so to speak, as to what would happen. The skilled performer learns to conserve energy and to cut away unnecessary movement. Similarly, the skilled reader learns to cut away the unnecessary responses in constructing an expression. The skilled reader does not need to construct and articulate each letter, word, and phrase of the complete expression. The skilled reader has learned short cuts. The skilled reader is still responding, but the responses are not as overt and grossly varied as those a beginning reader needs to produce. The initial overt responses, however clumsy and unnecessary they now seem, were nevertheless essential for obtaining this result.

Progressive differentiation. Behavior also develops in the direction of increasing refinement and adaptability to different situations. An erroneous explanation for this development is sometimes given in terms of accumulated links of atomic units of behavior. Teaching then becomes a task of joining together previously isolated parts in a part-to-whole buildup. It has been claimed that this also reflects how we think, synthesizing isolated component concepts into new concepts.

The history of American pragmatism and operant psychology provides exceptions to the view that we begin with isolated bits and pieces of thought and then put them together to form a whole. C.S. Peirce (1839-1914) expressed it this way: "What really happens is that something is presented which in itself has no parts, but which nevertheless is analyzed by the mind, that is to say, its having parts consists in this, that the mind afterward recognized those parts in it. . . . When, having thus separated them, we think over them, we are carried in spite of ourselves from one thought to another, and therein lies the first real synthesis" (6). This is a whole-to-parts-to-whole procedure.

Similarly, in language, smaller units emerge from larger units of behavior: "From responses such as *I have a . . .* and *I want a . . .*, a smaller unit response *I* emerges. Small functional units may, of course, be separately learned, particularly through the educational reinforcement supplied by those who teach children to speak, but they also appear to emerge as by-products of the acquisition of larger responses containing identical elements . . ." (7). Larger units also emerge from smaller units: "In general, as verbal behavior develops in the individual speaker, larger and larger responses acquire functional unity . . . It also seems reasonable to suppose that, as a verbal environment undergoes historical development, it reinforces larger and larger units" (8). Both processes contribute to an evolution of language skills in which overall refinement and organization develop: "In general, operant behavior emerges from undifferentiated, previously unorganized, and undirected movements" (9.), according to B.F. Skinner.

This progressive differentiation from the view of operant psychology contrasts with perceptions of language as a simple part-to-part-to-whole buildup of contiguous connections, e.g., in chaining one letter sound to another to produce reading or one letter form to another to produce writing. The part-to-part buildup presumes that the building up of letter sounds leads to the building up of word comprehension, which leads to the building up of responses to meaningful texts. Similarly, the building up of handwriting leads to word spelling, which leads to complete compositions. Again, the accumulation of these separate fragments will presumably "jell" at the end, unless the student lacks inner motivation or talent.

In progressive differentiation, there is not just one response change, there are several. Many of them seem to occur spontaneously as well as simultaneously. And many of the responses seem to become stimuli for other responses. Progressive differentiation has been referred to as "nature's way." For example, the human embryo develops in successive stages. It is always a whole. And all of its parts develop in a parallel fashion, interacting with the other parts. It never waits for a fully elaborated nose to develop before beginning the growth of a hand. This strikes us as a silly impossibility. As a biological principle, the development of increasing complexity through simultaneous differentiation and integration is taken for granted.

Several investigators of child development have observed that the acquisition of specialized and refined skills has been preceded by more global capabilities and refined into specialized skills within an integrated system. The development of any one particular skill tends to be accompanied by the simultaneous development of other related skills. The generalized movements of the infant become specialized. The child learns to inhibit parts of his or her motor system while exercising other parts. Both of the child's hands may become increasingly adept at grasping and manipulating. Later on, one hand may become dominant in performing fine movements, while the other hand assists in the grasping and holding of the object worked upon. Similarly, progressive differentiation from holistic, complete responses can be found in the development of speech from babbling and holophrases as well as in the development of drawing and handwriting from scribbling and holistic enclosures such as "sun" figures (10). Ever finer differentiation also occurs in judgments of same and different. At first children tend to judge things the same if they are in proximity, then gross discriminations of shape are made, e.g., open or closed, then fine discriminations, e.g., the number of sides or orientation (11). This general principle of progressive differentiation can be considered as a pervasive and systematic principle of human growth and development (12).

Evidence points to the right cerebral hemisphere for a dominant role in global integration and organization of gross to fine motor movement and the left cerebral hemisphere for a dominant role in analytic selection and differentiation (13). The global responses are characterized by relative quickness, simplification, coherence, proportion, and articulation, while the analytical responses are characterized by their complexity in a bit by bit, to and from, series of matches and mismatches that take longer to complete (14).

Instruction designed to serve only one of these functions seems clearly inadequate. It is possible, for example, to isolate small domains of language skill for instructional purposes, teaching one area independent of learning in another area. It is also possible to teach each skill as a serial construction of one fully developed response after the other. Much of formal traditional approaches in education that have been fragmented into distinct considerations for "reading" and "handwriting" seem to show this separate serialist approach. It is as if instruction were only designed for half of the child's brain, using half of the teacher's brain (the serial, analytic half). This approach could be characterized as "half-brained" and more pejoratively as "half-witted."

There is no need, however, for a basic incompatibility between the holistic and analytic development of language skills. A satisfactory description of progressive differentiation would seem to rely on a harmonious integration of both functions. It would seem much more enlightening, considering the evidence, to have available methods of instruction appropriate to the whole child that allow for the inclusion of progressive differentiation whatever the level of the task being learned. A holistic written narrative by the child, for instance, may be short and simple, or it may be an intricately complex work of art. A complete expression may be one word or an entire book.

Some characteristics of writing and reading. Writing is the result of a variety of behaviors that have been selected because of their previous effects on readers. Unfortunately, many misconceptions about writing and reading simply ignore the nature of writing and its direct relationship to reading. One misconception gives preeminent importance to those characteristics of writing which have a direct correspondence in speech. Attention is given to producing writing as a transcription of speech, as in spelling the words a teacher calls out, and to teaching reading as a direct decoding of letters into sounds. Other important characteristics of writing which reveal how it is produced and how it is responded to are ignored. Important as the similarities between writing and speaking are, no thorough understanding of writing and reading responses are possible under this restriction.

The popular conception of the development of writing skills (often supported by direct experience and observation) is that speaking develops first, then reading, then writing. It is tempting to assume a neat linear connection, that writing is merely speech written down and that learning to read is simply a matter of

decoding writing back into speech like a word-for-word transla-
tion. This is a misleading perception. It is possible for a child to
acquire reading skills before speaking (15). And it is common to
observe children who show an interest and ability in writing before
reading and to recommend that instruction in writing should aid
or precede instruction in reading (16).

A better understanding of writing can be had by temporarily
suspending some of the popular and traditional preconceptions
about it. An examination of the differences between writing and
speaking, the influence of writing on speech, and the importance
of visible language can then reveal quite a different conception.
Writing has a nature of its own.

1. Some differences between writing and speaking: Writing has
never been simply speech written down: "Writing can never be
considered an *exact* counterpart of the spoken language. Such an
ideal state of point-by-point equivalence in which one speech unit
is expressed by one sign, and one sign expresses only one speech
unit, has never been attained in writing. Even the alphabet, the
most developed form of writing, is full of inconsistencies in the
relations between sign and sound" (17). The highly sophisticated
writing of mathematical formulas illustrates how separate the
conventions between sight and sound can be while still being
related. These formulas can convey meaning through their signs in
an order and form which do not follow the conventions of
phonetic writing. The positions of mathematical symbols in
various combinations of horizontal and vertical arrangements show
little effort to approximate a sound stream. While these formulas
can be read aloud, visual considerations clearly predominate. It
would seem obviously inadequate to attempt to explain the
writing of mathematical formulas as speech written down.

There are many aspects of writing which have no correspondence in speech: e.g., punctuation marks like capitals or the
systematic spacing between letters, words, sentences, paragraphs,
etc. Even the concept of a word is more of a unit peculiar to
writing than speech. The utterances of speech have no clear
breakdown into words. And children may require an exposure to
writing before they acquire the concept of a word (18).

Grammatical analysis is a visual-spatial construction and process that uses diagrams and "branching trees."

In contrast to the temporal relationships of speech, writing is a system based on spatial relationships. Written symbols can be scanned simultaneously and in any directional sequence, skipping from one point to any other point. Space itself plays a role in organizing and grouping graphic symbols that far exceeds signals of temporal separation and organization in speech. Space separates written letters, words, sentences, lines, paragraphs, chapters, and books. In general, the larger the unit, the larger the space. Speech, on the other hand, is composed of utterances that flow together with much less indication of separation. The pauses between utterances are used more to check on reception and to gain time for composing the next utterance than to indicate units of organizational structure.

Speech relies on the common present experience between speaker and listener, with all the gestures and any other nonverbal supplemental communication that may be there. It has less need and is less suited to show complex organization. Writing often needs, and is used, to supply much more contextual detail to make its meaning clear to readers who are not present during the writing. Much of writing is a hierarchical organization of clusters of meaning, from small detailed units at the lower levels to thematic organizations at the higher levels. Space, position, syntax, inflection, punctuation, and word markers serve to organize systems of units: the relationships between units on the same level and the relationships between organizational levels above and below. Grammatical analysis explicitly exposes some of the immediate constituents of the organization with diagrams or branching trees. The grammatical analysis simply makes use of the indicators of organization that are already there. The reader has an organizational map before him or her, a reference guide, through which the reader can systematically hunt for the information needed. There is nothing comparable in speech to the elaborate layering of composition in writing.

2. The influence of writing on speech: Many people have wished that writing would directly reflect the sounds of speech so that

spelling a word would be a cinch. But there are good reasons why writing should resist the influence of speech. Much of our writing structure enhances visual meaning correspondence at the expense of sound correspondence. Similar meanings may have similar visual forms, although the pronunciation is different, e.g., *marine/mariner, advantage/advantageous, nation/national, sign/signify*. The final *s* of *hats* and *rugs* represents the plural form for both words, although the endings are pronounced differently. Different meanings may have different forms, although the pronunciation is the same, e.g., *rite/right/write/wright, rose/rows/roes/row's/roe's, new/knew/gnu*, and *isle/aisle/I'll*. The plural form of *spies* and the possessive form of *spy's* are written differently, although they are pronounced the same. As a consequence of this close relationship between meaning and visual form, the relationships of meaning between words are usually more apparent in the written form of the language than in the spoken form.

This resistance of writing to influences from pronunciation is accompanied by a susceptibility in speech to influences from writing. In other words, our writing structure influences a pronunciation change more than our pronunciation influences a spelling change, as indicated by the older pronunciations (between slash marks) for *Wednesday*/wenzdy/, *victuals*/vitlz/, *certain*/sartin/, *housewife*/hozwif/, and *often*/ofn/. And it is more economical to derive phonology from orthography than to derive orthography from phonology (19).

3. The importance of visible language: Some of the most important features of writing are those that it shares with other forms of visual communication. Visible language in general has played and continues to play a dominant role in human communication. Interestingly enough, communication through visible language has been taught to subjects who would be expected to have the greatest difficulty in acquiring symbolic expressions, to chimpanzees through sign language (20) and plastic shapes (21) and to extreme retardates using Premack's approach with plastic shapes for words (22). The methodological orientations which produced these dramatic results were those of ethnology in the case of the Gardners and behavioral analysis in

the case of Premack. Like the features inherent in written records, both methods emphasize the particular performance of the individual over time with a high degree of interactive communication and the production of visible language.

The advantages of visible language expression are also illustrated in deaf children who have learned manual language skills. There is evidence that these children have higher writing and reading achievement than children without a manual language and that early visual language leads to higher oral language skills as well. Manual sign languages have features that are also found in the historical development of writing and in the child's development of prewriting and writing skills:

> Three characteristics of manual systems, at least those used in the United States, which are of potential pedagogical importance are (1) the iconic nature of many common signs; (2) the motoric, or enactive nature of many signs; and (3) the use of spatial dimensions. Because of the transparent, or easily interpreted, nature of such signs, it is possible that many children are able to receive and express some information at a younger age than children who rely primarily on the auditory-vocal channel.... Work in progress by Moores and associates suggests that the first word appears in deaf children of deaf parents at an earlier age than it does with normally hearing children. (23)

Any graphic production, of course, will also use spatial dimensions, and the icons or pictures drawn by adult and child in their early forms of graphic communication may depict gestures and other behavioral indicators of action (although perhaps not so vividly as manual languages can).

Functional Consequences

Explanations in terms of consequences distinguish biology from the physical sciences. The consequences in the environment determine which species will survive, which physical structures; and behaviors prove adaptable when they produce consequences that enhance their survival. To have goals, intentions, meanings, and purposes is a highly human characteristic. People act for the future.

Language, like other behavior, is determined by consequences.

A full account would include the effect of consequences on historical and genetic sources for language development as well as the effects of consequences on everyday usage. Even within a narrow span of time, the consequences of speaking and listening are highly varied. Many things may happen in response to a spoken word. People may stop, look, ask questions, follow directions, make comments, engage in conversation, and behave in a variety of ways that show they were responding to what they heard. They may do this immediately and some time later. Considering how varied and interactive the consequences can be in a discussion, it is not surprising to find the evolution of highly complex language skills in all existing cultures as well as in the development of language skills in children.

In the everyday discourses of spoken language, the child can engage in and listen to many vocal transactions. People talk back and forth, requests are made and answered, cries and exclamations are given and responded to, comments are made, and questions are asked for clarification. Speakers become listeners and listeners become speakers in a rapid exchange of roles. There is rich and frequent feedback of various kinds, verbal and nonverbal. Most children develop rather complex skills in speech without formal instruction. We tend to take for granted a normally rich interactive process for spoken language, even though problems arise when feedback is inadequate. Distorted or inadequate feedback will hinder speech. A deaf person has difficulty in articulating speech.

In writing and reading, there is much less natural interaction and feedback. A response to a written message is often considerably delayed. Interaction cycles in writing are typically much longer and less frequent than in speech. In order to improve the feedback on writing, deliberate attention often needs to be given to arranging circumstances that provide feedback. Otherwise, the writer may be left to rely entirely on assuming the role of the writer and reader himself or herself, providing his or her own internal interaction and feedback. Realistically simulating another person's perceptions and reactions, however, is not an easy task for a child, or for many adults for that matter. Learning to do this well depends upon actual exposure to the reactions and feedback from others. An essential task of instruction in writing, then, is to design *functional* writing experiences that have consequences and feedback. This emphasis on consequences stands in contrast to the emphasis on antecedent structures, particularly in the form of rules. When instruction in writing is confined to the rules for correct letter formation, spelling, etc., then subsequent consequences are typically limited to whether or not the rules were correctly followed.

Similarly, reading instruction is often presented as a set of rules that the pupil is to follow in decoding a text. If the task of the child is to read a passage aloud, the child's feedback is typically limited to the accuracy of his or her immediate responses to the text. But there are many other responses to a text beyond what immediately follows a person's exposure to it. A text may be talked about, discussed, written about, and used in thinking new ideas, answering questions, and performing activities long after the text is available. Likewise, there are extended consequences that may in turn follow these responses to a text. These responses, as well as the text, may be talked about, discussed, written about, and used in thinking new ideas, answering questions, and performing activities. Since the writer is not likely to be present, the reader needs exposure to the reactions of others in order to check his or her perceptions. And readers need functional consequences to follow their reading responses, consequences which show that how they read makes a difference. This contrasts with reading instruction that has been limited to getting students to follow directions for reading aloud or to recall passages that answer questions which are largely paraphrases of that passage. When the reader's response to a text is made under these conditions, feedback has often been limited to whether the response was correct or incorrect.

There are some distinctive features in the functional causality of learning to write and read that distinguish it from instructional efforts based on simple structural cause-and-effect chains. (1) The consequences to a behavior determine the future probability of further behavior. (2) This further behavior is a functional, not a structural, response class. Functional response classes are defined by their common extrinsic consequences and need have no common topographical or structural features. Structural response classes share common intrinsic features but need not have any consequences in common. The functional response class for making a path includes retracing steps, putting down stones, hiring someone to lay a cement walk, and any one of a variety of different behaviors that produce a path to walk on. The structural response class of making a clenched hand includes pounding a hammer, throwing a ball, shaking a fist, and a variety of other behaviors with a common topography but perhaps quite different consequences and functions. Functional causality includes various forms of responses, i.e., the variety of alternatives for producing a particular consequence. (3) The functional causality involved in social communication is two-way. There is mutual or reciprocal causality affecting each of the participants in verbal behavior. Thus, under the conditions of mutually reinforcing and highly interactive exchanges, a rapid evolution of functional responses may occur. The response made by one speaker is a consequence for the other. Each consequence in turn affects the probability of future responses. Sometimes that consequence may be a specific signal for the next response, e.g., "Pass the salt." Sometimes it may be a relatively open-ended signal, e.g., "What do you think?" And (4) instruction that seeks to use functional causality must be concerned with consequences, with providing for new consequences and supplementing those that already exist in order to make them more conspicuous. The responses and consequences of writing and reading can be conveniently augmented through the use of progress records over time. Collections of actual products produced, stickers for performances, and symbolic check marks and frequency counts can serve this purpose.

Occasions That Are Natural Settings

We tend to take natural settings for granted. When we examine the uses of language, we find it naturally occurs in a rich context that includes the extended environment, past experiences, the person being addressed, the language used, reactions to that language, the physical surroundings, the materials in those surroundings, and other particulars of the setting. Language originally developed and continues to be practiced in natural settings on extended occasions. Natural uses of language occur within a variety of occasions and are in response to a variety of stimuli within those occasions.

We can contrast this rich natural setting with the restricted artificial setting that is required for taking standardized tests in school. In this test condition, each student is typically treated as though the student were in an isolated environment deprived of all stimulation except the test paper before him or her. The student is to behave as though nothing else in the environment existed. The student is to be controlled exclusively by the written rules that the student is to follow in the test. Even the student's marks on the answer sheet are designed to be as brief as possible, furnishing little additional stimuli to respond to. The student is discouraged from looking back at previous sections in order to re-examine them. The student is to be brought under the control of a narrow selection of stimuli that the student follows. The student must confine his or her attention to a narrow sequence of isolated stimuli and respond only to them. The student must then *re*-call and *re*-peat what the student has learned about language in the form of the answers to questions that have one best response. Each question itself is a narrow, isolated structural form to which another isolated structural form (the correct answer) is to be attached (as indicated by the student's mark on the answer sheet).

Most people would agree that this is no way to learn language skills. This is only a way to sample a small area of language achievements, and a very restricted area at that. Yet, formal instruction in school is often conducted in imitation of these test conditions. Students are frequently required to work on language skills in a highly isolated and restricted fashion. They must behave as though nothing else in their environment existed except their textbook or workbook. They must confine their attention to the directions. They must *re*-member, *re*-call, and *re*-cite a particular structure. Their responses are limited to indications that match the structure of the answer to the structure of the question, often in direct imitation and copy of the language structure. Such an artificial setting confines student responses to the isolated tasks of language that can be conveniently sampled in this manner. There is little variation among the occasions for learning language in this kind of formal schooling and little variety of stimuli within any of these occasions. Many, if not most, people would agree that this is no way to learn to write and read.

When all that needs to be learned is to follow a rule, then that is all that may be learned. If you are intently following one of the colored lines on the floor of a hospital corridor, then you have no time to notice the rest of your surroundings, e.g., the rooms or the people whose desks you pass. And you are likely to find that the next time around you still have to follow that line because you have not learned to respond to the other things in your surroundings. Learning that is confined to following rules or structures is like that. The rule substitutes for the natural setting.

It is sometimes forgotten that the original structural form could never have been produced by simply following that structural form. The farmer may have produced a straight and narrow path on the land that we can closely follow by confining our responses to the narrow path before us. But the farmer must have responded to a variety of stimuli in constructing that path, to the shape of the land, to the boulders in the way, to where he or she wanted to go, etc., and the farmer must have produced a variety of responses to that variety of stimuli rather than a series of simple structural responses to a series of simple structural forms. Similarly, the poet must have been responding to a richer variety of stimuli when the poet wrote the words than when we copied them. Structural forms represent past achievements. They do not show how these achievements were acquired. Learning that is based on following structural forms leaves out learning how these forms were acquired and how to produce new forms that are successful on new occasions. Writing and reading limited to following and imitating structures of language are similarly confined. The student may find that what he or she learns in school about writing and reading is of little help in writing and reading successfully for the natural occasions that the student encounters outside of school.

Writing and reading instruction in the schools should assure that naturalistic settings are provided so that the student can learn to respond to multiple sources of control rather than just simple isolated structures. This means providing for occasions of instruction in the classroom where the student has available and has access to a wide variety of resources. Opportunities for writing and reading in school should also be extended to a wide variety of occasions, many of which with a wide variety of stimuli to respond to. Some people may still find it is desirable to retain some test-like conditions in order to prepare students for standardized tests which are based on reference to a normal distribution (i.e., the "curve of error," or the "normal curve" as it is somewhat euphemistically called). Such conditions, however, should only be one component of writing and reading in school. The most useful student learning will occur in naturalistic rather than artificial settings.

Discussion ·

There are extensive implications for parents and teachers who manage learning environments. (1) There should be an emphasis on (developing *overt* responses that are relevant to writing and reading.) This means a high productivity of writing responses in particular and any response that "shows" a child can read in general. Instruction should begin with complete units of behavior in meaningful, naturalistic contexts and then provide for the progressive differentiation of subsequent behavior. This means beginning with complete texts in natural settings and moving to words and letters while including the building up of letters and words for texts. (2) In addition, students must learn from the future by producing conspicuous consequences with their writing and reading. They can learn to make their writing a conspicuous consequence of what they directly see and do. They can also make direct and conspicuous consequences by graphing, charting, and discussing what they write and read and then responding further to these consequences. And (3) there are many sources of control for writing and reading. Effective instruction should provide a variety of occasions for these sources of control. This includes providing occasions for writing and reading which are like those which occur in natural settings outside the classroom, e.g., when children write a note to a friend or read or listen to reading for pleasure.

This process should be seen as naturally integrated and reoccurring. The behavior of the student under the control of the immediate natural environment of the classroom begins naturally by being free to act and act again in many different directions. Without prohibiting constraints, the child can look and look again, speak and speak again, write and write again, read and read again. The child begins his or her learning by dwelling within the multiple sources of control of the immediate environment. The child's behavior is then selected and altered by the consequences it produces. Repeated recordings of what the child writes and reads will amplify subsequent responses to the child's behavior and its consequences. This results in the selection for survival of functional classes of writing and reading behaviors and their stimulus controls. When rules are derived from the selected behaviors of children in various environmental conditions, these rules then become part of the total antecedent occasions to which a response can be made. Rules may serve to replace some or all of the immediate environment for controlling a response. This process may be repeated until effective student performance in writing and reading is achieved. The child's initially gross behavior becomes progressively refined. The teacher may not be aware of all the contributions to this process in the child's learning, but this does not prevent the teacher from designing effective instruction. The teacher participates in a similar cycle of teacher behavior and continues until effective instruction is achieved.

In order for this process to progress systematically, the teacher must respond to the larger contexts of the classroom environment as well as to specific learning tasks. This includes the physical conditions and materials established in the past, the social climate of the present, and the available feedback of the future. It is especially in the feedback that the teacher provides effective instruction for students—in the displays, collections, charts, and other consequences for student performance—that a functional approach is applied in the classroom.

In a practical application of this approach, much of the above would come down to a dramatic emphasis on extended "writing" behavior. Writing in its broad sense belongs at the beginning of education. Leaving traces is the beginning of writing. Primitive writing produces marks that make records. Writing skills begin to develop as soon as a child can make a mark in the world and continues when the child collects and makes records of any events.

SUMMARY

A functional approach to writing and reading pays special attention to consequences and how consequences affect future behavior. It is an approach oriented to the future, differing dramatically from approaches that rely on unfolding revelations in the present or links to causal chains in the past. Approaches that rely simply on the maturational unfolding of skills from within the child are vague on the details of instruction. Their major thrust is to provide the child with nourishing surroundings of rich stimuli with ready acceptance for whatever and whenever the child expresses interests in writing and reading. Approaches that rely simply on the child recalling and following structures from the past narrowly restrict the details of instruction to isolated forms and rules for following them correctly. Maturational views of self-expression may then be pushed back into the world of preschool or play. A fully functional approach, however, includes the holistic concern with a naturalistic setting expressed by some maturationists, but it provides much more detail about what this means. It also includes the concern for precision and exactness that structural views find necessary, but this is placed within a far broader context. All the worthwhile sources of learning from the present, the past, and the future need to be included for effective instruction in writing and reading. And a fully functional approach does this.

To begin with, we want the behaviors (B) of writing and reading to emerge in all of their rich variety. The extended consequences (C) of writing and reading will then select those behaviors which are more successful. The writing and reading achievements that

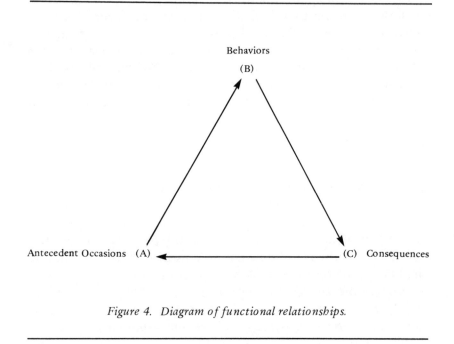

Figure 4. Diagram of functional relationships.

were consequences then become antecedent stimuli (A) and part
of the occasion to which another cycle of behavior responds. This
is represented schematically in Figure 4.

It is natural for us to notice the behaviors (B) we see before us
and to talk about them. And it is easy for many of us to talk at
length about what we want students to do. Schools have identified
the antecedent occasions (A) for some of these behaviors in
specific, if not restricted, detail. But the functional consequences
(C), which make this three-way relationship turn in a fully
evolving cycle, have been neglected.

Functional causality is so natural to human nature that we may
not even notice it occurring when learning happens easily in
speaking and listening. Yet, when difficulties occur in writing and
reading, it is easy to show that functional causes are lacking. And
it is to this functional causality that teachers must address
themselves.

REFERENCES

1. Smith, N.B. *American reading instruction* (1934). Newark, Delaware: International Reading Association, 1965, p. 189.

2. Dewey's pedagogical creed. In W.H. Goetzmann (Ed.), *The American Hegelians.* New York: Knopf, 1973, p. 317.

3. Chaney, C.M., and Kephart, N.C. *Motoric aids to perceptual training.* Columbus, Ohio: Charles E. Merrill, 1968.

4. Piaget, J. *Biology and knowledge.* Chicago: University of Chicago Press, 1971, p. 8.

5. Baer, D.M. In the beginning, there was the response. In E. Ramp and G. Semb (Eds.), *Behavior analysis: Areas of research and application.* Englewood Cliffs, N.J.: Prentice-Hall, 1975, pp. 16-30.

6. Peirce, C.S. *Collected papers of Charles Sanders Peirce* (C. Hartshorne and P. Weiss, Eds., Vol. 1). Cambridge, Mass.: Harvard University Press, 1931, p. 204.

7. Skinner, B. *Verbal behavior.* New York: Appleton-Century-Crofts, 1957, p. 120.

8. Skinner, B. *Verbal behavior.* New York: Appleton-Century-Crofts, 1957, p. 336.

9. Skinner, B. *Verbal behavior.* New York: Appleton-Century-Crofts, 1957, p. 464.

10. Kellogg, R. *Analyzing children's art.* Palo Alto, Calif.: Mayfield, 1970.

11. Taylor, J., and Wales, R. A developmental study of form discrimination in pre-school children. *Quarterly Journal of Experimental Psychology,* November 1970, *22*(4), pp. 720-732.

12. Werner, H., and Kaplan, B. *Symbol formation.* New York: Wiley, 1963.

13. de Quiros, J.B., and Schrager, O.L. Postural system, corporal potentiality, and language. In E.H. Lenneberg and E. Lenneberg (Eds.), *Foundations of language development: A multidisciplinary approach* (Vol. 2). New York: Academic Press, 1975, pp. 297-307.

14. Abercrombie, M.L.J. Learning to draw. In K. Connolly (Ed.), *Mechanisms of motor skill development.* New York: Academic Press, 1970, pp. 307-325. Bamber, D. Reaction times and error

rates for "same"—"different" judgments of multi-dimensional stimuli. *Perception and Psychophysics*, 1969, *6*(3), pp. 169-174. Kinsbourne, M. Looking and listening strategies and beginning reading. In J.T. Guthrie (Ed.), *Aspects of reading acquisition*. Baltimore: Johns Hopkins University, 1976, pp. 141-161.

15. Steinberg, D.D., and Steinberg, M.T. Reading before speaking. *Visible Language*, Summer 1975, *9*(3), pp. 197-224.

16. Chomsky, C. Write first, read later. *Childhood Education*, March 1971, *47*(6), pp. 296-299. Chomsky, C. Beginning reading through invented spelling. *Selected papers from the 1973 New England kindergarten conference*. Cambridge, Mass.: Leslie College, 1973, pp. 1-8. Durkin, D. *Children who read early*. New York: Teachers College Press, 1966. Durkin, D. A six-year study of children who learned to read in school at the age of four. *Reading Research Quarterly*, 1974-1975, *10*(1), pp. 9-61. Hall, M., Moretz, S.A., and Statom, J. Writing before grade one—A study of early writers. *Language Arts*, May 1976, *53*(5), pp. 582-585. Hildreth, G. Early writing as an aid to reading. *Elementary English*, January 1963, *40*(1), pp. 15-20. McCarthy, L. A child learns the alphabet. *Visible Language*, Summer 1977, *11*(3), pp. 271-284. Price, E.H. How thirty-seven gifted children learned to read. *The Reading Teacher*, October 1976, *30*(1), pp. 44-48. Torrey, J.W. Learning to read without a teacher: A case study. In F. Smith (Ed.), *Psycholinguistics and reading*. New York: Holt, Rinehart, and Winston, 1973, pp. 147-157.

17. Gelb, I.J. *A study of writing* (rev. ed.). Chicago: University of Chicago Press, 1963, p. 15.

18. Downing, J., and Oliver, P. The child's conception of 'a word.' *Reading Research Quarterly*, 1973-1974, *9*(4), pp. 568-582.

19. Householder, F.W. The primacy of writing. In his *Linguistic speculations*. London: Cambridge University Press, 1971, pp. 244-264.

20. Gardner, R.A., and Gardner, B.T. Teaching sign language to a chimpanzee. *Science*, 15 August 1969, *165*(3894), pp. 664-672.

21. Premack, D. The education of S*A*R*A*H: A chimp learns the language. *Psychology Today*, September 1970, *4*(4), pp. 54-58.

22. Anders, F. If you can teach an ape to read, can you do something for my retarded child? *The New York Times Magazine*, 1 June 1975, pp. 14-15, 47, 50, 52, 54-59. Deich, R.F., and Hodges, P.M. Learning from Sarah. *Human Behavior*, May 1975, 4(5), pp. 40-42. Premack, A.J., and Premack, D. Teaching language to an ape. *Scientific American*, October 1972, 227(4), pp. 92-99.

23. Moores, D.F. Nonvocal systems of verbal behavior. In R.L. Shiefelbusch and L.L. Lloyd (Eds.), *Language perspectives— acquisition, retardation, and intervention*. Baltimore: University Park Press, 1974, p. 395.

Chapter II

How We Naturally Acquired Language Skills

Although children can master the intricacies of spoken language with ease, it is commonplace to observe that students should have learned to write and read better than they do. The failure to learn these skills adequately is particularly troublesome when we reflect that the evolution of human culture from primitive beginnings has produced highly sophisticated language skills without a notable dependence on schooling. We might profit then from examining those conditions where language skills were learned naturally in order to consider similar conditions for children to learn writing and reading in school.

In the following, a parallel will be drawn between an outline sketch of the evolution of language and the development of language skills in early childhood by pointing to examples of activities in which children can and do engage. Some of these activities are fairly common experiences for most children. Other activities might be introduced more frequently into their experiences.

This theme of parallel development in language acquisition is also pursued between and within different language areas. It is not a neat, ordered, linear development of one elementary unit of language followed by another. Rather, it is a development by progressive interaction and differentiation.

THE ORIGINS AND EVOLUTION OF LANGUAGE

Numerous theories for the origins of language have been proposed. Many of these seem plausible as a partial contribution to the evolution of language but inadequate as a total account. Reflecting this inadequacy, trivial names have been given to theories of language origin that have no doubt been regarded as trivial explanations. Hewes (1) has presented the following categories into which language origin theories may be classified: (1) interjectional or *pooh-pooh* theories point to emotional or attitudinal vocal exclamations as a source of language development; (2) onomatopoeic or *bow-wow* theories point to the imitation of a sound the object makes, e.g., bees *buzz*; (3) the *ding-dong* theories point to the imitation of sounds produced when objects are struck; (4) work-chant or *yo-he-ho* theories point to inadvertent and conventionalized expressions of sound a community would reinforce in performing a group task; (5) in mouth-gesture or *ta-ta* theories, the mouth parts imitate the movements of hands, arms, or other body parts; (6) *babbleluck* theories point to associations between spontaneous infant babbling and environmental events; (7) in *instinctivist* theories, language suddenly appears at a particular level of cognitive evolution and is inborn thereafter; (8) in *conventionalist* theories, the community deliberately agrees to create language in order to improve its social life; (9) in *contact* theories, language is the natural outcome of man's social and communicative needs; (10) *divine or miraculous* theories consider language to be a gift of the Creator; (11) in *chance mutation*, language is the outcome of a random biological event; and (12) in *gestural sign* theories, communication was initially by hand and arm movements with vocal language appearing later.

Against this background, reticence in accepting any account of language origins and evolution is understandable. In 1866 the Societe de Linguistique de Paris even imposed a ban against papers dealing with language origins. Yet, some explanations are more convincing than others. The following gives an account of two major traditions in temporary and more enduring forms of communication as well as their uses in the evolution of signs (see Figure 5). These traditions undoubtedly influenced each other, and any particular state would reflect multiple sources of control not indicated by the simplified sequence in the outline of Figure 5. There is also a closer relationship between form and function than is suggested in the outline. Even though a form may be put to

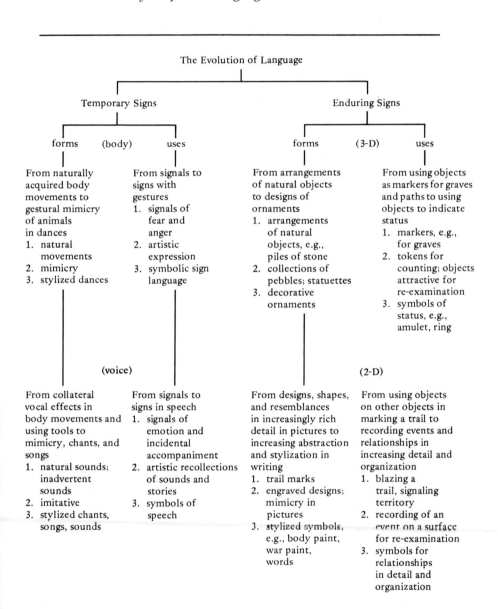

The Evolution of Language

Temporary Signs

forms (body) uses

From naturally acquired body movements to gestural mimicry of animals in dances
1. natural movements
2. mimicry
3. stylized dances

From signals to signs with gestures
1. signals of fear and anger
2. artistic expression
3. symbolic sign language

Enduring Signs

forms (3-D) uses

From arrangements of natural objects to designs of ornaments
1. arrangements of natural objects, e.g., piles of stone
2. collections of pebbles; statuettes
3. decorative ornaments

From using objects as markers for graves and paths to using objects to indicate status
1. markers, e.g., for graves
2. tokens for counting; objects attractive for re-examination
3. symbols of status, e.g., amulet, ring

(voice)

From collateral vocal effects in body movements and using tools to mimicry, chants, and songs
1. natural sounds; inadvertent sounds
2. imitative
3. stylized chants, songs, sounds

From signals to signs in speech
1. signals of emotion and incidental accompaniment
2. artistic recollections of sounds and stories
3. symbols of speech

(2-D)

From designs, shapes, and resemblances in increasingly rich detail in pictures to increasing abstraction and stylization in writing
1. trail marks
2. engraved designs; mimicry in pictures
3. stylized symbols, e.g., body paint, war paint, words

From using objects on other objects in marking a trail to recording events and relationships in increasing detail and organization
1. blazing a trail, signaling territory
2. recording of an event on a surface for re-examination
3. symbols for relationships in detail and organization

Figure 5. Parallel traditions in the evolution of language.

new uses that are quite different from the uses in its earlier evolution, these forms have still arisen and evolved as a result of previous functional uses.

As the outline indicates, visible sources for communication dominate audible sources. And writing is in the mainstream of that visible tradition. Writing is not simply speech written down, even though there may have been influences from one tradition on the other. The fact that speech can be transcribed into writing or that writing can be transcribed into speech is not an argument for the evolution of one form before the other. Rather, it points out the fact that functional uses can be made of relationships between different forms of communication. Figure 6 illustrates some of the different forms that will be described in the following.

Temporary Signs in Gestures and Sounds

We can imagine how important it was for a community, or any creature for that matter, to respond to the movements of other creatures. It would be critical to detect even slight movements that would signal what the next movement might be. Mistakes in misreading "intentions" could easily be fatal. And the members of a community would soon learn how other creatures would respond to the movements that they themselves made. There would be an early and natural evolution for detecting movements in others and revealing movements in self.

The evolutionary line for language in such gestural signs, with hand and arm signals before the elaboration of vocal signs, has had support over the years from several anthropological studies. Additional support comes from recent studies with chimpanzees and gorillas in which surprisingly sophisticated language skills have been developed through the use of manual gestures, plastic symbols, and keyboards—all visual media of communication (2).

Chimps naturally show a wide range of gestural signs, from body posture in attention-orientation or leading individuals to arm and hand gestures and facial expressions. Although it is difficult for human observers to interpret much of this, it seems clear that higher animals are able to "read" the signals emitted by other species, prey, and predators, as well as by the members of their

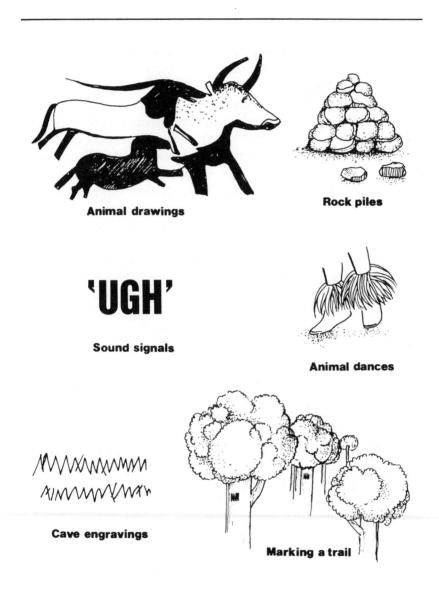

Figure 6. Some ways of communicating in the early evolution of language-related skills.

immediate social group. There is obvious survival value in anticipating the actions of others by "reading" head and neck positions, flicking the ears or tail, general body stance, and other characteristic poses or movements.

In the early development of a human community, the "here and now" detection of subsequent action was undoubtedly a major influence in shaping an effective community that could cope with prey, predators, and other environmental pressures through coordinated efforts. Immediate contingencies would have had a powerful influence in shaping gestural communication among early hunters and gatherers, who depended on food sharing and cooperative efforts for survival. Those members who gave signs that were "read" by their fellow members would be discriminatively reinforced by their fellow members' actions for doing so.

One kind of sign that must have been reinforced in early communities is given by mimicry or imitation. The young in many species quickly imitate their elders. The imitative skills of chimps have frequently been exploited in commercial entertainments. And recent hunting peoples still perform dances consisting of highly accurate imitations of animal movements. Animal mimicry is also found in the narration of hunting episodes and is apparently represented in some Upper Paleolithic paintings. Given the prevalence of animal dances in ethnographic dance literature, it is not difficult to imagine the development of accompanying stylizations and standardizations for communication through dance and story telling. A gestural tradition for representing events that had passed could easily be shaped by an appreciative audience who derived pleasure in "reliving" significant events of their lives under safe circumstances. The benefits from observing performances with structural resemblances to past events in the form of dance, story, or play have been extensively discussed in the literature of Western culture from the time of Aristotle's *Poetics*.

Just as the imitation of some characteristic movement of another animal can be a sign for that animal, so too the imitation of the characteristic movements in making or using a tool or a weapon can be a sign for that activity (process) or its consequence (product). We still learn much of our use of tools and instruments through direct observation and imitation with occasional guidance. And we still use that as a means of communication in games like Charades, or when we only communicate visually (e.g., when there is too much noise to be heard or when we do not wish to be overheard).

Another development that must have received considerable reinforcement in early communities was the use of the hand as an instrument to point, to touch, to mark, to shape, to hold, and to use and make other instruments. The organization of the brain, the extensive area controlling the hand, the specialization of left and right hemispheres, and the peculiarly human association of right-handedness and left-hemisphere dominance for both language skills and precise manual manipulation suggest an extensive history of environmental pressures leading to a distinct separation and development of the precision grip for finely detailed marking and manipulation from the power grip for holding and placing the substance or context to be marked or manipulated.

This distinction is exceedingly pervasive. We examine a conspicuous figure against a less conspicuous ground. We consider a broad topic and make a comment upon it. The main subject of our sentence has a predicatory comment. A head word in our sentence has a modifier. Cerebral lateralization may be the most striking structural product of selective environmental pressure for more sophisticated tool manipulation, for more observational sensitivity to left-right consistency in responding to landmarks and other signs, and for more extensive use of all language forms.

Although vocal communication may have had a substantial evolution before the use of tools (3), Hewes speculates on the following evolution of speech sounds from a gestural base. In the mouth-gesture theory, the lips, mouth, and tongue roughly "imitate" hand movements or other body-part movements when they are used to manipulate or communicate. We frequently observe such movements of the tongue and mouth when children and adults attempt to thread a needle or perform some other concentrated effort. Use of the lips, tongue, and teeth in tasting and testing objects is quite prominent in infancy and early childhood and rarely completely suppressed in adults. The vocal sounds that accompanied mouth gestures may have formed a rich pool of sound variations that were discriminatively reinforced over time. Even today, high front vowels are associated with smallness, while low back vowels are associated with flatness or large size. Sharp and pointed things are more likely to be associated with *t* or *k* sounds, while soft and smooth things are associated with *l* or *m* sounds. The artificial words *takete* and *maluna* are a conventional test pair to which people in widely different cultures respond almost identically. Once discriminative responding to vocal sounds began, there would be strong environmental pressures for their expanded development.

Selection of vocal sounds as signs is possible because any incidental or collateral sound that accompanied a movement or an event could become a signal for that event. We continue to regard many vocal cries today as signals for an immediately present state of affairs. When we are sufficiently involved in the context of conditions that brought forth the cry, we understand what the cry meant. It meant surprise, anger, fear, joy, grief, etc. In another context, we might infer it was a general call for help or for something or someone. Such signals could also be used as signs in communicating events that were no longer present. They may have evolved originally as adjuncts to primarily visible or gestural forms of communication.

The rapid expansion of vocal sounds as signs is made more likely when visual communication becomes deficient in fulfilling its established functions. Visual communication depends upon sufficient illumination, absence of intervening objects, and freedom in the use of the hands. When daylight fades, more and more people find it difficult to get a clear view. And when task demands increasingly occupy the hands, then environmental pressures for increasing vocalization are similarly increased. It also takes longer to communicate by gestures than by speech. The upper limits of a manual-sign lexicon may be around the same number of signs as there are in modern sign languages for the deaf, about 1,500 to 2,000 items, without counting finger-spelled words. By contrast, the use of a limited subset of elements like vocal phonemes permits a large vocabulary of words to be formed without taxing the ability of people to remember different units such as mastering a code of 1,500 to 2,000 different word signs does. The development of speech would have been given a sharply increased impetus as it gained advantages over gestures as a means of quick, easy, and efficient communication.

Enduring Signs

Enduring remains and traces permit a more detailed inspection than temporary signs in gestures and sounds. An instance of droppings, bones, tracks, or other traces left behind by a creature may be examined at leisure with various and repeated responses. Members of a culture could then see the effects that these traces had on other members, and they could learn the effects that their own traces had on others. However, there is often a longer time gap between leaving an enduring record and seeing its effect on another than there is between making a temporary movement and seeing its effects. It may take longer to learn more about enduring signs.

Objects and pictures. Displays of objects have long served as enduring signs whose primary function is to refer to something else. Arranging piles and gatherings of sticks and stones could be used to mark the terrain and for burial sites. Collections and sequential accumulations of pebbles could be used for counting and recalling objects and events.

Some of these objects could be marked and shaped by tools. And some of these objects may have a value in themselves in addition to referring to something else. Amulets, pendants, beads, etc., have long been used as symbolic artifacts in social roles and ceremonies. Similarly, in the engravings and images marked upon the surfaces of objects, there may be value in the forms beyond a specific reference to something else. An art object may be cherished and prized to an extraordinary extent. What it refers to and the relationship of the structure to that reference may fade from view as the structure of the object dominates the original function it served in communication. Possession of the jeweled crown may seem more important than possession of the role that went with it.

An early example of intentional engraving on a surface dates back to about 300,000 B.C., and an "extraordinarily sophisticated" image of a Vogelherd statue, a carved horse of mammoth ivory, dates back to about 30,000 B.C. This is quite a bit earlier than the similarly sophisticated cave paintings of animals at Lascaux and Altimira of around 18,000 to 15,000 B.C. (4). It would be a bit of an oversimplification, however, to assume that this reflects a simple invariant evolution from "abstract" or "scribbled" engravings to detailed art. Rather than the one being followed after the other, abstract design and concrete image often had a close temporal and physical proximity. Some of the early representations of images had abstract designs written on them or alongside them. The production of images was not always in the direction of becoming more detailed and refined. Sometimes the images became increasingly stylized and abstract. The function of a symbol in referring to something else does not require the detail to be prized for itself.

One way of communicating about something which is not present has been to tell a story or an idea with pictures. A drawing on a rock near a steep trail in New Mexico shows the picture of an upright mountain goat and an upside-down picture of a man on a horse. This design warned horsemen that a mountaingoat could climb up the rocky trail but a horse would tumble down. Its purpose was to communicate that information. It lacks the embellishments which are an important part of an artistic picture, containing just those elements which are important for the transmission of the message. This has been termed a descriptive-representational device by Gelb (5).

In the winter counts of the Dakota Indians, a picture of a buffalo hide represents the year 1816-17, when buffaloes were very plentiful. The Sumerians and Babylonians also named their years after outstanding events. As a figure of speech, putting a part in place of the whole—the crown for the king, fifty sails for fifty ships—is called synecdoche. Signs like this that are associated with much larger events are called an identifying-mnemonic device by Gelb when they are used to represent the larger event.

Pictures can be adapted for different uses. They can be used to represent things seen, e.g., a picture of the sun can represent the sun, or things not seen, e.g., a picture of the sun with seven marks can represent a week. Abstract relationships can be represented by pairing pictures of objects together, e.g., a picture of a woman plus a picture of a son might represent love, or a drawing of an object associated with an abstract concept might be used, e.g., the drawing of a peace pipe, which was smoked as a symbol of peace, can represent the concept of peace (6). Early uses of signs could also identify the contents and ownership of containers storing food and valuables.

At one point, the paintings of the artist and the writings of the author may have had a common origin. Expression through pictures may then have continued to evolve at an artistic level of holistic imagery, while an off-shoot of expression through pictures may have evolved into analytic symbols. The artist striving for realism is likely to include more detail. The writer striving for speed and economy is likely to include less.

What seems to have occurred with writing is a progressive differentiation from larger units (a picture of an event or for an event) to smaller units (the alphabet) with each stage capable of a complete expression. When written language acquired the alphabet, it acquired an efficient coding system by which a limited number of elements could be combined to form a large number of words. Analysis in alphabetic systems can be detailed much more precisely. Complete expressions in the beginning were comparatively ambiguous. The earliest known correspondence between speech sounds and writing goes back to around 3,000 B.C. Correspondence between speech sounds and letters goes back less far to the Greek alphabet of about 1,000 B.C. Some, if not all, of our letters are the outcome of centuries of stylized evolution of images resulting in smaller units for writing and a correspondence with smaller units of speech.

Functional origins in recording and trail-marking. It is hard to imagine a more fundamental need for the survival of man and other animals than the ability to distinguish the signs of prey from the signs of predators. Are the tracks those of the hunters or the hunted? When did they pass? How many were there? In a community of hunters, it would become essential to follow the trails left by fellow members of the community as well as by prey. There would also be selective reinforcement in making a trail conspicuous so that it could be more easily followed. The marking of trails would secure safe passage through the territory of a community for young and old alike. A common theme in many tales of folklore involves the marking of a trail, such as the trail of bread crumbs left by Hansel and Gretel that was eaten by the birds, or the trail of Ariadne's thread that Theseus used to find his way through the labyrinth. Maps of a territory imitate trails. Conspicuous stimuli are constructed so the "reader" can find his or her way. People can also construct plans, theories, formulas, recipes, rules, laws, reports, etc., by constructing discriminative stimuli that make the next move easy to follow. The architect's plan, the chef's recipe, or the scientist's report is considered well constructed if it can lead to a replication of the behaviors and product for which it was designed.

The construction of conspicuous stimuli for guiding people has advantages in (1) bridging the gap when natural signs of the terrain are unavailable as a guide, (2) economizing effort by making it easier for new members of the community to follow a desirable path, and (3) leading to new discoveries by extending the range and speed of exploration.

One simple method of mapping or recording is to use tokens based on a one-to-one correspondence with the things they represent. Many kinds of tokens widely distributed in time and space are found among early communities. Tokens have been used to keep count of herd animals—each animal represented by a token deposited in a basket. To keep track after changes of pasture or shepherds or when animals were shorn, they could simply be transferred from one basket to another. The Romans used small pebbles or "calculi" as counters, and present-day shepherds in Iraq still keep track of their animals with pebbles. Hand-made clay tokens of different shapes could stand for different things or for different numbers of things, e.g., cones for 1 and spheres for 10.

Hollow clay balls or *bullae* appeared around 3500 B.C., shortly before the appearance of clay tablets. When broken, they are found to contain tokens. The *bullae* appear to have served as bills of lading accompanying products that were sold or transferred. When a middle-man was used to ship goods, the recipient could check the accuracy of the shipment upon arrival by breaking open the *bullae*. Since the *bullae* hid their contents, any verification at any point required breaking them open. Some *bullae* have been found that overcame this difficulty by having the shape of the tokens inside impressed on the outside. Thus, the *bullae* could be read at any time without breaking them open. Of course, the tokens inside the bullae were now superfluous, and clay tablets bearing the signs of tokens soon appeared. It is interesting to note that these signs did not represent the shape of the items but rather the tokens of the previous recording system.

Schmandt-Besserat (7) summarizes this evolution from communicating with separate objects to communicating with marked surfaces as follows. In the first stage (8500 B.C.), a system of recording based on tokens is used. In the second stage (3500-3200 B.C.), hollow clay balls or *bullae* hold the tokens of a particular transaction. In the third stage (3500-3200 B.C.), signs are impressed on the surface of the *bullae*. And in the fourth stage (3200-3100 B.C.), clay tablets appear with impressed and incised signs. Indeed, the convex profile of early tablets may be a morphological feature inherited from the spherical bullae as well as the use of clay for a writing surface, a soft and easily smeared medium that must be dried or baked if it is to be preserved.

Since the impression of tokens on tablets did not allow for much precision, the invention of specialized tools or styluses permitted more complicated shapes to be made accurately. Totally abstract signs and lifelike pictographs could then exist side by side. The repertory of first signs has been estimated to consist of around 2,000 words, with abstract shapes for all the numerical signs and a score of commodities of daily use. The subsequent invention of the alphabet in writing led to a more efficient way of encoding language and an increased vocabulary, but the signs for numbers have remained at the word-symbol level. Since then, enduring visible traces have become "the preferred mode for advanced propositional communication in higher mathematics, physics, chemistry, biology, and other sciences and technology, in the familiar forms of algebraic signs, molecular structure diagrams, flow-charts, maps, symbolic logic, wiring or circuit diagrams, and all the other ways in which we represent complex variables, far beyond the capacity of the linear bursts of speech sounds" (8).

THE DEVELOPMENT OF LANGUAGE SKILLS
IN EARLY CHILDHOOD

The development of language skills in children can be viewed in parallel to the evolution of language skills in our culture (see Figure 7). Even in cases where the parallel is not as close as it might be in the experiences of all young children, there are instructional activities that have been used which would fill in the gaps. The early behavior of young children is highly expressive both in temporal gestures and sounds as well as in the manipulation of objects and in making traces. They eagerly produce forms and acquire increasing skills in producing them, and they eagerly explore and acquire skills in the functional uses of different structures. These activities are the forerunners of speaking, listening, writing, and reading. See Figure 8 for some illustrations of the ways children use language-related skills in their early development.

The Temporal Stream of Behavior

The shaking, crying infant begins interaction with the environment through relatively unorganized behaviors. Over time, increasingly refined language skills emerge from originally undifferentiated, unorganized, and undirected behaviors. Generalized bodily movements of shaking arms and kicking feet become differentiated into crawling, walking, and fine motor movements with hands and fingers. Scribbles become pictures and letters. The stream of a baby's babbling becomes progressively differentiated into speech.

The sequences of how any particular child's behavior is filled in, however, may vary. Some children walk before they talk. Some children talk before they walk. Some children master speech sounds or letter writing in a different order than others. When the

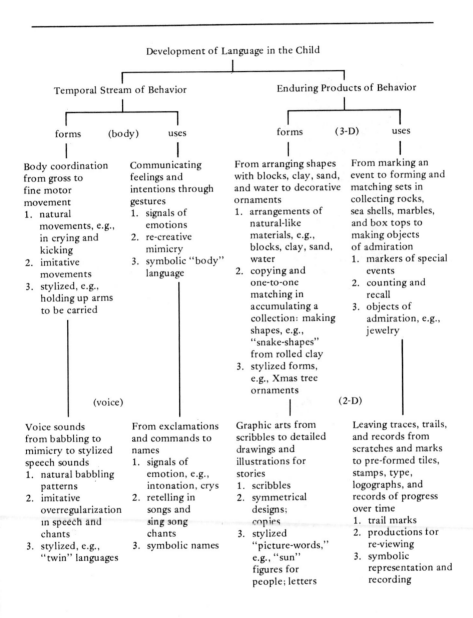

Development of Language in the Child

Temporal Stream of Behavior

forms   (body)   uses

Body coordination
from gross to
fine motor
movement
1. natural
   movements, e.g.,
   in crying and
   kicking
2. imitative
   movements
3. stylized, e.g.,
   holding up arms
   to be carried

Communicating
feelings and
intentions through
gestures
1. signals of
   emotions
2. re-creative
   mimicry
3. symbolic "body"
   language

(voice)

Voice sounds
from babbling to
mimicry to stylized
speech sounds
1. natural babbling
   patterns
2. imitative
   overregularization
   in speech and
   chants
3. stylized, e.g.,
   "twin" languages

From exclamations
and commands to
names
1. signals of
   emotion, e.g.,
   intonation, crys
2. retelling in
   songs and
   sing song
   chants
3. symbolic names

Enduring Products of Behavior

forms   (3-D)   uses

From arranging shapes
with blocks, clay, sand,
and water to decorative
ornaments
1. arrangements of
   natural-like
   materials, e.g.,
   blocks, clay, sand,
   water
2. copying and
   one-to-one
   matching in
   accumulating a
   collection: making
   shapes, e.g.,
   "snake-shapes"
   from rolled clay
3. stylized forms,
   e.g., Xmas tree
   ornaments

From marking an
event to forming and
matching sets in
collecting rocks,
sea shells, marbles,
and box tops to
making objects
of admiration
1. markers of special
   events
2. counting and
   recall
3. objects of
   admiration, e.g.,
   jewelry

(2-D)

Graphic arts from
scribbles to detailed
drawings and
illustrations for
stories
1. scribbles
2. symmetrical
   designs;
   copies
3. stylized
   "picture-words,"
   e.g., "sun"
   figures for
   people; letters

Leaving traces, trails,
and records from
scratches and marks
to pre-formed tiles,
stamps, type,
logographs, and
records of progress
over time
1. trail marks
2. productions for
   re-viewing
3. symbolic
   representation and
   recording

Figure 7. Parallel developments in the language of the child.

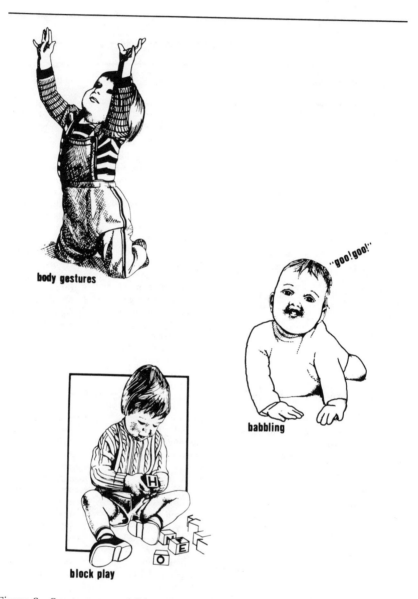

Figure 8. Some ways children use language-related skills in their early development.

Figure 8 (continued)

scribbling

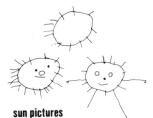

sun pictures

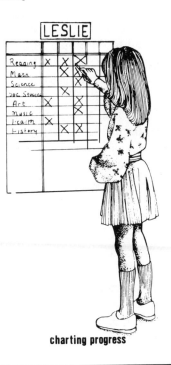

charting progress

child can frequently interact with an environment that is rich in feedback to his or her responses, the child's developing behaviors seem to fill in naturally. When the contingencies for a child's actions are defective in producing effective behavior, we often seek to augment or supplement the feedback. If our intervention is sufficiently formal, e.g., with models, prompts, and other guides, we may refer to it as instruction. Sometimes, however, the focus on rules that govern behavior in a step-by-step sequence may, perhaps unwittingly, exclude attention to assuring feedback from natural contingencies. When this happens, the resulting behavior of the child is often disappointing.

Body movements. Undifferentiated bodily movements accompany a baby's crying. Everything may seem to be moving at once. Undifferentiated movements can also be seen when the baby is excitedly gurgling or babbling as well as when the baby is making few sounds. When one limb moves, the infant seems unable to inhibit the other limbs from moving along with it.

A primary task for young children is to gain control over their body and to develop a sensitivity for its orientation in surrounding space. Chaney and Kephart (9) have presented a developmental sequence covering gross motor, fine motor, listening, eye movement, and speech skills. Harrow's taxonomy (10) presents a developmental sequence based on the levels of Bloom's taxonomy from simple to complex skills. Following Harrow's taxonomy, Flinchum (11) provides applications for movement education for children two to six years of age: from reflex movements, basic movements, perceptual-motor movements, physical abilities, skilled movements, to creative movements.

Some gross motor activities can involve all of the children in interactive movement and exploration of space and relationships. In parachute play, for example, the children can be variously involved in the lifting up and down of an old army surplus parachute, running under and into and out of the billowing cover as it rises and descends, running on top of the fallen chute and into and down on the captured pockets of air.

Other movement activities may focus on parts of the body, exercising and showing what the feet, legs, arms, and hands can do. Records may narrate movements for children which are set to music. The Kodaly method (12) has been successful in teaching music to young children by relating music and body movement through the use of hand and arm gestures. In creative dramatics, children might enact the movements of a fanciful machine, each child moving some parts of his or her body in articulated movements with another child, while following the "story" told by a narrator-choreographer.

The development of bodily gestures for communication can proceed in many different directions, from dancing to musical rhythms to creative dramatics, from specific role playing to open-ended make-believe. These activities can be related to other forms of communication. Children, for example, can write or dictate their own plays and incorporate a large cast of active characters in them. These stories can then be read aloud and enacted by other children using extensive bodily movement and gestures in response to the story being read.

Vocal sounds. The stream of sound emitted by a babbling infant is highly varied. During their first year, infants seem capable of emitting all the sounds possible for humans to make. This is not a characteristic of other primates, who are relatively quiet in this respect.

Following Jakobson, other investigators (13) have been struck by how the development of speech sounds can be considered as a successive differentiation of contrastive features in which highly contrasting distinctions subsequently subdivide into finer and finer ones. Within babbling, the child first begins to differentiate between the production of closed front sounds (consonants) and open sounds (vowels). Early consonant sounds may then be contrasted between a stop like /p/ or a continuant like the fricative /f/ or the nasal /m/. Sounds made with the mouth may be contrasted with sounds made by the lips (labial) and those made by the teeth (dental). In mouth sounds (oral), when the contrast of voiced or unvoiced is made with the lips, we have unvoiced /p/ and voiced /b/. When the contrast of voiced or unvoiced is made with the teeth, we have unvoiced /t/ and voiced /d/. Sounds made with the nose (nasal) may also be differentiated between sounds made with the lips /m/ and tongue behind the top front teeth /n/. From this we find early differentiated pairings in *papa, dada,* and *mama.* Once these expressions occur, it is easy to understand how parents might appropriate these sounds for themselves and reinforce such meanings.

Phonemes that are rare among the languages of the world, e.g., the /ae/ phoneme of English, are among the last to be acquired. Even though the /ae/ phoneme is fairly common in English (*bat, glad, sad, at*), it is acquired later by the child. Apparently, frequency of exposure is not as critical as is the stage of progressive differentiation. There are more or less universal similarities in which this differentiation occurs throughout the languages of the world.

An initial organization of vocal behavior seems to occur with single word speech or *holophrastic speech.* Highly contrasting sounds seem to be learned first, usually with repeated syllables (consonant-vowel or open syllables). Inferences as to the conditions or meanings of these utterances are vague. The expressions seem to be sentence-like, related to the child (e.g., his or her feelings or actions) or the actions of someone around the child. When such speech forms more identifiable words, nouns are used rather than verbs, e.g., "dog" may mean the object or its action. Whatever meaning there might be is heavily context dependent.

Later, children of one and two years of age or more will use two and three word utterances in *telegraphic speech.* The words are mainly content words like nouns and verbs and fewer function words like articles, prepositions, conjunctions, and auxiliaries. Typical examples are *I see, no bed, all broke, all gone juice, fall down there, bye bye papa.* In general, one grammatical structure can be described as a "pivot" word that makes a comment like an adjective, e.g., *no, all, more, pretty, my, a, poor, the, dirty, that.* This is coupled to the other grammatical structure, an "open" word class containing the topic, often a noun, e.g., *boy, sock, boat, pretty, see, baby, mommy, daddy, milk.*

The initial word classes will subsequently subdivide again and again until the word classes resemble those of adults. Subject and predicate structures will become more distinctly detailed, e.g., subjects like *it* and *airplane* will be linked to predicates like *doggie, all gone, see train, more hot.* By age three, the average length of sentences is about four words.

Progressive differentiation occurs in various other developments in language, like inflections and the verbal auxiliary, negatives, and questions. The first inflections to be acquired are plurals, then possessives, and finally verb inflections. Interestingly enough, irregular verb inflections are used correctly at first, e.g., *He ran, I did, We came.* And then overregularization of the past form produces *He runned, I doed*, and *We comed.* Overregularization also occurs with plurals, e.g., *feets*, and possessives, e.g., *mine's.* The *-ing* auxiliary emerges along with *have, will* and /-ed/ with verbs in the predicate, and then the copula (*to be*) is acquired, e.g., *Doggie is here.* After the initial appearance of these new verb forms, most children's sentences have the subject as well as the full predicate. The first negatives are used as outside tags, *no bed, touch the snow no.* Later, the negatives are used within the sentence, e.g., *You didn't caught me, This not ice cream.* Questions develop as follows: (1) At the two-word stage, intonation at the end is used, *ball go?*, with rising pitch, like a *no* tag at the end of an expression. (2) Later, /Wh-/ words are used for beginning questions, e.g., *Where my mitten?*, *Why you smiling?* (3) And then there is inversion of /Aux/ and subject in the first transformations used by children to produce adultlike word order, e.g., *Does the kitty stand up?*, *Did I saw that in my book?*, *Can I have a piece of paper?* Later, inversion with /Wh-/ words will be acquired in the next few months by most children, e.g., *Where is he going?* At the two-word stage, children can only generally question a thought or an action. Soon they can ask for a missing object, person, location, or cause. Between three and four years of age, children are nearly as specific in their questioning as adults, although they have not yet mastered /Wh-/ word question inversion and the use of the indefinite *any* (Don't you want any?).

In general, the development parallels the hierarchical analysis of language by linguists, from sentence (one word holophrases) to subject and predicate (pivot and open class) to ever finer distinctions like auxiliaries with verbs. The behavior that emerges is increasingly organized, directed, and refined.

Enduring Products of Behavior

Children can acquire direct experience in forming complete expressions of some duration in a visible language from the time they can move, manipulate, and arrange objects. The expressions they construct can stand by themselves, and they can be followed by meaningful responses and consequences. Spatial arrangement and sequence, from blocks to pictures of murals with comic-strip narrative balloons, may be developed. Skill in using pictographs by themselves may be followed by using rebus pictures mixed with letter symbols (14). Instructional procedures that build on the early levels of the child's development can provide a gradual transition from expression in blocks, to pictures, to written symbols. Many of these activities are considered natural, if often independent and isolated, tasks of early childhood. In close articulation, these activities can be seen to belong to a coherent development of early skills in language. They can also be seen in rough parallel to the evolution of language.

Constructions produced by hand and eye. An old saying has it that "the hand is quicker than the eye," which refers to a sense in which movement occurs before perception can follow. Much of perceptual-motor concerns focus on the relationships between motor movement and sensory perception. Rosner (15) emphasizes a progressive differentiation approach that moves from sensory-MOTOR to SENSORY-motor. The capitalization indicates that relatively more importance is given to the capitalized term of a tightly reciprocal interaction between action and observation.

Whether playing with blocks or drawing on paper, children first show an interest in manipulation and arrangement for its own sake. They are interested in their constructions in themselves, rather than in what their constructions might resemble. Even when resemblances begin to appear in their constructions, the production of a faithful copy often seems a secondary consideration, as when children draw arms and legs radiating from a face without a body.

Playing with blocks is an engaging activity for developing early skills in hand-and-eye coordination. It is an activity that lends itself to many variations and also many interconnections with other skills. From an initial holding and carrying of a block, the child can begin to collect and arrange them. Children can refine their capability to place one block on top of another without its falling down, a result with clear and immediate feedback. They can make bridges with blocks, a rather complex problem for the young child to solve. They can focus on increasing size or length in one dimension at a time. They can learn about one-to-one correspondence, counting, matching, sorting, fitting spaces, fractional parts, etc. They can work alone or with others in developing creative new forms and acting out fantasy in dramatic play. They can cooperate in the building of "roads," "houses," "towns," etc. They can show, describe, and tell stories, carrying, arranging, and rearranging. Blocks can also be used to form letters, words, and sentences. Blocks for letters or with letters written on them (single letters or meaningful clusters of letters) can be used to form words. Blocks for words or with words written on them can be used to form sentences.

Working with a plastic material like clay or play-dough can develop more refined motor skills. Chernoff (16) describes how to make animals, like snakes and frogs, ornaments, like pins and pendants, toys, and letter signs from play-dough by mixing one-third cup of water a little at a time to one cup of all-purpose flour and one-half cup of salt. Objects can be dried in the air or the oven (at 225 degrees, 15 minutes for small objects on each side, an hour on each side for big objects). The finish can be protected with three coats of nail polish. Children can decorate their products, collect them, and exchange them with other children, much like early pottery makers.

While the high fluidity of water and sand play lend themselves to more temporary arrangements, blocks and clay can be a little more enduring. Permanent displays of blocks and clay can be made from nailing or gluing blocks and materials together or "firing" the clay. Permanent records, however, can be made of even the most temporary arrangements by taking pictures.

Cooking can provide a variety of experiences for motor skill development in rolling, shaping, and cutting dough, measuring, pouring, etc. Pouring, measuring, and mixing can also develop many of the skills associated with science: doing something and seeing what happens; using precise descriptions that can replicate the results the next time, making a prediction and seeing if it comes true. As suggested by the saying that "the proof of the pudding is in the eating," the consumption of the product can provide clear feedback from several consumers. For those children ready to learn to do so, reading and following recipe directions is a fairly exacting demonstration of comprehension with meaningful consequences. Some of these directions can be written very simply in rebus-like forms that are designed to make it easy for young children to follow. Composing and writing such recipes, recalling the details with precision and completeness, would also be a fairly rigorous test of communication with tangible consequences. Wilms (17) lists recipes with fruits, vegetables, eggs, dairy foods, spices and herbs, and grains that children can follow, as well as providing suggestions for relating cooking to vocabulary building, math, science, and reading. *Cook and Learn* (18) provides clear illustrations and rebus-like standardized pictures for each step in the recipe directions.

The transition from working with three-dimensional objects and representations to two-dimensional forms and pictures is a big one for young children. Tactile manipulation is lessened, and orientations like left and right now become critical. Working with manipulative picture puzzles can be helpful in making this transition. Initial puzzles might be solved with tactile feedback if the edges of the pieces are formed so that they will fit together in only one way. Gradually a transition may be made to puzzles requiring visual feedback for their solution when the edges do not fit distinctively into each other. Cutting and pasting can serve as another transitional activity in making collages, scrapbooks, murals, puzzles, thematic collections with labels, sequences of pictures that tell a story, etc. The various shapes and illustrations can be cut from books or constructed by the child. Considerable tactile feedback may be used in assembling the parts on a flat surface.

Although there are substantial differences between concrete manipulative arrangements and pictorial images, they may share underlying principles in common with symbolic forms. Each level, for example, may show hierarchical complexity. Even manipulative play may be composed of pilings and subassemblies that have some parallel with linguistic development. The copying strategies of children may even be viewed in terms of a grammar of action (19).

Graphic arts include representation, decoration, and writing on flat surfaces. This is a vast domain. A variety of materials can be used to decorate or draw upon a flat surface (20). Designs can be "drawn" in glue, for example. Different colors of sand, jello, seeds, salt, or sugar can be sprinkled on, shaking off whatever does not stick to the pattern. Colors may be put on the material before the application by pouring sand into dixie cups of water and food coloring and then draining to dry or simply mixing in dry jello or coloring with salt or sugar. And colors may be painted on afterwards. Anything that sticks can be used. Cut-up broom ends or pieces of straw can be arranged in a variety of designs, decorations, pictures, shapes, letters, etc.

When a child begins to manipulate instruments that leave traces, he or she leaves a scribble behind. Stages of development within scribbles have been noted; and these can be used as indicators of progress in scribbling, from tangled mazes of lines to broken patterns with dots, lines, and curves in the direction of writing or to symmetrical patterns and "sun" figures in the direction of pictures (21). (In the beginning development toward writing, scribbles of children may show no evidence of organization. The first signs of organization may appear as zig-zag lines of little variation which are written in a horizontal orientation so that one zig-zag line may appear below the other. A later stage shows better articulated forms with more variation of structure that is not yet broken up into smaller units by spacing. These forms may resemble a very badly scrawled cursive script that might seem potentially decipherable. Later on, spacing is used to divide the elements, and the elements are increasingly differentiated. Clusters of lines may form a recognizable letter or look as though they could be reassembled to form a recognizable letter. Problems of orientation may be the last to disappear. Articulations of parts of the letters may be reversed. And reversals of entire letters may persist for some time. These reversals are less likely to occur originally if the child does not have to lift up the writing instrument so often in forming a letter, as in recent D'Nealian manuscript writing.

(A scribble can stand for a communication simply by saying what it represents. Hand the child a note with a scribble on it and tell the child it says, "Shut the door." When the child hands you a scribble, ask the child to tell you what it says. A scribble can also be a pattern set to rhythm or a mosaic of different colors, like a stained glass window, after the child colors in the spaces. When the scribbling has differentiated to the point where the child can produce curving lines across the top of the paper with slanted lines beneath, the child can show the rain falling from the clouds. This may be the start of further picture drawings of houses and figures (that, incidentally, contain all the elementary shapes and parts of letters). Or, it may be the beginning for letters like *o* and *l*.

The function of making records and marking trails. Anyone who has observed children for long is aware of their fascination in collecting things and leaving traces behind them. Like little pack rats, children will collect marbles, string, bottle caps, stickers, stamps, cards, dolls, cars, soldiers, comic books, or almost anything else that is collectible. They will absorbedly make a mess in mud, sand, paint, flour, powder, or anything else that leaves a trace of their trail. They are fascinated by the imprints their hands and feet make, their own recording of themselves. They delight in seeing the traces made by their feet on smooth sand or in wet mud. They turn around to examine their trail, to see where they have been and where they have come, before continuing on again. They cannot resist tracing their fingers across frosted window panes or fogged car windows in spite of parental protests against leaving grease marks.

They will readily take to more sophisticated recording and trail marking. Children love to count. They will count almost anything that can be counted. They will make a game of counting things they see while riding in a car. They will count how long they can hold their breath. They will compare their counts with one another. They will try to improve upon their previous personal records. Given the opportunity, they will keep records of their progress to see where they were and how they are doing now. They will mark a spot on a cellar doorway to record their height at various times. They will record their personal experiences in a diary. They will collect examples of their work, model airplanes they have built, or pictures they have drawn. If shown how, they will chart and record their progress in various activities, using checklists, point-to-point graphs, or some other convenient marking system. Teachers have long been aware how children love to collect stars, stickers, or stamps on and for their work. When the recording method is clear and meaningful to children, they also enjoy making and marking their own records of progress, to see where they have been, what they have done, and how they are doing.

They learn that marks "stand" for things that happen, whether an x or a word. They learn that written words have an advantage in distinguishing one type of mark from another. And they learn that words can bring them in contact with experiences they may or may not have had.

Many language arts activities lend themselves to functional uses as records and trail markers. Personal diaries, notebooks, and scrapbooks serve that function admirably. Collecting new vocabulary words or spelling words on cards or keeping track (or count) of the number of words/stories/books that are read or written also serves that function.

One of the most sophisticated and useful recording functions is filled by the written project report. A description of the problem and its history, an account of the methods and procedures followed in the project activity, and a discussion of specific results are essential ingredients of project reports in all fields of endeavor. Such reports "set the record straight" or "blaze a new trail" of investigation.

In order to leave a symbolic mark, a child has often been required to make his or her own construction from scratch or from relatively undifferentiated materials. The child creates the forms from the raw materials of blocks, clay, or pencil. However, the development of skilled behavior in using these materials often requires an extended period of time for the child. The child may have much to say, but lack the motor development to write it. Or, the child's attention and efforts may be so absorbed in the construction of symbols that the child cannot attend to what he or she would like to say. There are ways to overcome this difficulty. Some of what the child would have to construct can already be constructed for the child.

Deich and Hodges (22), for example, worked with eight institutionalized retarded children who had not had prior speech therapy and who were described as having mental ages equivalent to that of chimps. The children constructed sentences with nonpictorial symbols for words, one symbol for each word. They matched symbols to the picture of an object, e.g., food, and used a magnetic board for three- to seven-word sentence construction and responding. Neither mental age, I.Q., nor chronological age predicted which of the retardates would learn faster.

The symbol units being used were pre-formed representations for words with which complete expressions were constructed. As with a typewriter, the pupils did not have to struggle with motor-visual skills for the formation of individual letters. Nor did they have to struggle with the formation of individual words. Both handwriting and spelling skills were by-passed. They could go directly to forming complete expressions by selecting the word that would form a sentence. They could thus form complete expressions with "stylized" pictures for words before they could write by hand or spell. The use of these permanent visual symbols helps to simplify a complex process:

> The use of permanent visual symbols, rather than gestures or sounds, circumvents the short-term memory problem, makes possible the use of errorless training along with the introduction of one unknown at a time, and does not depend upon elaborate motor learning (causing a particle to adhere to a board is something primates do readily). When each new word is taught by arranging it so that its introduction at a marked location in a string of known words has the effect of completing the sentence, three primary sources of difficulty are eliminated: (1) only one new word will be present, so the subject cannot err in choice of

words, (2) the blank location in the (potential) sentence is marked (with the interrogative marker) so the subject cannot err as to where in the sentence to put the word, (3) the completing operation always consists of addition, rather than addition plus the possibility of deletion and/or rearrangement. (23)

The rationale behind this method of learning language expression is a persuasive argument for using language instruction with children at the sentence completion level, even though they are not yet able to write by hand or to spell words. It would be an easier introduction to the naturally meaningful use of symbols in our written language than requiring children to construct words before they can use them.

When symbols for words or ideas have a strong image resemblance to other things, the term used in referring to such symbols may be *pictogram*. Kolers (24) has pointed out some formal characteristics of pictograms: (1) Caricatures that emphasize distinguishing features are easier to recognize than photographs of the object or event represented. (2) Pictorial representations thus commonly use synecdoche that substitutes a part to indicate a whole. (3) Pictograms can make use of inferences based on synthetic experience and/or empathy, e.g., a saw-tooth line may depict a resistor in a diagram of electronic circuits. Here the functional consequence of jagged edges that resist movement is used for the concept of resistor. (4) Compound elements may represent conceptual commonness, even when the elements are more conventional than pictorial, e.g., a curved arrow with a slash mark across it that means "do not turn." (5) Similar shapes can stand for similar classes. Like other writing systems, pictograms can be used to symbolize objects or their locations, convey instructions, and comment upon or evaluate information. For these reasons, pictograms may offer special advantages in their use by young children to acquire visible language skills.

When the signs for words or ideas do not have a strong image resemblance to other things, the term used may be *logograph* (or *ideogram*). In a broad reference, both *pictogram* and *logograph* may be applied to references that are highly pictorial or highly conventional. In either case, they are minimal units of expression and cannot be decomposed into smaller components such as the letters of the alphabet. In any particular usage, the meaning of a *logograph* or *pictogram* depends upon its integration within a complete expression.

It would not be advisable, however, for a child to remain only at this level of unit identification. A language whose smallest unit of construction is a picture word (or ideogram) is limited in total vocabulary. There is a limiting memory load on the number of separate pictures that can be remembered and used conveniently. Eventually this places pressure to shift to smaller units of word construction (which the child must be able to handle as smaller units). The order here is significant. In all known historical developments of writing, the formation of expressions with word signs precedes any shift to an alphabetic system. This is even the case with the history of some modern writings created under the stimulus of advanced cultures among primitive societies, as in Cherokee Indian and African Bamum writings (25).

In the beginning, the child does not need to depend on either dictation or words previously written for him or her in order to move directly to producing complete expressions. In addition to arranging objects, the child can construct stories out of pictures as the Indians did. The child can systematically be taught "Indian Writing" by using more or less stylized pictures to represent events. The child can draw the pictures or use pre-formed pictures from a rebus collection and paste them on. The child's vocabulary may be quite simple at first, then gradually increase. A lot can be done with a dozen or so signs for expressing ideas. If the child has plastic rebus shapes that are readily attached to a magnetic board, the child can easily engage in constructing requests as well as in constructing stories. Plastic rebus shapes provide the child with an opportunity to play at arranging and rearranging expressions. Children can easily exchange communications with these expressions, taking turns, playing a game, having fun. The child could decide when to add new images. The child could also decide when to replace images with written words and when to replace plastic forms with forms that the child draws.

The evolution of natural languages has never evolved from a step-by-step buildup from letters to words to complete expressions. Similarly, requiring a child to follow a step-by-step buildup from letters to words may be an "unnatural" direction. It may come at the expense of directly understanding a complete and meaningful expression. It is certainly not the only choice of directions available for instruction. If pictograms or logographs make it easier for children to form complete and integrated expressions, a variety of ways could be pursued for encouraging this.

IMPLICATIONS FOR TEACHING WRITING AND READING

We observe children developing many of their language skills, such as speech, in response to natural contingencies that require no planned intervention. However, when we examine some of the practices of teaching writing and reading in the schools, we often notice some striking differences between responding to the natural contingencies of the environment and the planned intervention of schooling:

1. In schools, there is often much memorized rule learning and recitation, e.g., the names and sounds of letters, rules of spelling, and rules of grammar. More complex language-related experiences are often only a temporary activity without follow-up or an opportunity to show progress—whatever is learned is almost incidental to simply experiencing the activity. Integrated experiences are lacking for learning the uses and constructions of written language in a gradual development of effective communication through social interaction.

2. In schools, tasks are often organized into hierarchies to be learned from the bottom up, beginning and mastering the smallest component units before moving up to combine them at the next level. e.g., first letters, their names, sounds, or handwriting; then words, their names, syllables, and spelling; then sentences, their grammatical classification, parts of speech, and construction. More creative activities are often presented as a one-time occurrence, disconnected from learning skills. This stands in contrast to much naturalistic learning, which leads from the top to the bottom, beginning with complete and meaningful expressions, however gross and undifferentiated, and moving down to increasingly finer

distinctions and smaller component units (e.g., from babbling to holophrases to sentences, from scribbling to drawing patterns to drawing recognizable pictures, from holding a block to arranging blocks in patterns to constructing castles).

3. In schools, the subject matter of language is often taught in separate and isolated parts, e.g., in reading, spelling, and handwriting periods taught separately from each other and from the rest of the curriculum. Even class plays, which obviously call upon a wide variety of language skills, are often presented in isolation from the rest of the curriculum. In contrast, learning a language by exposure to natural contingencies continually finds occasions for tying together the different aspects of language.

4. In schools, the separate subject matters of language often sample only a narrow domain of that subject, e.g., reading may focus primarily on reading a text aloud and recalling the words in the text. The child's capability in complex performances, like writing a poem or a story, may be sampled at only infrequent intervals. By contrast, effective learning in response to natural contingencies involves a much fuller sampling of a wide variety of responses to a wide variety of stimuli.

There is a need to bridge the gap between relying merely on rules or incidental learning activities. More naturalistic contingencies can be designed into school environments so that learning is more like a continuous progressive differentiation. A rich supply of resources in space and materials increases a child's freedom and variety of interaction. Increased cooperative social interaction in sharing and exchanging notes and comments on prominently displayed language efforts provides more realistic consequences. Collections and displays of products, progress records, and tokens of achievement can substantially increase the feedback available to children. The behaviors included for development in language skills can be expanded to fill the gap between memorized and creative behaviors. Attention to the wide range of natural-like contingencies will reveal whether and how a rule or an incidental learning activity is an aid or an obstacle.

SUMMARY

The origins of language can be traced to both temporal and

enduring traditions of signs. The temporal traditions of gestures and vocal sounds evolved with a close interaction in tool using. More enduring traditions of visible language arose with objects, pictures, trail-marking, and other functional recordings. The development of language skills in early childhood can be traced to a temporary gestural and sound stream, more enduring arrangements of objects and graphic expressions arranged by hand and eye (with and without the aid of pre-formed parts, with and without sound stimuli), and an evolving trail- and record-making. The parallel between the evolution of language and the development of language skills in early childhood illustrates that language does not develop naturally as a linear sequence of one elementary unit after the other, building up into higher complexities as it goes along. Rather, there are multiple, parallel developments of language skills. Any particular skill gets filled in as part of a parallel development of progressive differentiation from wholes to parts within wholes. To the extent that these evolutionary and developmental processes contribute to the acquisition of sophisticated language skills and to the extent that these processes can be identified and applied to the environment of early childhood learning, much of the child's progress in language may occur more naturally and easily.

REFERENCES

1. Hewes, G.W. Primate communication and the gestural origin of language. *Current Anthropology*, February-April 1973, *14*(1-2), pp. 5-24.

2. Gardner, R.A., and Gardner, B.T. Teaching sign language to a chimpanzee. *Science*, 15 August 1969, *165*(3894), pp. 664-672. Patterson, F. Conversations with a gorilla. *National Geographic*, October 1978, *154*(4), pp. 438-465. Premack, A.J., and Premack, D. Teaching language to an ape. *Scientific American*, October 1972, *227*(4), pp. 92-99. Rumbaugh, D.M. (Ed.) *Language learning by a chimpanzee: The Lana project.* New York: Academic, 1977.

3. Falk, D. Language, handedness, and primate brains: Did the Australopithecines sign? *American Anthropologist*, March 1980, *82*(1), pp. 72-78.

4. Marshack, A. Implications of the paleolithic symbolic evidence for the origin of language. *American Scientist*, March-April 1976, *64*(2), pp. 136-145.

5. Gelb, I.J. *A study of writing* (rev. ed.). Chicago: University of Chicago, 1963, p. 29.

6. Ogg, O. *The 26 letters* (rev. ed.). New York: Thomas Y. Crowell, 1971, p. 37.

7. Schmandt-Besserat, D. The invention of writing. *Discovery*, June 1977, *1*(4), pp. 4-7. Schmandt-Besserat, D. An archaic recording system and the origin of writing. *Monographic Journals of the Near East: Syro-Mesopotamian Studies*, July 1977, *1*(2), pp. 31-70. Schmandt-Besserat, D. The earliest precursor of writing. *Scientific American*, June 1978, *238*(6), pp. 50-59.

8. Hewes, G.W. Primate communication and the gestural origin of language. *Current Anthropology*, Feb.-April 1973, *14*(1-2), p. 11.

9. Chaney, C.M., and Kephart, N.C. *Motoric aids to perceptual training*. Columbus, Ohio: Charles E. Merrill, 1968.

10. Harrow, A.J. *A taxonomy of the psychomotor domain: A guide for developing behavioral objectives*. New York: David McKay, 1972.

11. Flinchum, B.M. *Motor development in early childhood: A guide for movement education with ages 2 to 6*. St. Louis, Mo.: C.V. Mosby, 1975.

12. Chosky, L. *The Kodaly method: Comprehensive music education from infant to adult*. Englewood Cliffs, N.J.: Prentice-Hall, 1974.

13. Dale, P.S. *Language development* (2nd ed.). New York: Holt, Rinehart, and Winston, 1976. Jakobson, R. *Child language aphasia and phonological universals*. The Hague, The Netherlands: Mouton, 1968. McNeill, D. *The acquisition of language: The study of developmental psycholinguistics*. New York: Harper and Row, 1970. Pflaum, S.W. *The development of language and reading in the young child*. Columbus, Ohio: Charles E. Merrill, 1974.

14. Ferguson, N. Pictographs and prereading skills. *Child Devel-*

opment, September 1975, *46*(3), pp. 786-789. Richards, B. Mapping: An introduction to symbols. *Young Children*, January 1976, *31*(2), pp. 145-156. Woodcock, R.W. *Rebuses as a medium in beginning reading instruction*. Nashville, Tenn.: Peabody College for Teachers, Institute on Mental Retardation and Intellectual Development, 1968, *5*(4). Woodcock, R.W., Clark, C.R., and Davies, C.O. *The Peabody rebus reading program: Teacher's guide*. Circle Pines, Minn.: American Guidance Service, 1969.

15. Rosner, J. *Perceptual skills curriculum: Introductory guide*. New York: Walker Educational Book Corp., 1973.

16. Chernoff, G.T. *Clay-dough, play-dough*. New York: Scholastic Book Services, 1974.

17. Wilms, B. *Crunchy bananas*. Salt Lake City and Santa Barbara: Sagamore Books, 1975.

18. Veitch, B., and Harms, T. *Cook and learn.* Menlo Park, Calif.: Addison-Wesley Publishing Company, 1980.

19. Goodson, B.D., and Greenfield, P.M. The search for structural principles in children's manipulative play: A parallel with linguistic development. *Child Development*, September 1975, *46*(3), pp. 734-746. Ninio, A., and Lieblich, A. The grammar of action: "Phrase structure" in children's copying. *Child Development*, September 1976, *47*(3), pp. 846-850.

20. Lambert, C., and Christensen, S. *What a child can do*. Boulder, Colo.: Pruett, 1964.

21. Gibson, E.J., and Levin, H. *The psychology of reading*. Cambridge, Mass.: The MIT Press, 1975. Kellogg, R. *Analyzing children's art*. Palo Alto, Calif.: Mayfield, 1970.

22. Deich, R.F., and Hodges, P.M. Learning from Sarah. *Human Behavior*, May 1975, *4*(5), pp. 40-42.

23. Premack, D., and Premack, A.J. Teaching visual language to apes and language-deficient persons. In R.L. Shiefelbusch and L.I. Lloyd (Eds.), *Language perspectives—acquisition, retardation, and intervention*. Baltimore: University Park Press, 1974, p. 372.

24. Kolers, P. Some formal characteristics of pictograms. *American Scientist*, Autumn 1969, *57*(3), pp. 348-363.

25. Gelb, I.J. *A study of writing* (rev. ed.). Chicago: University of Chicago Press, 1963, p. 203.

Chapter III

Writing Complete and Creative Expressions

Simply having pupils duplicate constructions or giving them opportunities to express their feelings in writing is inadequate. This leaves complex writing skills either to the tail-end of a long process of mechanical skill development, which the pupil often never reaches, or to a mysterious, innate talent that we are presumably born with or without. It assures that the mystery of writing complete and creative, complex expressions is preserved and made inaccessible. But do we want to make it difficult or easy for young children to produce complete and creative expressions?

BACKGROUND

A written expression is complete when we are satisfied to stop, stand back from it, and give it space, as it were. An interruption before we are finished leaves us dissatisfied and we return to complete our work. Although perfectionists never finish completing their work, we are often easily satisfied to complete our work (for the time being). We do not accept a complete expression as something that must be mysterious, nor should we accept a creative expression as something that must be mysterious.

A creative response is a new response. Sometimes it is one we have never seen produced by anyone. It may excite wonder by its uniqueness. A new response may also be one that we have never seen produced before by a particular child, even though we have seen it done by others. Originality is relative, and there is little point in setting a level for acceptable originality so high that we ensure it cannot occur very often. See Figure 9. A creative response also produces valued consequences. Sometimes it is a

71

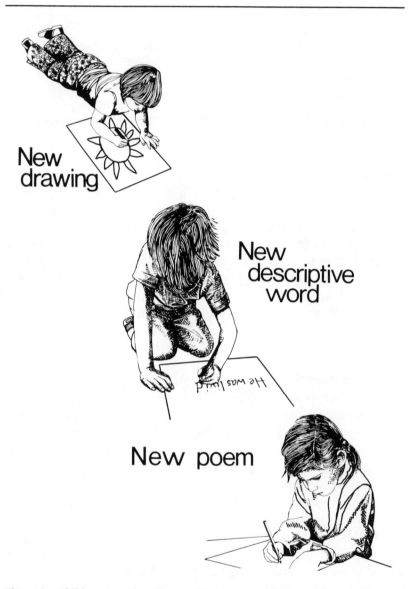

Figure 9. Children continually produce novel and creative responses for themselves.

value represented by a competitive auction involving millions of dollars. Sometimes it is a value in the comment made by another child who reads the writing. When we arrange for more valuable consequences to occur more often for what is written, the value of that writing is thereby increased. A creative response also needs a situation where something more is demanded than an imitative response. Situations that simply require repetition or duplication, e.g., in copying or recalling, allow no opportunity for creativity except by a happy accident that breaches the routine. Rather than wait for happy accidents to occur, we can design environments and show children how to arrange their surroundings so that happy accidents are much more likely to occur.

APPLICATION

We can, therefore, increase creative writing, and any other complete expressions the child is learning, by increasing the *variety* of writing behaviors, the *consequences* to this writing, and the *occasions* or situations for this writing.

The Variety of Behaviors in a Writing Curriculum

In the drawing of a picture, there are natural resemblances to concrete events, with some deletions and interpolations. Images are tightly bound to the here and now and past remembrances. They present a tightly knit view of concrete particulars that are linked together, all of a piece. The distinctive features of a pictorial representation lie in the relationship between what is visibly present and what is resembled. In modern writing, the visual appearance of symbols and their resemblances are subordinate to the conventional usage of language. Words can mean whatever it may be useful for them to mean, with much less dependency on concrete events. The substitutions and transformations of words are relatively free of the concrete, contiguous binding of pictures. Words lend themselves to talking about alternatives and abstract future possibilities.

This leaves a domain of writing that extends from picture writing that tells a story with some conventional symbolism, e.g., a setting sun for death, to stylized pictograms where the original visual image is no longer recognized, e.g., Chinese writing. Within this range, anything from a brief mark, e.g., a signatured x, to an elaborate text, e.g., a multi-volume saga, may be included. See Figure 10.

Access to this domain is made easier for children when they do not have to produce many units of writing or when they do not have to produce each individual unit solely by themselves. Children may begin with complete expressions that are very brief, e.g., *I* or *me* signed to a self-portrait drawing. In writing, complete expressions are bounded by indefinite space. Additional considerations of completeness may include whether the writer is finished composing or whether the reader would have the writer include more. To make it easier for children, we can allow them to begin with their own criteria for meaningful closure.

When parts of the task are accomplished by someone else, the complexity of the task and the dependency on other skills are also reduced for the child. For example, children may use letter tiles or word cards for their expressions. If this is too difficult, children can dictate stories that are transcribed into print. In order that a child may "read" his or her dictation more easily, rebus shapes might be included in the transcription, either in place of or above key words. The rebus forms may then be removed when the child no longer needs them to identify the words. Various procedures for writing down children's oral expressions have been actively pursued in language experience approaches with young children (1). See Figure 11.

Both a language experience and a language arts approach emphasize the integration of children's experiences, including their previous experiences with language. Instead of teaching reading, handwriting, and spelling as relatively distinct and independent skills, they can be taught in relationship with other varieties of language skills: e.g., creative dramatics, journalism, typing, etc. Activities like class plays, for example, which can involve reading, composition, oral interpretation, creative dramatics, proofreading, and editing would be highly recommended. In such activities, the close interrelationships between language skills are maintained under conditions that permit frequent feedback. Examples of

**Collections of stories,
words, and letters written**

Words identified

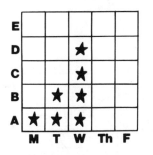

Letters written

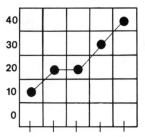

Graph of words written

Class mural

Figure 10. Some writing records.

Dictating a story

**Drawing
a story with pictures**

**Selecting word symbols
on cards**

Figure 11. Some ways a child can produce a visible story.

integrated language arts approaches have also been given in detail (2).

Such holistic approaches move away from confinement to rigid, stereotyped, and fragmented performances in isolated skill areas and toward imaginative problem solving and creativity. Holistic completeness and comprehension is a value from the start, in complete thoughts, complete expressions, and complete stories in books or phrases. A variety of writing behaviors can occur early and continue throughout the child's education.

Consequences for Evaluation

The consequences of writing can be increased by increasing the feedback from readers. If any reading behavior that reinforces the writer's responses is increased, then that writing behavior will also increase. This requires that readers make responses and that the writer gets the feedback. The writer must be aware of the reader's responses if they are to be useful to the writer. These reading responses include discussing the work, summarizing it, editing it, writing a story about an idea suggested by it, doing an illustration for it, following the directions, doing something about an idea in it, mailing a copy to a friend, referring to it, selecting it for a collection, asking questions about it, and so on. See Figure 12.

The frequency of these reading responses can be increased, in turn, by providing reinforcing consequences for the readers. Give conspicuous consequences to those who comment, discuss, and act on a text at any time after their exposure to it. Consequences to the reader's responses may be discussing them, recording them, collecting them, placing them on prominent display, doing something about them, referring to them, acting on them, etc.

All of these consequences contribute to the evaluation of writing. Any particular evaluation can focus on the final product, the cumulative record of products over time, the stages and revisions in developing a product, or on any parts or aspects of the written expression. Evaluation is easier when the consequences of the writing are conspicuous to the writer and when there are many situations in which the writer can be made aware of the effects of his or her writing and its values. Evaluation is particularly effective

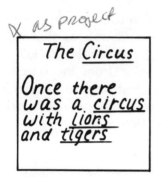

Display of story

Selecting words from story

Read and act out story

Figure 12.   Arranging consequences for producing stories.

when it can be managed by the writer to give the writer the kind of feedback the writer needs when the writer needs it. This includes a far richer range of feedback than a globally obscure "good" or "bad."

To begin with, it is useful to have some idea of the component parts of writing that can be identified for feedback. This should not lead to a focus on isolated parts that becomes an end unto itself. Rather, it should lead to a focus on the relationship of a particular part within the whole. The function of writing should always receive priority over the structure of writing.

Identifying component parts for feedback. A focus on those aspects of writing to receive attention for development can be introduced into the writing activities themselves as well as some time after the writing has been finished. Once the creative expression has been produced, it is available for examination and analysis at leisure. Methods are available for detailed analysis of the pictures that children draw and the sentences they dictate (3). The child's progress in any component of writing can be monitored by the teacher or the child.

There is little evidence of any necessity, however, for children to have a fully detailed development in one area before moving on to another. Children do not need to produce standardized spelling before they produce stories. Nor do they need to produce letters by fine motor control of a pencil (they can use a typewriter, pre-formed letter tiles, or dictate). In terms of sequencing opportunities for a child's growth and development, it may be worthwhile to consider initiating writing development with complete holistic expressions in stories, poems, and phrases, then moving on to word formation, and finally taking up letter formation. The child can thus develop his or her skills in progressive differentiation as the units become smaller and smaller, from story to word to letter. Each step in such a sequence could then provide the opportunity for a reintegration into a larger context which has already proven meaningful to the child. This does not mean that the child needs to be held back from development in any one area. Simultaneous development may occur at all three levels of complete expressions, words, and letters. Each new advance in a lower level can be integrated into the higher, more comprehensive levels. Descriptions illustrating the development of children's writing are available in collections and interpretations of children's stories (4). Gardner, for example, points out the greater creativity of children's art between the ages of three to five, the similarity between creativity and problem solving, and examines six aspects of storytelling: the occurrence of events, counterforces, control of resources, role of organizing affect, creation related to the literary tradition, and creation related to external events.

Any complete written expression can be analyzed at various levels. Stories can be analyzed in terms of changes in a critical part, e.g., the main character, the goal, the obstacle, the result, the ending. A theme may be analyzed in terms of a change in the beginning, the middle, or the end. A paragraph may be analyzed in terms of the topic for its opening sentence and the following comment sentences. At the sentence level, one method practiced in Montessori schools is to take a pair of scissors and actually cut up a sentence into its constituent parts. The subject can be cut from the predicate. Then the noun can be cut from the adjective in the subject part. The adverb can be cut from the verb in the predicate part, and so on, depending on the complexity of the sentence. Another constituent analysis that serves the same function is diagramming by drawing branching lines, e.g., "trees," instead of cutting the paper.

One way to develop skills in producing the parts of a complete expression is to have the child fill in the part which is missing from a complete expression. This "fill-in-the-blank" approach is popular in many areas of language analysis. It can be found in the blanks to be filled in of programmed instruction books (sometimes called frames). In reading, the *cloze* procedure leaves out a word, and the *maze* procedure supplies controlled alternatives for the selected position. In grammatical discussions, this is sometimes called a slot-and-filler procedure. A word is left out of a sentence, and one is sought to fill the empty slot and make sense out of the sentence. The list of words that can fill that slot and make a meaningful sense in some realistic context is limited. These word lists form categories or word classes. Depending on the particular sentence context and similar sentence contexts, word lists can be formed for very precise parts of speech. In fact, this is how parts of speech come to be defined—by describing the characteristics of the word lists. Moving from the more essential to the less frequently encountered parts of speech, children can have practice in gathering word lists for verbs, nouns, adjectives, adverbs, question words, prepositions, determiners, articles, conjunctions, coordinators, subordinators, interjections, etc. Given a model of a sentence which might be spoken by a native speaker, children may soon be able to form their own classification piles that might be substituted for each of the words in the sentence. After collecting words into piles, children may practice generating sentences by selecting words from the appropriate piles placed in the appropriate order. This can be done with deliberate selection of each word or by random selection from each pile in the same order. Some of the results may be commonplace. Some may be humorous and far-fetched. But they will all be recognized as possible English sentences. To illustrate the significance of word order, the results can be compared with words taken randomly when all the piles are mixed together. Many of those sentences would never be spoken by a native speaker and make no sense whatsoever.

"Opin" clozes permit alternative fits, all of which could make good sense (5): The boy climbed up the ladder . . . , showing he was nervous. *Quickly, hesitantly, shakily*, etc., could fit in here. Discussion can follow as to which is the better word. The context can be constrained by having a picture which the incomplete sentence describes. The picture and sentence match may be more or less ambiguous so that only one choice or many alternatives would fit the context. Even very subtle differences can be considered, such as which word fits best in a poem. The children can make their selections, then discuss among themselves which is the better. They may even consider their choice to be better than the word chosen by the author of the poem. The actual word selected by the author can be revealed later as feedback. It can be used as a standard against which comparisons can be made so the children can see how well they did.

The accuracy of a child's sentence completion can be further checked in describing a particular picture, e.g., one of two pictures. At first, the pictures may be very different, so that any description that is at all close will permit a reader or listener to pick one from the other. Later, the pictures may be similar globs that require a precise statement to determine which one is being described (6). Discussions can follow as to which words made a difference. An oral version of this activity can be played with young children describing cards of human-like forms composed of various shapes and features, e.g., a polka-dotted square body, a triangle head with an upsidedown nose (7). With more than one card displayed before them, the other children try to pick out the one being described. Accuracy in description can also be practiced in trying to guess if the description is a real experience or a pretend one as in the TV game show "To Tell the Truth." Or, the task of the other children may be to guess "Who would say that?," in response to a statement written by another child. Can the children guess who the child is who did the writing? They can be told that it was written by one of two children or that it was written by someone in the class. These situations ask children to determine the context that the writing fits. Examples like these show how producing a description that clearly demonstrates context sensitivity can be easy or demanding.

Many of the above analytical procedures can be applied with the use of "made-up" or nonsense words. Lewis Carroll's poem "Jabberwocky" is a well-known illustration. The words are strange, but they are the kind of words (often signaled by the ending) which could fit in that space. We try to make sense out of it from a previous experience with words that fit in those places. Often we feel we succeed rather well. To come up with a good explanation of the meaning for a nonsense word requires sufficient context and sensitivity to that context. The following is an example:

Mean Song

Snickles and podes,
Ribbles and grodes:
That's what I wish you.

> A nox in the groat,
> A root in the stoot,
> And a gock in the forbeshaw, too.
>
> Keep out of sight
> For fear that I might
> Glon you a gravely snave.
>
> Don't show your face
> Around any place
> Or you'll get one flack snack in the bave. (Anonymous)

Children's ability to describe the meaning for any of the above words depends on their sensitivity to the context and the words that could be substituted for it. The list of words that could be substituted for a nonsense word form a word class. For example, in the last line, *bave* could be replaced by *face, head, ear, eye, mouth*, etc., all common nouns. Making sense out of nonsense can be sound grammatical analysis.

Analysis of expressions can also be constructed as a game. There can be sentence completion games like Scrabble, e.g., "Who can add on the next word?" There can be bingo games, e.g., "Do you have a word on your card which would fit in this slot?" There can be games like 20 Questions in which students could construct their own "slot-and-filler" tests to determine the identity of a secret part of speech. And there can be open kinds of creative games to see who can construct the longest meaningful sentence from a given group of words.

Analytical procedures of some kind for highlighting the relationships of part to whole can be applied to any level of composition. They help determine which differences make a difference. As the children progressively differentiate their constructions, so too discriminations can be made from the more conspicuous and obvious to the more subtle and refined. While some analytical activities may require no more than a token pointing response from the child, others may have the child construct highly involving responses that are sensitive to a wide range of stimuli and rich in feedback.

The records of progress in such skills may be in the form of simple categorical checklists or frequency counts over time. Checklists are useful for indicating the current level of a child's ability in these skills. Frequency counts are sensitive to slight changes in the child's performance—its speed and accuracy—which are useful in diagnosing the more effective instructional conditions. In the production of a complete expression, however, there are often so many components that the teacher may be undecided as to which alternative to choose as an indicator of progress. This problem can be easily resolved by simply picking one and then seeing how well it serves the purpose. Observing the child's progress and responding to its context can determine the adjustments that are to be made.

Providing conspicuous feedback on progress. One way to ensure conspicuous feedback on progress in any aspect of writing is to use varied and frequent record-keeping. Activities in the classroom can be designed so that they increase the likelihood of feedback and record-keeping. Cumulative charts can reflect progress in the formation of letters, words, and phrases. They might simply reflect the quantity produced or the stages in a sequence of developing complexity. For example, the total number of letters written might be recorded for each day, or a check might be placed beside each letter that the child learns to reproduce accurately. Anything that can be explicitly identified and counted can be used. Any activity that results in a visible product is easy to count and record. Enduring visible expressions lend themselves to record-keeping by their very nature.

The child's work provides a record in itself. A note indicating the number accomplished or the percent correct can be attached to the work and kept in a cumulative folder for periodic survey and recording. A summary of developmental changes can be made by listing any differences in quantity, forms, or other details between one production and another.

Children can make collections of their own work in alphabet books, word books, wish books, or story books of their own making. They can also construct their own instructional aids, which are a record in themselves. They can make their own books and their own dictionaries, adding words and pages as they learn.

When feasible, a class newspaper makes for an excellent collection of children's work over time. The high visibility of the writing and the many copies available are advantages in securing feedback from a variety of sources. Students can produce their own newspaper if they have access to a typewriter or can write directly onto ditto masters. Ideas for creative writing with the news can be found in *Teaching with Newspapers*, a newsletter published by the American Newspaper Publishers Association Foundation.

Games are another convenient method of record-keeping. Scores in games can be kept. Children can also make their own games. They can make a spinner or die, a game board, or cards. On the game board, they can make a path with bonuses and penalties. They can then pick up a card from the appropriate deck (decks can be substituted to make the game easier or more difficult, or the child may choose to select a card from a deck of his or her own choice). The deck can contain high and low valued cards. Some may give the child extra moves. The child may need to produce a match from his or her own card collection, or from a letter, a word, or a phrase in order to move ahead.

Peer tutoring activities tend to have on-going feedback built into them. And one child can easily do the recording for the other, exchanging roles as it becomes convenient. Children can also be seated in arrangements that encourage pair interaction, e.g., sitting at the corners of tables, or chaired in pairs. Study buddies can build on the informal feedback they naturally provide one another to where they help chart and record each other's progress. The informal comments that children make on each other's work can be recorded and collected. This can be particularly helpful for creative work which is difficult to analyze.

Increasing opportunities in which children will seek feedback. It is not enough to just have feedback available on the different aspects of writing. Children must also *want* to receive it. They will seek feedback when it results in pleasant experiences. They will avoid it when it results in unpleasant experiences. The unpleasant experiences of many people with writing can be traced to practices like the heavily red-marked pencilings on their papers that list all their faults and shortcomings with little notice paid to accomplishments or improvements. Students soon learn that avoiding writing also avoids red pencil marks. The red pencil mark has become virtually synonymous with negative feedback that points out errors, but typically with little indication of what would be better.

Consider the unfortunate history of Linda's experience with early writing (8). It is a classic example of the results from "red penciling" a beginner's early efforts. An early draft of hers reads:

> Spring is here
> and I like it
> it flowers all over

The repetition of "it" run onto the last line creates a perhaps accidental but nevertheless vivid and creative image by making "flowers" an active verb. Her teacher, however, did not attend to this "happy accident" but to the "mistakes." For example, the teacher put periods at the end of each line, crossed out the second "it," capitalized "flowers," and inserted an "are" between "flowers" and "all," making "flowers" a noun instead of a verb. The teacher's written comment was, "Please finish. You have a good beginning." The third-grade teacher's red markings through this and eight other drafts are reproduced by Suhor. The markings are used to indicate, as red pencil markings traditionally do, what was wrong. It may be suspected here and elsewhere that developing a set for "what is wrong" may lead to seeing frequent and sometimes questionable instances of "what is wrong." Linda's final draft reads:

> Spring is here I
> like it Flowers
> are all over, around me.
> They snell
> so mice.

The end-result is scarcely an improvement over the original. The drafts by Linda showed her frustration, e.g., in her peripheral markings on the paper, in her ignoring of the feedback. The teacher, similarly unreinforced, also lapses into ignoring "mistakes." Two people have learned to avoid interacting with one another. Both the production and the reading of the writing have become an unpleasant task, something to be avoided in the future.

This is a sad tale. Unfortunately, it seems to have been repeated over and over again, in one way or another, in many a classroom.

Many of us have learned to have strong aversive reactions to the whole notion of evaluating writing because of the association with the red-penciled corrections that came back to us. We have been shaped into perceiving evaluations and conspicuous comments on our writing as aversive. It is rather curious, isn't it, how the eagerness of a young child to show everything he or she writes is so often matched by the reluctance of the adult to show anything he or she has written.

In order to be sought for and used, conspicuous feedback needs to be reinforcing. There must be ample positive reinforcement in the attention and comments given to writing. Good things must happen afterwards. If the consequences make it easier for the child to be successful in attaining valued goals, if they make it easier for the child to see how he or she is doing and to make improvements, then the child will seek and use those consequences. Evaluations can take a very favorable and sought for connotation when they are linked to positive consequences.

Giving positive feedback on what was successful gives the child a foundation upon which the child can build, and it increases the writing productivity of children. Further self-management advantages follow when the child can request the feedback as the child needs it. In the beginning, feedback to the child on what the child does right is more informative and useful than feedback on what the child does wrong (since there are just so many more ways in which a beginner falls short of the expert). As the child becomes more aware of the conditions under which he or she can receive different kinds of feedback, the child can develop increasing self-management skills in selecting one condition more than another and in selecting one kind of feedback more than another.

Occasions for Instruction

The frequency of situations for writing can be increased by having more and briefer moments for writing with shorter written responses required, e.g., exchanging notes in class, writing short comments, short poems, labels, and brief descriptions. It is important for these occasions to be followed by reinforcing consequences if they are to increase. One way to make reinforcing consequences more likely is to make the consequences more conspicuous, e.g., talking about them, posting them, decorating them, etc.

The opportunities for writing can be made pervasive throughout the curriculum, e.g., in the areas of math, science, health, social studies, expressive arts, as well as in language arts. These occasions can be increased further by increasing the students' own control over arranging their environmental circumstances for writing opportunities, e.g., forming writing groups, science projects, editing newspapers, journals, booklets, etc., on all topics across all areas of the curriculum.

The environmental conditions that support these occasions are a variety of resources in the physical setting, cooperative interaction and complex problem-solving tasks, and extensive feedback. (1) Resources that include paper, pencil, pen, typewriters, space for writing centers, both individual and group centers, people, peers, tiles of print, typesetting materials, walls for writing, areas for posting writing, time for writing when the student chooses to write, etc., contribute to increasing the occasions for writing. (2) A verbal community is an essential ingredient in language development and effective communication. The writer can be provided with a verbal community that the writer can be effective with when social interaction is basically cooperative, helpful, highly interactive, with students working together on writing projects, editing and commenting on each other's works, reciprocally exchanging roles of reader and writer, directing specific comments, suggesting particular areas of confusion, possible alternatives, personal private responses, etc. Higher-level complex problem-solving tasks require the student to examine alternatives before discovering a resolution. The student may be presented with problems to be resolved: research problems, ecological problems, human relations problems, personal problems. The student may generate his or her own problems for resolving. Learning to define the problem carefully, articulate alternatives, choose a reasonable resolution, discuss the points of interest, and summarize the entire paper contributes to increasing skills and providing opportunities for varied, interesting, and meaningful issues on which to write. (3) Feedback that refers to individual progress, that shows collections of works, that is specific to a particular part of the writing, that makes consequences conspicuous (in individual, small-group, and large-group conditions), and that builds on previous work can increase the likelihood of further writing with increasing differentiation and sophistication.

Three major categories of writing situations are writing for responses, writing stories, and writing throughout the curriculum. One of the most elementary functions of writing is to write in order to produce a response. Producing stories has long intrigued adult and child. And writing throughout the curriculum optimizes the natural classroom setting for learning the functional effects of writing.

Writing for responses. Writing that increases the likelihood of a response by others gives the child feedback to learn from as well as consequences to reinforce him or her. Some writing leads naturally into being followed by a response which shows how the writing was understood. If we write a recipe, as with cooking, we can sample the product. We can see if the directions are followed. Written requests and commands have a similar consequence.

Children can be encouraged to write notes to each other in class, exchanging messages among themselves and the teacher. With a few guidelines, frequent notewriting is a good practice to encourage, not only to show to others but also as a reminder list for the writer. Children can write notes, cards, and letters to their friends outside of class. They can compose a group postcard or greeting card. They might write a giant greeting card to their school cook, expressing what they liked about the cooking and await what responses occur.

If it is easier or more interesting, children can write their messages in telegraphic style, sending themselves and their friends telegrams. Words may be cut for them to paste on. At first, they might copy complete sentences. Then they may be given slots in sentences for which they are to select the words to complete the telegram. Later, they can construct their own complete telegrams, perhaps in groups at first, then singly.

In the beginning, children may write rather blunt messages for a response that appear as commands or orders (and there are appropriate conditions for encouraging this). Later they might write direct questions and requests. Eventually, they will learn the conditions under which a request is most effectively phrased one way or the other. They can learn how a descriptive statement, e.g., "I am hungry," may be more effective in producing a response than a direct request, e.g., "Give me something to eat," as well as learning when a direct question is more effective. Increasing sophistication and skill in using language to produce a response will be acquired if children have frequent opportunities to engage in a wide variety of such writing for responses and if they receive frequent feedback on the effectiveness of their requests or instructions. When the classroom climate encourages children to write informally like this, the children may begin to create their own ideas. In one kindergarten, for example, the children began spontaneously to write down each other's orders for food while playing the roles of waiters and waitresses.

Writing stories. Descriptive writing is easily begun with stories that are dictated or briefly jotted down under a picture. Such writing may be very open in terms of expression and may be thought of as embodying the essence of creative writing, leading so easily to novelty and wonder. But stories also have patterns and variations that permit novelty and wonder to occur. There is a beginning, a middle, and an ending to every story. And there is a beginning, a middle, and an ending to every writing of a story.

1. Story Starters: Prewriting conditions set the stage for writing by giving children something to respond to. Some imaginative visual effects, for example, may be created with an overhead projector. The shapes formed by colored water or oil on a transparent surface can be flashed on the screen and shifted about to background music while the imagination creates an interpretation. The darkened setting and the focused light help to create a dramatic, theater-like atmosphere. The children can then record what they have seen or thought. One of these ideas can be used to write a story.

A more specific stimulus can be provided by having the children listen to or watch a story. The story itself may be produced by the children. In a "shadow theater," cut-outs may represent characters in a story. Using an overhead projector and a transparent sheet, the shadow outlines can be projected against the sheet. Like puppets, they can be moved about and different objects can be introduced, e.g., a house, a tree, or an airplane (9). Much can be left to the imagination and to the subsequent writing by the children.

Stimulus support that involves children in vividly imaginative activities may contribute to a high degree of interest and the generation of meaningful responses in which the children are eager to receive feedback. Block play and picture drawing can provide immediate and on-going concrete support for a story about what the child produced. Storytelling, fantasies, and creative dramatics can also be deliberately designed as story starters. Children can be read a story or a fantasy for them to imagine and respond to with limited movement (10). Additional details may involve the use of music and movement and longer sequences of events, e.g., the life cycle of the butterfly, and dramatization of songs, stories, and poems with beginnings, middles, and endings (11). Use can also be made of comics and myths (12).

Preparation for involvement in a highly visual display can be a source of motivating stimulation in itself. Children can pool their collective resources, interacting with one another, in making a story mural that stretches around the room, hallway, or school-yard. The mural can involve a map of "our town" with illustrations and a sequence of events described and depicted in following the path from one child's house to another. Seasons may change. Individual stories may be told. Past events may be re-enacted. Details may be added, forming a collage effect in places. Little narrative balloons can be expanded beneath the pictures. Additional descriptive details and explanations can be continually added to this "story starter." Mezey (13) gives suggestions for resolving the practical problems of more ambitious murals.

Another way to get children started is to provide them with a story pattern as a guide. Variations on the pattern may be as simple as changing a word or as complex as taking the point of view of the wolf in "Little Red Riding Hood." They may rewrite a favorite story like "Goldilocks and the Three Bears," "The Three Little Pigs," or "Snow White." They may imagine themselves as a character in the story or change the ending. Story line lead-in's may be written on strips of paper to get things started, e.g., "Once upon a time . . .," "If I had a wish, I would like . . .," "I was walking along when suddenly I saw . . .," etc.

2. Story Development: In the beginning, the child can act out his or her stories or use three-dimensional objects like blocks and toys to express his or her representations. Much of children's play is a kind of story making. They can play with and arrange blocks, dolls, and cars freely and creatively. In moving to two-dimensional expressions on a surface, children can rearrange and restructure the objects on a surface to produce their own variations and reintegrations of objects and events.

Figure 13 illustrates a collection of "picture words" that children might use in constructing visible expressions. Children could be allowed to collect them as tokens or "mixes" that indicate progress in their accomplishments (14). They could be encouraged to play with them and to see what they could do with them. What is another way of putting them together? In one expression, a picture may have one meaning. In another expression, that same picture may have a different meaning. For example, the word for *hilltop* may be formed from a picture that could mean *hill* or *mountain* in combination with a picture that could mean *on* or *top*. Articles and verb agreement inflections may be given separate picture symbols or simply be implicit in the arrangement of the "picture" words. Distinctions can be added as needed. Children can invent their own signs. Various card games could be played with them. Children could match two or three of a kind in similar sound or meaning. They could construct a series of short sentences. They could see what substitutions or additions they could make to other children's "hands." Colors and animal figures can enhance the attractiveness of the signs and help in the transition to abstract symbols. *The Peabody Rebus Reading Program* illustrates one way of commercially packaging "picture words" that lead to more abstract, symbolic words in language expression. *Let's Do Some Cooking* illustrates the use of picture

Figure 13.   A collection of "picture words."

words for following directions and producing something to eat (15). The direct, concrete involvement in using picture words for cooking is highly motivating for even very young children.

Children can produce stories with symbolic writing by dictating them and having stories displayed on large sheets of paper hanging from the classroom walls or collected into booklets. It is difficult to imagine a more useful early learning experience than for children to collect their work in booklets and to construct story booklets of their own. Not only is this a record which provides opportunities for feedback to the child on his or her progress, but these booklets can also be used as learning materials themselves. An exceptionally wide variety of skills can be integrated when a meaningful story is produced by children. They may then illustrate the story, act it out on their own or with puppets, reread sections of it with others, and discuss it.

An easy way to introduce the production of story booklets by children at an early age is to have them take turns dictating the parts of the story. Each child's dictated part then appears on a separate page with that child's illustration for the part that child dictated. Children may first be given background information about authors and how books are written. Then, as a demonstration for the entire group, all the children may be led through the procedure for telling a story, each child telling a part, the next child picking up where the other child leaves off. Then the children can be divided into small groups for producing their story booklets. This time, as each child tells his or her part of the tale, it can be recorded on tape or notes can be made. The children are told to remember what they said and to draw a picture for their part of the story. The teacher or aide then writes down what the child said beneath the child's illustration. These pages are then stapled together in the story line sequence, and the covers are decorated by the authors (16).

These booklets may be used to develop a child's awareness of the different components of stories, e.g., one child tells about the main character, another the goal, another the obstacle, and another the result. And they can also be used to lead the child into producing story booklets all by himself or herself. Children may later examine in more detail the formula patterns of the fairy tale, the adventure story, the mystery, the soap opera, etc. They may be given an abbreviated "skeleton" of a story to fill in. They can construct variations of patterns on these formulas and invent their own story lines in a progressive development from one story project to the next (17).

The continued production of booklets can actually be used in all of the curriculum areas, math, science, social studies, and art, both as group and individual activities. These booklets can then become part of the classroom's permanent resources. They can become sources for learning facts and concepts and for making further revisions. All of these booklets would be rich sources for learning about words and their relationships, their spelling, and their meaning.

Any story booklet, or other kind of booklet, can be developed through progressive stages. Gradual expansions, deletions, and editing can be incorporated along the way, from the first rough outline to the final published version embellished with cut-out pictures, book covers, and advertising blurbs. Publication may run into copies of different editions and into the class anthology. The publication enterprise itself may be one the children learn to perform for themselves, doing their own writing directly onto ditto masters for reproduction, their own editing, and so forth. The history of notes and revisions on the conception and production of the story may even be kept in the child's own personal journal.

At any one stage, the child may deal with wholes with more or less stimulus support from the context of the activity in which the child is working. Drawing on immediate and previous personal experiences, children can dictate stories as a group or individually. The personal experience story might be a simple "me" self-portrait or a series of "me" self-portraits, showing what the child did next, what happened to the child next. Details may be added and labeled as desired. Stories may involve the child, the child's family, or the community in which the child lives with personal accounts of events the child has experienced or imagined.

The first stories produced by a child may be a single picture or a series of pictures without words. Words may be added later by dictation or by the child's own labeling, with cut-out letters or the child's own handwriting. The child's picture book may be a narrative of likes and dislikes, wishes, the things the child wants to do, and the things the child does not want to do. Some of the items in the series may be described with a terse comment. Others may be described more elaborately. The common theme holds them together.

More organized stories can develop around the child, the child's family, or perhaps a fantasy, e.g., "If I were . . . ." The child may be stimulated to imitate another tale he or she has heard, perhaps a scary tale about a monster where the monster is afraid of a child. The stories can be organized as little novels or plays, e.g., "The Adventures of . . . ." Other children can help act out the different roles of the child's story. The child who wrote the story may be the director and selector of the cast. Another child or teacher may narrate the story aloud while the cast acts out their roles. Hats or costumes can be used to embellish the roles (18). Sound effects, music, and dance may be added. The story can be rehearsed and done again with the children rotating their roles.

The story form may even be a vehicle for introducing letters within a context of images of sights and sounds. Stories can be made up about the letters. After exposure to letters and words in a full and meaningful context, the child may then use them in other meaningful expressions. As Coleman and Morton point out, "There may be fundamental biological reasons for starting at the top, for having the child extract meaning from the very beginning" (19).

3. Story Endings: In a broad sense, the ending to a story may be considered to be whatever completes its meaning. Skill in doing this may be developed through pictorial as well as symbolic expression. A picture may be presented with something left out to complete a meaning that is implicitly or explicitly asked of the scene. There may be a picture of a crowd of people without an indication of what they are doing. Revealing captions or clues in the picture can be cut out. The children can be asked to express their own captions or explanations for what is happening in order to "complete the story." There are several levels of description

that may be involved here: "In any picture, there are several different levels of description: what is shown, what is going on, what has happened, what is about to happen" (20). Alternative endings can be discussed, considered, and selected. Newspaper pictures or illustrations from a book may be used. As a learning experience, however, the writing of a story is never complete without the follow-up and feedback from readers of the story.

Writing throughout the curriculum. Writing is not an activity to be confined to particular periods of the school day under a collective label of language arts. It makes as little sense to restrict writing in this way as it would be to restrict speaking. Writing skills in math, science, social studies, and expressive arts, for example, need be no less sophisticated than those in language arts periods. And the opportunities offered by those other subject areas may be considered as essential to the development of effective writing. In writing, it helps to have a subject matter to discuss. And it helps to have meaningful uses for what we write about. The organizational features of the British Infant School serve as one example for centering the curriculum around writing:

> The integrated day is characterized by project themes which are integrated with regular curricular subjects. Mathematics, language arts, science, and social studies are taught within the framework of various unifying themes. Based on student interests, they are often chosen by individual teachers or by the faculty of a small school together. The generality of an overall theme allows for the development of individual pupil interests and for varying ability levels.
>
> An integrated day program, by its very existence, requires writing to become a part of the children's total learning and living experience. Writing in an integrated classroom is not something to be done on Thursday afternoons when all academic work is completed. Writing *is* the physical work to be completed, and in order to accomplish it, the other intellectual work of reading, thinking, and doing will also be done.
>
> Vertical grouping facilitates growth in writing ability. Older children help beginners with their writing. (21)

Part of the argument here is that if writing is taken care of, then much of the other curricular concerns will be taken care of also.

Math: Mathematical concepts can be expressed through the use of token counters, visual hand signs like those in the finger counting methods of Chisanbop, and symbolic marks. Communication through mathematical symbols shares common similarities with other sophisticated visible languages in the abstract nature of its elements and its many levels of organization. Teaching mathematics through graphing is especially appropriate for developing relationships with other language skills. The horizontal and vertical axes must be labeled. The scale must be identified, as well as what the recorded events were and when they occurred. The discussion and interpretation of these charts provide further language-related activities in meaningful situations.

Science: In science, descriptions are written for all sorts of observations. Some of these observations may be from a recent field trip. Others may be directly from a present on-going event. Children, like scientists, can write and collect descriptions of the ecological world around them, about geology, the weather, plants, animals, and the food they eat. Children can list different features by which they sort out buttons, rocks, leaves, plants, animals, human behavior, and anything else they might collect and sort. Later on, the collections of their recorded observations can document the growth and development of plants, animals, and behavioral skills over time.

Nutrition, as an example, may be addressed in a simple fashion in the beginning and then move on to more complex writing skills. Writing on nutrition can involve the classification and grouping of foods the children are familiar with and have had personal experience with, as well as less familiar foods. Children can sample a food, experience how it looks, feels, smells, tastes, sounds (Is it crunchy?), and write about it. Later on, writing simple food recipes can include all the basics of scientific report writing.

The basic descriptive principles can be applied to descriptions of how to do carpentry work, how to work with animals (how to feed the goldfish), plants (how to water them), machines (how to start them), electricity, magnetism, math, measurement, etc. From examples like these, children can learn to generate their own list of basic questions. What is it? What are its parts? What are its properties? How does it work? What happens when . . .? Did it float? How do you explain that? What other questions do you have? A child can also learn to answer these questions, in short terse statements at first, then later in more elaborate detail.

In many ways, the language used in scientific endeavors reflects the language of everyday use in a close connection to the natural world. Skills in observing, classifying, measuring, communicating, inferring, organizing, predicting, and evaluating are valued in both scientific endeavors and in everyday language use (22). As early as 1893, Joseph Rice observed "by far the best reading in the schools in which the pupils were taught to read through science lessons, and by far the best—not infrequently incredibly good—results in written language where the children began to express the results of their observations in their own words in writing, as early as the fifth or sixth month of school life" (23).

The most natural way of learning about language and its uses may be to begin with the uses of language in science and science-like endeavors where children can see the close relationships between symbolic words and concrete contexts. There the children can directly see the differences between *in/out, open/ close, top/bottom, before/after, more/less, hot/cold, wet/dry, soft/hard, white/black*, etc. Increasing skill in introducing the background for a problem, describing the procedures of an investigation, listing and organizing the data, and discussing and evaluating the outcomes can be indefinitely refined and applied to any subject area.

Social Studies: Children can describe their personal thoughts and feelings. They can narrate their fantasies, tell what they like and do not like, and say what their wishes are. This process can help clarify their private events and thinking about things. By so doing, children's values may be clarified as well as the goals they wish to work for in life.

In interaction with other children, they can write about behaviors they identified, their consequences, and the conditions when they occurred. They can write about who did what to whom. They can write about how they felt when this happened. They can check and clarify their perceptions with others, discussing, paraphrasing, restating, and writing them down for inter-observer agreement.

Children can write interviews with a friend in class, a member of their family, someone they know in the community, or someone they have never met before. They may write up the interview as a group. They can compare notes and their agreement as to what was said and how to express it. Showing the written interview to the person interviewed provides another opportunity to check on its accuracy. Even subtle shifts in meaning and emphasis can be brought out then. The relationships between spoken and written language can be highlighted in a context that provides feedback on how well one form of communication can express another. The relationship between what people say and what they mean can also be brought out as the writer seeks to make what the writer heard comprehensible and the person interviewed re-expresses his or her original thoughts.

The interviews can be structured so as to encourage short or long responses covering familiar or unfamiliar topics. "What is your favorite food?" "How do you prevent accidents?" As with any other learning task, the beginning stages can be simply constructed. At first, there may be little more than a recording of a one-word dictation with a picture. Later, more and more alternatives and complexities can be allowed.

Expressive Arts: There are various ways for bringing writing into the other expressive arts. Plays and musicals may incorporate all forms of writing, movement, and music, whether with puppets or costumed students. Letterforms may even be used as a graphic designer would use them to teach art basics (24). Examples may be printed initials on planes of a box, trail writing on construction paper with flowers and paste, a central initial surrounded by objects that start with that letter, calligrams (shaped writing), a hissing cat made of *S*'s, a collage of *B*'s to form a bee, distortions and variations, personalized wild flower letters, etc. Free form arrangements of words may similarly be used.

Words that are expressed to music or used to form visual effects beyond their symbolic reference move close to the realm of poetry. Where the line is drawn will be somewhat arbitrary, but practicing poets will typically grant themselves more freedom of expression than the models of poetry typically taught in the classroom. Koch (25) even recommends against rhyming lines because this is too confining and restrictive for children. He suggests some constraints to get children started, but he tries to use ones that permit easy variations. For example, every line should contain a color, a comic-strip character, and a city or country; every line begins with "I wish . . ."; strange comparisons, something big to something small; question games, "How does a bee go? What sounds like a bee but doesn't mean anything like buzz?"; a strangely composed object; "I used to . . . but now I . . ."; or some other similar constraint.

Playing with letters, words, and phrases is invaluable for developing a creative attitude in exploring alternatives. Insisting on restrictive, standardized ways of writing letters, words, and phrases directly inhibits creativity. Children acquire an entirely different attitude toward written expression when they find out it is something they can play with and use to suit all sorts of purposes instead of being merely a set of standardized forms to which they must mold their expressions.

SUMMARY

Creative writing and any new development of complete written expressions can be increased by increasing the variety of writing behaviors that may be considered as creative, by increasing the consequences for this writing, and by increasing the occasions, situations, or opportunities for this writing. These aspects of variety, consequences, and occasions can be considered in each of the traditional areas of curriculum, evaluation, and instruction. This perspective leads toward a dramatic "freeing up" and generation of complete and creative expressions that can follow a natural and orderly evolution in the development of each child's abilities.

REFERENCES

1. Hall, M. *Teaching reading as a language experience* (2nd ed.).

Columbus, Ohio: Merrill, 1976. Lee, D.M., and Allen, R.V. *Learning to read through experience* (2nd ed.). New York: Appleton-Century-Crofts, 1963. Stauffer, R.G. *The language-experience approach to the teaching of reading.* New York: Harper and Row, 1970.

2. Moffett, J., and Wagner, B.J. *Student-centered language arts and reading, k-13: A handbook for teachers* (2nd ed.). Boston: Houghton Mifflin, 1976. Moss, J. A general language arts program in an informal classroom. *The Elementary School Journal*, January 1975, *75*(4), pp. 238-250.

3. Goodnow, J. *Children drawing.* Cambridge, Mass.: Harvard University Press, 1977. Harris, D.B. *Children's drawings as measures of intellectual maturity: A revision and extension of the Goodenough draw-a-man test.* New York: Harcourt, Brace, and World, 1963. Kellogg, R. *Analyzing children's art.* Palo Alto, Calif.: Mayfield, 1970. Lee, L. *Developmental sentence analysis: A grammatical assessment procedure for speech and language clinicians.* Evanston, Ill.: Northwestern University Press, 1974.

4. Ames, L. Children's stories. *Genetic Psychology Monographs*, May 1966, *73*(2), pp. 337-396. Bergold, S. Children's growth of competence in storytelling. *Language Arts*, September 1976, *53*(6), pp. 658-662. Burrows, A.T., Jackson, D.C., and Saunders, D.O. *They all want to write: Written English in the elementary school* (3rd ed.). New York: Holt, Rinehart, and Winston, 1964. Clegg, A.B. (Ed.) *The excitement of writing.* New York: Shocken, 1972. Gardner, H. *The arts and human development.* New York: John Wiley and Sons, 1973.

5. Greene, F. An opin and cloze case. Paper presented at the meeting of the North Central Reading Association Nineteenth Annual Conference, Ann Arbor, Michigan, October 1976.

6. Patten, D. Using student-student feedback to improve information sending. *The Reading Specialist*, Spring-Summer 1975, *11*(3), pp. 22-23.

7. Eddy, T. Personal communication, 1976. Thiagarajan, S. Monstrously teaching concept teaching. *Simulation/Gaming/News*, January 1973, *1*(5), pp. 10-12.

8. Suhor, C. Linda's rewrite. *Learning*, August/September 1975, *4*(1), pp. 20-25.

9. Moxley, T. Personal communication, 1976.

10. de Mille, R. *Put your mother on the ceiling: Children's imaginative games.* New York: Viking, 1973.

11. Adams, D. The great honey swamp and peanut butter lake: Imaginative creative dramatics activities. *Learning,* February 1976, *4*(6), pp. 28-33. Chambers, D.W. *Storytelling and creative drama.* Dubuque, Iowa: Wm. C. Brown, 1970.

12. Kohl, H. Comics and myths. *Teacher,* November 1974, *92*(3), pp. 6-12.

13. Mezey, P. Mural making. *Learning,* May/June 1976, *4*(9), pp. 12-17.

14. Sacks, A.S., Moxley, R.A., and Walls, R.T. Increasing social interaction of preschool children with "mixies." *Psychology in the Schools,* January 1975, *12*(1), pp. 74-79. Walls, R.T., Moxley, R.A., and Gulkas, S.P. Collection preferences of children. *Child Development,* September 1975, *46*(3), pp. 783-785.

15. Rodgers, F.A., and Larson, K.A. *Let's do some cooking.* Champaign, Ill.: Continuing Education Publication Co., 1977. Woodcock, R.W., Clark, C.R., and Davies, C.O. *The Peabody rebus reading program: Teacher's guide.* Circle Pines, Minn.: American Guidance Service, 1969.

16. Pinkney, S. Personal communication, 1980.

17. Cawelti, J.G. *Adventure, mystery, and romance: Formula stories as art and popular culture.* Chicago: University of Chicago Press, 1976. Propp, V. *Morphology of the folktale: Bibliographical and special series of the American folklore society* (Vol. 9). Philadelphia: American Folklore Society, 1958.

18. Davis, M. Personal communication, 1973.

19. Coleman, E.B., and Morton, C.E. A modest plan to raise the national intelligence. *Educational Technology,* September 1976, *16*(9), p. 9. Hitchcock, F. Amy ape ate apples. *Grade Teacher,* October 1971, *89*(2), pp. 61-63.

20. de Bono, E. *Lateral thinking: Creativity step by step.* New York: Harper and Row, 1970.

21. Davis, F.R.A. Writing development in some British infant schools. *Young Children,* March 1977, *32*(3), p. 60.

22. Barufaldi, J.P., and Swift, J.W. Children learning to read

should experience science. *The Reading Teacher*, January 1977, *30*(4), pp. 388-393.

23. Rice, J.M. *The public school system of the United States* (1893). New York: Arno Press and The New York Times, 1969, p. 25.

24. Walklin, C. Letters, art, and children. *Visible Language*, Winter 1977, *11*(1), pp. 53-62.

25. Koch, K. *Wishes, lies, and dreams: Teaching children to write poetry*. New York: Random House, 1970.

Chapter IV

Spelling

We consider feats of spelling any spoken word quickly and correctly without any help to be extraordinary. Our culture bestows local and national honors on those who win "spelling bees." Writing words that are spelled correctly is often considered the hallmark of an educated person. If we marvel at the ability of those who can accomplish such a difficult task, we might also marvel at why spelling should be so difficult. Considering the alternatives that are available for producing visible words, there are many easier ways to form words than the traditional "spelling test" approach.

BACKGROUND

A traditional way of teaching spelling has relied on the test-setting in which the teacher dictates words to a group of children from word lists in spellers. The child writes down the word without help. The child must rely on how well he or she has memorized the spelling, on how well he or she can guess at the sound-to-print relationships, and (presumably) his or her knowledge of spelling rules. The pupil's response is either correct or incorrect, typically without partial credit for those letters that are correct or for those letters that are possible variants of the sound stimulus. Approximations do not count. The outline of this test-activity may be described as follows:

Typical Classroom Spelling Tests

1.0. Intention: To produce words with standard spelling when needed.
2.0. Performance: The student writes out words in standard spelling.

105

3.0. Conditions:
    3.1. Words are selected by the teacher from the spelling book.
    3.2. Words are dictated orally by the teacher.
    3.3. One isolated word is written down after another by the student.
    3.4. Frequently with an earlier opportunity to memorize the word and the rules of spelling.
    3.5. Without access to a dictionary or other resource aid.
    3.6. The entire class responds under a set time limit for everyone.
    3.7. Without credit for coming close.
    3.8. Often without a chance to respell the word after feedback.

Like a manufactured part, one word is to follow another at a set rate, with a penalty for defective parts. The student is expected to learn how to spell from repeated exposure to this test-activity. Interestingly enough, this way of learning how to produce words is confined to the classroom.

The production of written words *outside the classroom* proceeds in quite a different fashion, which may be outlined as follows:

Typical Word Production Outside of School

1.0. Intention: To produce words with standard spelling when needed.
2.0. Performance: Words are produced by dictation and typing as well as by handwriting.
3.0. Conditions:
    3.1. Words are self-selected.
    3.2. The words responded to are more often seen than heard.
    3.3. The words are typically produced in the context of other words that form meaningful texts.
    3.4. There is frequent reliance on visual memory and on writing the word down and seeing how it looks.

3.5. A dictionary or another person may often be consulted.

3.6. The production of words is self-paced.

3.7. Coming close to standard spelling makes a difference in producing less uncertainty and distraction for the reader.

3.8. There is frequent opportunity to respond to how the word looks and to make changes. Proofreading may continue indefinitely.

The task of producing written words is less restrictive for the adult outside the classroom than for the pupil inside the classroom. The adult has more options. The adult has several sources of control to respond to in producing a word, but the student is left to be controlled by the voice of the teacher, the form memorized, and the rules of spelling.

It would seem that a more appropriate educational approach would make skill in word production easier and more common instead of preserving it as a rare talent. When we consider the primary function spelling serves in producing written words for sentences, some alternatives to the formal traditional approach are worth considering.

APPLICATION

Alternative Behaviors for Producing Written Words

There are a variety of ways for producing words and a variety of conditions under which they may be produced. Words may be produced by selecting from words already formed, e.g., words (or logographs) printed on strips of paper. They may also be produced by combining parts of multi-syllable words with picture words of one syllable, e.g., the many varieties of rebus forms (1). And they may be produced by arranging letters already formed, e.g., tiles and type. In none of this is the ability to write by hand a prerequisite. Handwriting as a skill is largely irrelevant to spelling. However, if it is required, then the complexity of the task of handwriting becomes an additional difficulty on top of the task of spelling. Even if handwriting is required, there are still ways to make spelling easier. See Figure 14.

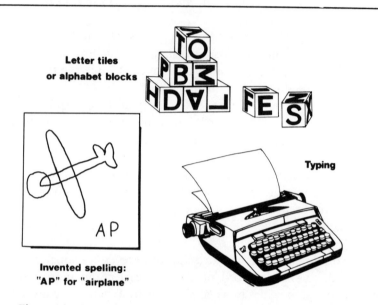

Letter tiles or alphabet blocks

Typing

Invented spelling: "AP" for "airplane"

Figure 14. Some ways it is easier for children to produce words.

Letters in tiles and typewriters. Variations of alphabet blocks and Montessori tiles have long been used by young children of many cultures. With letters printed on their surface, these blocks and squares can be freely manipulated by children to produce a variety of arrangements. The typewriter introduces a constraint on the order and spacing of printed letters so that only a firm touch by the child is needed to produce a string of letters one after the other. With a typewriter, the child's word formation skills can be largely independent of the fine motor coordination involved in handwriting.

In an age where typewriters, hand calculators, and computer terminals are ever more commonplace, keyboard literacy allows children to make use of powerful tools for communication. When these instruments are available, there are ways to design learning programs so that advantages can be taken of these instruments for learning about visible language. Some fairly detailed guidelines to using typewriters in the classroom with young children are available and indicated below. These guidelines provide recommendations ranging from detailed directions in the mechanics of typing to the organization of school-wide typing programs across the entire curriculum.

Among studies in the educational literature, the research on the use of typewriters is strikingly consistent in reporting favorable results in a multitude of studies since the turn of the century. A two-volume report on the Elementary School Typewriter Investigation, which was conducted during 1929-1931, is one of the earliest and largest studies of the use of the typewriter in the classroom (2). This study involved nearly fifteen thousand pupils and over four hundred teachers during the first year. About 6,000 children from kindergarten through the sixth grade constituted the experimental group, which used portable typewriters provided in a proportion of roughly one machine to three children. The typewriters were used for arithmetic, social studies, science, and art as well as for reading, spelling, and composition. The two volumes are singularly rich in concrete examples of what the children produced on the typewriter, all of which was collected and saved. The authors of the study wrote a favorable summary of the benefits from using typewriters:

> The study as a whole presents strong evidence (1) that it is feasible to use the typewriter in the conduct of the ordinary work in the elementary school, (2) that the use of the typewriter in the informal fashion in which it was employed in this study produces an average typing speed approximately equal to the average handwriting rate in each grade, and also yields a very considerable degree of typing accuracy at the end of one year's use, (3) that the use of the typewriter stimulates elementary school pupils to produce more written material than they would otherwise produce, (4) that the classroom typewriter, as used in this experiment, entails no loss in handwriting quality or handwriting rate, (5) that it very probably raises in some measure the level of achievement in some of the fundamental school subjects, without observable loss in any subject, and finally (6) that the teachers regard the typewriter as a valuable educational instrument and approve its use in their own classes, while the pupils enjoy typewriting and look upon the typewriter with marked favor. (3)

Even before electric portables, the high productivity in producing words turns out to be a theme that continues to run throughout much of the literature in using typewriters.

Subsequent studies have found new uses and new benefits from using the typewriter even with young children: "A little girl of five happily pecks away at a specially designed automated typewriter and composes a poem. A two-and-a-half-year-old teaches herself to read and write by banging the jam-proof keys of a similar 'talking typewriter'" (4). The Talking Typewriter, developed by O.K. Moore, is an elaboration of the standard typewriter with colored keys, a small speaker, a display on which printed matter can be seen with a red pointer, a projector resembling a miniature TV screen, and dictation equipment. One of the things this machine does is to name aloud the letter or punctuation mark of whatever key the child presses. The machine can also lock all the keys except the one for the letter pointed to by the red arrow. When the child presses the matching key, the voice names it again. Later, the child may be shown a series of letters which must be pressed in the correct sequence for the keys to be unlocked. One day the child suddenly realizes that the letters determine words. "Overwhelmed by the revelation, he [or she] is likely to run out of the booth ecstatically—a reaction the Lab has witnessed over and over again" (5).

A conventional electric typewriter instead of a Talking Typewriter has been successfully used in a subsequent adaptation of Moore's approach: "At the New Nursery School in Greeley, Colorado, three- and four-year-old disadvantaged children typed words and stories. Some of their achievement can be attributed to the fact that they spend up to 20 minutes daily playing in a special environment booth with an electric typewriter, a Language Master, and tape recorder" (6). The booths were modeled after Moore's but used the conventional electric typewriter to reduce the cost. Before entering a booth, the child's fingernails were painted to match the colors of the typewriter keys. The child learned the accepted fingering system by hitting the colored key with a finger of the matching color. The children progressed through four stages: (1) free exploration, (2) search and match, (3) typing words, and (4) writing a story. In free exploration, the child plays with the typewriter while the booth assistant tells the child what the child is doing and the typewriter shows the child what the child has done. The "game" in search and match is for the child to find the letter on the keyboard that matches the one on the chart and strike it. For typing words, the procedure is to ask the child what word the child would like to type, then print it on a card, tape record it, and let the child type it. When the child knows 15 to 20 words, the child is ready to write a story, which is first dictated and recorded; then it is later typed by the child.

Innovative programs have also used conventional typewriters with little other supplementary equipment than instructional booklets. The Flanders programs (7), for example, use a behavioral-based analysis of the skills required to achieve mastery in learning how to type and in learning how to read through typing. The tasks are broken down into small steps, self-paced, with immediate feedback, systematic practice, and recapitulation. *Di*rect *co*mparison (Dico) is made by typing directly underneath the stimulus print, which shows errors immediately. The child begins by learning how many words can be made with the letters *a* and *s*. When a new letter is added, it is combined with previously learned letters to form *fat, fit, let, lit, rat, sat, set*. After 11 letters have been introduced, little phrases and sentences are typed. Both booklets are available through Smith-Corona.

From 1904-1963 some 900 studies or reports were done on research in typewriting (8). The results of these and subsequent studies (9) consistently report advantages to using the typewriter with rather minimal negative findings. One of the areas reported to benefit most from the use of the typewriter is spelling. Despite this overwhelming accumulation of empirical data, the use of the typewriter has tended to be ignored until high school and then limited to specialized formal skills in typing speed and accuracy. It is especially curious that many school practices and programs (including expensive ones) continue to exist with far less (if any) empirical support, while so well-researched and useful a tool as the typewriter continues to be neglected.

A striking exception is the public school system in Hawaii:

"Typewriting stations with one machine for 30 children are provided in the nongraded K-3 classes throughout the state" (10). Although learning to type was a voluntary activity, a survey made during 1968-1969 disclosed that 91 percent of the children chose to learn to type. When asked during individual interviews why they like typewriting, most children replied, "Because I can do it!"

One of the reasons given for the early use of the typewriter was "To support the development of the child's reading ability." Several advantages were listed for having instruction in typewriting precede instruction in reading:

> Whereas some language specialists theorize that reading serves as an introduction to writing, a further step suggests typewriting before reading so that children receive an introduction to print through print. Children in this program have demonstrated that they are able to develop a fair amount of typing skill using correct fingering before they begin to read. The child masters many pre-reading skills through the automatic operation of the typewriter, such as the left-to-right progression of letters . . . the visual discrimination process of letter recognition is separate from the often confusing, audiovisual recognition process. . . . Young children, ages 5-7, sometimes type for an hour or two, getting much relevant practice in paying close attention to differences among letters, syllables, and words. An advantage of using the typewriter is that the child gets immediate visible feedback from what he [or she] has typed. (11)

Other reasons for early use of the typewriter included motivating a child in learning to use the graphic symbols of our language; offering a faster and more legible method than handwriting for producing stories, songs, poems, and letters; supporting the development of handwriting ability through improved finger dexterity and muscle and eye coordination; and helping the child become an independent learner through self-evaluation when the child compares his or her own typed copy with that in the text.

Data from two preference surveys reported by Oksendahl revealed that typewriting was the children's favorite language activity. Parents reported that their children preferred typing to all other language skills activities. This often meant taking their children to school early so that they could type before school started, since the machine in the classroom was constantly in use during the language arts period. The children also retained high enthusiasm for tutoring others in how to type. Children would happily copy stories, songs, and poems at the typewriter, using correct fingering, while as yet unable to read. Typewriting was also used for publishing the children's own newspaper. In an ungraded K-3 class with six typewriters for 21 children, five-year-olds, according to the teacher, would dictate their stories to those who had completed the key location exercises.

One electric typewriter per five children was recommended for an individualized classroom permitting children free access to a machine throughout the day, or in a learning center, or in a typewriting laboratory. Tryouts indicated that primary children do not really need any larger type than pica size, ten spaces per inch. Although other experiments had utilized the larger "primer" type, which has six spaces per inch, with heavy classroom usage this typeface eroded within a year. Both the SCM 250 and the IBM Selectric proved to be successful with young children.

The use of a typewriter vividly illustrates what can happen when children are freed from dependency on handwritten letters. Instead of having their responses tied up in the fine motor control required to form letters of the proper size, shape, and slant, children can now respond directly to the task of forming words with letters. Their responses can be more strongly controlled by the word formation task itself.

Special aids to forming words the way they sound. Another approach to letter selection is to change the writing symbols into a more direct transcription of English pronunciation through a modified alphabet like Pitman's Initial Teaching Alphabet (i.t.a.) or some diacritical marking system such as dictionaries use. SRA's DISTAR alphabet uses joined letters, bar lines over long vowels, and a minimal amount of changes from standard letter shapes in providing a unique sound for each symbol. This allows children to write readable writing early and to be encouraged to write more than they would with the standard alphabet. Later, they make the transition to spelling in standard English orthography. While there is evidence that this transition can be made successfully (12), the evidence to date is somewhat inconclusive as to what advantages are retained for children who first learn through a phonetic system and then make the transition. The use of such a system, of course, does not need to exclude traditional orthography. Diacritical marking keys can be written under texts written in traditional orthography, and children may be permitted to use mixtures of phonetic and standard symbols in their writing.

In an analysis of research on transitional writing systems, Gillooly drew some interesting interpretations on the role of phonographic and orthographic relations in the acquisition of reading skills. There seems to be a change in the reading responses from the beginner to the accomplished reader that is tied to attending to ever-larger information-bearing units for more efficient information processing. Writing systems which stress orthographic relations may be more attuned to the later responses. Eventually, experienced readers seem to learn how not to be limited by these writing system differences:

> In the beginning stage (grade one), children using a writing system employing more simple and direct grapheme-phoneme correspondence than ours (that is, writing systems such as German or the *initial teaching alphabet*) have an advantage in terms of word recognition skills. However, the advantage is not sufficient to increase their reading comprehension.
>
> At intermediate levels of reading skill (grades four and six), an advantage in terms of reading speed with no loss in comprehension was found to emerge in favor of our traditional English orthography.
>
> Finally, at advanced levels of reading (from college on), no differences in either eye movements or reading speed have been found among those using widely different writing systems. (13)

As an aid to reading, a writing system in a language with direct grapheme-phoneme correspondence need not have any advantage over our traditional English writing system for the skilled reader.

Any particular advantage of special alphabets with grapheme-phoneme correspondence may actually lie more in the ease with which children can select letters to produce words. Anything they say, they can write down in a form that can be recognized by those familiar with the special alphabet. This increased productivity in forming words may justify the use of special alphabets or alphabetic markings.

Invented spelling. When the traditional English alphabet is used, children may be allowed to develop their spelling skills in natural stages. Given the opportunity, children will invent spellings in a systematic development of stages that have their own regularity: (1) writing the first letter for each word or syllable, e.g., *TB* for *toybox*; (2) adding the final letter or phoneme of the word or syllable, e.g., *HL* for *hill, RT* for *rabbit, WZ* for *was*; (3) separating short vowel sounds from surrounding consonants, e.g., *DORRDY WOTAR* for *dirty water*; and (4) digraphs like *sh*, *ch*, and *th* appear and spelling moves closer to the standard forms (14).

In this development, children seem to explore alternative constructions of spellings. Gradually, the generalized and inter-changeable productions become more differentiated. "When the children wanted to spell a short vowel sound, they seemed to give the vowels that were formed similarly in the mouth equal value and to use them interchangeably as a sort of marker" (15). The children seldom invent the same spelling twice, but they easily substitute standard spellings later. These early word formations can be made with type, plastic letters, blocks, tiles, or pencil for notes children write or for labeling their drawings. In these early stages, children seem primarily interested in the expression or production of writing, showing disinterest or difficulty at first in reading what they write (16).

Even after the child has acquired the ability to produce standardized spelling, he or she may be deliberately encouraged to create new and innovative communication with alternative spelling inventions, e.g., *Decembrrr, v-cancy, Sun Kist* (17). Inventions that successfully communicate a relevant meaning are hardly likely to be haphazard. They would reflect, in fact, a more thorough understanding of phonographic and orthographic relationships in word formation. Simply producing a standardized spelling need reflect no more than memorized recall. Like word reading or word calling, it need not reflect any substantial comprehension of the English word formation system and its relationship to sound and meaning. Goodman (18) has shown that an analysis of how observed oral reading responses differ from expected oral reading responses can provide insight into the child's understanding of what he or she is reading. Similarly, spelling deviations, like reading deviations, can provide insight into the child's understanding of word formation which can be used for later instruction. Interestingly enough, the deviations *must* occur in order to obtain this information.

In order to respond to and make use of the visual information in a written word, children should be encouraged to write down an alternative spelling. This would facilitate the child's use of orthographic information in conjunction with phonographic information (which is insufficient by itself):

> The data and theory give no encouragement to the idea that pupils should learn sophisticated rules for phoneme transcription. Most of their errors cannot be corrected by phonemic information. Instead, what is largely lacking is sufficient visual information about spelling—either in the form of direct associations or in the form of recognition information—to filter out the errors caused by phonetic ambiguity.
>
> Perhaps the most valuable phonetic experience for pupils would be experience in generating possible *alternative* transcriptions for testing by recognition. This experience can be given without requiring pupils to learn complex systems of rules, since what is wanted are *lists* for each phoneme, and not unique transcriptions . . . . spelling will only be learned if sufficient visual information is also available. . . . It may be effective to make students explicitly aware of the generate-and-test technique for spelling and to encourage them to try out alternatives rather than to arrive immediately at the "one correct spelling." (19)

Indeed, adults typically write down alternative ways for spelling words they are unsure of. Or, they may try to imagine the word as a visual printed image in order to see it first before they write it. The sequence here is revealing: first, produce a word formation, constructing it as an explicitly written form on paper or as a mental image; then read and select the form to be used.

Unfortunately, traditional spelling instruction in schools has placed so much emphasis on producing correct spellings in one step that it may be difficult for some people to even entertain the notion of encouraging or allowing alternative spellings at any stage of development. Printed manuscripts of a few centuries ago, however, showed much less concern for regularized spelling, with different spellings occurring for the same word on the same page. The early portfolios of Shakespeare are not models of spelling consistency. Why then insist that children must begin at the last stage of the process toward standardization?

Filling in the missing letter. A simple spelling exercise for developing sound-to-print relationships is to fill in the missing letter of a word that the child hears pronounced. The child is shown a word with a letter missing, e.g., _ip, _at, b_t, sl_d, fla_, ca_, and is asked to indicate or produce the letter for the word he or she hears pronounced. This can be presented and handled as a typical spelling exercise as well as in other ways. It could be played as a bingo game with some key sounds, e.g., vowels, already printed on bingo cards. One student could pronounce known words and sentences aloud while the other children covered an appropriate letter on their bingo cards for representing that sound. This analysis of sound to print is initially more meaningful than trying to analyze from print to sound. It would provide some information about print to sound as well as exact information about sound to print. It can also be used for minimally meaningful discriminations, e.g., *bit/bet*. The choices for the child to consider can be so few that if the child does make a mistake, the child knows what the right way must be: e.g., tell the child to point to *i* or *e* when you say "bet." Since the child is quickly acquiring skills in selecting alternative letters for a sound, the child can apply this directly to looking up words in a dictionary. A related variation might use "maze" spelling, e.g., *b/c a t, p/c o t, b i/e t, t a/o p*, and have the child cross out the incorrect letter. These spellings could be contained within a meaningful sentence or paragraph. Such an activity has advantages over having the children respell the entire word they hear pronounced in that it is easier for the children to be successful and easier for the teacher to control what is being learned. It also provides accurate diagnostic information to the teacher and precise feedback to the children on their progress.

Consequences

The consequences of spelling that follow from the proofreading, publication, distribution, reading, and discussion of a school newspaper may not require any particular intervention. Good instruction designs for activities with natural consequences like this to occur. However, natural consequences often need to be arranged and to be augmented with a record system in order to make their effects more conspicuous.

Having children collect what they produce is a simple way of increasing consequences. Children can be encouraged to "sign" their drawings, to label them, and to identify or write about what they have drawn. They can do the same for pictures they cut out and paste. And they can collect what they produce. They can collect their own production of names for their favorite food, for animals, for parts of the body, for wishes, or for anything else that interests them. These collections, which may be kept in a folder, made into a booklet, or listed on a chart, provide their own feedback on the child's progress in forming words. See Figure 15.

Self-correcting feedback may be introduced for the child to make use of as the child needs. Letter cards may be coded on the back to reveal their proper combination for a word: a picture of a car, for example, may be drawn across the back of all three cards with a letter for *c, a,* and *r* on the front of each separate card. When the letter cards are in the proper order, the parts of the pictures on the back fit together. After selecting a letter to complete the word, the child can check on the back. Such codes, of course, have to be formed for each separate word.

Various forms of feedback through public display of a child's works, to stickers that record achievements, to charts that the child makes of his or her own progress can be built into the learning situation until the child can be successful and comfortable in his or her spelling achievements. The more this feedback is in harmony with the consequences for spelling that a child finds outside the classroom, the more useful the child should find what he or she learns.

Occasions for Instruction

Every item in the room is an opportunity for a sign or a label. Any experience or event can serve as an opportunity to construct a word. There is no want of potential opportunities for spelling

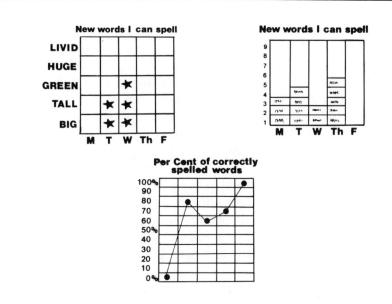

Figure 15. Spelling records.

words, but the occasions must still be provided. The following illustrates some occasions for the word formation behaviors described earlier.

Tiles and type. Providing children with time at the typewriter gives them the opportunity to arrange letters easily and rapidly. Once the child selects a letter on the keyboard with his or her finger, the machine automatically takes over the task of placing the letter in the next space on the paper. By using colored fingernails to match their fingers with the colors on the keys for proper fingering, even young children can learn to discriminate letters, to match them, and to copy them. They can learn to type up dictation, from another student or from a tape recorder. They can learn to produce master copies for duplication and for a class newspaper. When the equipment is available, children can learn to use computer keyboards and even to write computer programs that would provide them with precise feedback on the accuracy of their communication. A high output of word production with a high rate of reactions to those words produces a rich, enduring, and evolving source of feedback on children's spelling.

There are also more simple ways of producing symbols mechanically. A rotating letter wheel, for example, can be constructed out of cardboard circles of different sizes with letters written along their perimeter. The wheels can be fastened together at their center so as to allow one or more wheels to be turned. The wheels can then be turned to line up a desired display of letters highlighted by some device, a straight edge or a window frame attached to the center. Two wheels of letters might be held constant while a third wheel is turned to form different words, e.g., *pan, can, tan, man.* One wheel might have a middle vowel and a final consonant printed together so that only an outer wheel needs to be turned to form words, thus simplifying the choices even more. Different wheels might be designed for different purposes. The children can copy a given letter pattern for a word, or they could arrange and rearrange letters. If they ask, "Is this a word?," the teacher or another child can respond. If they ask, "How can I make this word?," they can be shown.

Letter cards, letter blocks, or letter stamps with ink pads can be used in many game-like variations to produce letter arrangements: e.g., searching for pairs of letters, three of a kind, three in a row; copying a word; or making up a word. These games could be played as a form of "Fish," "Rummy," or some simplified "Scrabble." Vowels and consonants may be color coded for easier placement identification. The rules of the game determine which letters or combinations of letters shall be allowed to count as "words."

Aids for transcribing sounds. Once out of the classroom, adults typically have access to resources—someone they can ask or a dictionary—to help them spell the words they have chosen to use in their own writing. Why not then allow children to develop proofreading skills for their own writing and have access to resources like a dictionary, a written one or a human "talking dictionary" who would give them the information needed on request? (20) Even if it is determined that the child has to learn to spell words from memory, the word can be of the child's own choosing, which the child may collect and accumulate on word cards at the child's own rate of progress. These cards then become a resource for the child to consult and use.

Various other guides and references can be provided for the child's assistance on request. The teacher or another child can respond to the request "How do you spell . . .?" The answer may simply be written on the chalkboard. Transitional writing systems or diacritical marking systems can be made available for the children to consult in some convenient reference format, e.g., a chart on the wall or a list on a sheet of paper. The children need only a few aids to construct a few words and only a few more letter aids to construct a few sentences. The children can write in a phonographic script, e.g., using i.t.a. or diacritical markings, or they might write in their own mixture of traditional orthography and transitional script, inventing their own script just as they can invent their own spelling. They could even construct their own mini-dictionary on a theme, e.g., Halloween. They can illustrate it and record the regular spellings and the sound transcriptions side by side.

Invented spelling. Using the typewriter, letter stamps, or their own handwriting, children can quickly begin to invent spellings. At first, children may only copy the initial to their name, but they can quickly put this skill to use in writing the identification for their places, seats, desks, mailboxes, messages, attendance, and whatever they produce. They can learn to use initials for other words. Then they may learn to write the first and last letters for their name and other words. Eventually they will learn to fill in the missing letters and that there are standard spellings for words.

If there is a high degree of interaction between the children's invented spellings and feedback from others, they can be expected to progress faster through the stages toward standard spelling. Frequent writing, frequent displays of writing, and frequent encouragement of comments on each other's writing provide children with the opportunity to learn more about alternatives. One child may ask, "What does that say?" Another child may say, "I write it like this."

Filling in the missing part. A programmed approach to spelling by Smith and Steslicki (21) focuses on making the parts of a spelling word visually prominent. First, the student must circle the letters of the word in sequence from rows of jumbled letters. Then the student circles the syllables in sequence from rows of jumbled syllable clusters. Then the student must write the word in a backward chaining fashion, first filling in the last part of the word, then the next to last plus the last part, and so on; e.g., for *etcetera* this might be *etceter_*, *etcet____*, *etc_____*, _____. This method is especially recommended for troublesome words that a student continually misspells.

Instruction can also be designed at an early level in order for children to learn how to match visual stimuli to the sounds they hear. Children may begin by matching pictures to comparatively gross discriminations, e.g., animal sounds. They may also match one picture to another picture that begins with the same sound. Then they can look for pictures that have the same rhyme. In matching a word to a picture, the task at first may focus on the beginning sound discrimination. Given the picture of a car and the word written with the first letter missing (e.g., _ar), does the child produce *jar* or *car* as a match? The child can then move on to filling in letters for other parts in words.

While the focus on individual subskills of word formation can be pursued in many ways, it is important to keep the context of subskills paramount. Since the primary function of word formation occurs within complete texts, the foremost instructional objective is for children to spell within complete texts that they produce. This means using the production of complete texts as opportunities for learning to spell. The primary occasions for learning to spell should be within complete and meaningful expressions.

SUMMARY

Children could be shown how to produce words much more easily than they are often allowed. Setting a criterion of spelling performance that requires correct spelling in one step for all children effectively delays productivity in writing. Insisting that the letters be formed by hand also delays progress in writing. Prohibiting the use of resources that would ordinarily be available outside the classroom increases the difficulty still further. Restricting spelling tasks to memorizing inadequate rules and unfamiliar word lists tightens the constraints on opportunities to develop writing skills even more. There are many alternative ways for forming words. Children can learn to use the typewriter, the dictionary, and many other ways for increasing their production of written words. Instead of being mired in mechanical problems of writing, which they can often never resolve, children can continue with the business of expressing themselves effectively in complete texts. Instead of word formation being an obstacle to writing more, it can become an aid for writing more.

REFERENCES

1. Rozin, P., and Gleitman, L.R. The structure and acquisition of reading II: The reading process and the acquisition of the alphabetic principle. In A.S. Reber and D.L. Scarborough (Eds.), *Toward a psychology of reading: The proceedings of the CUNY conference*. Hillsdale, N.J.: Erlbaum, 1977, pp. 55-141. Woodcock, R.W., Clark, C.R., and Davies, C.O. *The Peabody rebus reading program: Teacher's guide*. Circle Pines, Minn.: American Guidance Service, 1969.

2. Haefner, R. *The typewriter in the primary and intermediate grades: A basic educational instrument for younger children*. New York: Macmillan, 1932. Wood, B.D., and Freeman, F.N. *An experimental study of the educational influences of the typewriter in the elementary school classroom*. New York: Macmillan, 1932.

3. Wood, B.D., and Freeman, F.N. *An experimental study of the educational influences of the typewriter in the elementary classroom*. New York: Macmillan, 1932, p. 184.

4. Pines, M. How three-year-olds teach themselves to read—and love it. *Harper's Magazine*, May 1963, 226(1356), p. 58.

5. Pines, M. How three-year-olds teach themselves to read—and love it. *Harper's Magazine*, May 1963, 226(1356), p. 59.

6. Nimnicht, G. Low-cost typewriter approach helps preschoolers type words and stories. *Nation's Schools*, December 1967, *80*(60), p. 34.

7. Flanders, R.G. *Instant touch typing with the new dico system*. Eltham, London: Dico Education International, 1973. Flanders, R.G. *Type to read with the new dico system*. Eltham, London: Dico Education International, 1974.

8. Rahe, H. The research in typewriting. *Business Education Forum*, October 1964, *19*(1), pp. 17 and 23.

9. Oksendahl, W.J. Keyboard literacy for Hawaii's primary children. *Educational Horizons*, 1972, *51*, pp. 20-27. Sinks, T.A., and Thurston, J.F. Effects of typing on school achievement in elementary grades. *Educational Leadership Research Supplement*, January 1972, *5*(2), pp. 344-348.

10. Oksendahl, W.J. Keyboard literacy for Hawaii's primary children. *Educational Horizons*, 1972, *51*, p. 21.

11. Oksendahl, W.J. Keyboard literacy for Hawaii's primary children. *Educational Horizons*, 1972, *51*, p. 22.

12. Downing, J. The Bullock commission's judgment of i.t.a. *The Reading Teacher*, January 1976, *29*(4), pp. 379-382. Mazurkiewicz, A.J. ITA and TO reading achievement when methodology is controlled—extended into second grade. *The Reading Teacher*, May 1967, *20*(8), pp. 726-729.

13. Gillooly, W.B. The influence of writing-system characteristics on learning to read. *Reading Research Quarterly*, Winter 1973, *8*(2), pp. 167-199.

14. Paul, R. Invented spelling in kindergarten. *Young Children*, March 1976, *31*(3), pp. 195-200.

15. Paul, R. Invented spelling in kindergarten. *Young Children*, March 1976, *31*(3), p. 199.

16. Chomsky, C. Write first, read later. *Childhood Education*, March 1971, *47*(6), pp. 296-299.

17. Nilsen, D.L.F. The right to write wrong. *Language Arts*, September 1976, *53*(6), pp. 670-672.

18. Goodman, K.S. Analysis of oral reading miscues: Applied psycholinguistics. In F. Smith (Ed.), *Psycholinguistics and reading*. New York: Holt, Rinehart, and Winston, 1973, pp. 158-176.

19. Simon, D.P., and Simon, H.A. Alternative uses of phonemic information in spelling. *Review of Educational Research*, Winter 1973, *43*(1), pp. 115-137.

20. Rudman, M.K. Spelling flunks the test. *Learning*, August-September 1974, *3*(1), pp. 67-68. Wilhelm, R. Improving writing with a talking dictionary. *The Reading Specialist*, Summer 1972, *9*(6), pp. 12-16. Wilhelm, R., and King, W.A. *An exercise to improve the quantity and quality of writing: The writing dictionary*. Ann Arbor, Mich.: Office of Instructional Services, School of Education, The University of Michigan, 1976.

21. Smith, D.E.P., and Steslicki, J.X. *Programmed spelling for high school and college*. Ann Arbor, Mich.: Ann Arbor Publishers, 1967.

Chapter V

Handwriting

At the turn of the century, many people in both industry and education were enamored with following the "one best way" for doing things. This often meant bringing responses under the narrow control of a set of rules for efficient, standardized performance. It is easy to see the appealing simplicity of this method in handwriting, where every student's response was to be controlled by the rules for the one best way to form a letter by hand.

When pupils are simply to conform to the one best way, there is no need for them to be brought under the functional consequences for determining how one way is better than another. They do not need to respond to the consequences of which way is easier, more legible, and more attractive for themselves personally and for others. They need only produce a structure in conformity to the rules. In handwriting, these rules have provided almost ritualistic details on the correct slant, the correct sequence, the correct paper, the correct writing instrument, the correct grip, the correct posture, etc. Handwriting is then "all too often . . . a drill act requiring all children to make letters in *a* particular way" (1).

BACKGROUND

Presumably the justification for *a* particular way to write lies in simplifying the complexity of the writing task for pupil and teacher. The issue lies in how well the "one best way" succeeds in this. The complexity of letter formation as a task for the young child is greater than might first appear to the adult who automatically produces letters without conscious attention to how he or she will do it. The ideas that "logically" come to the adult's mind for simplifying and teaching this automatically are not necessarily well suited to the developing child.

Task Complexity

The demands in producing a letter far exceed those of discriminating one of the 26 letters of the alphabet from another. To recognize a letter, a child needs only to attend to the distinctive features that distinguish one letter from another letter (e.g., straight/curved, open/closed, horizontal/vertical). However, "to compose (produce) an 'A,' one must know not only how it differs from 'B' and the rest, but also how it differs from everything else. Thus, passage to a composition task automatically raises one's sights: to greater 'breadth'; to 'descriptive' adequacy; and possibly to greater 'depth'" (2).

The inexperienced child who must construct a letter on his or her own, using pencil and paper, is undertaking a task of substantial complexity. The child is continually faced with major and minor decisions on direction changes, continuations, junctions, intersections, etc., that will determine the legibility, proportion, and harmony of the result. The child must continually ask himself or herself (covertly or overtly), "Which way shall I make it? Which way shall I turn it?" (3)

The orientation of letters written by children illustrates the difficulty that can exist in selecting one of two alternative directions. Even children who have mastered considerable skills in letter formation will commonly reverse a letter. Depending on circumstances, both children and adults may reverse the sequence of letters as well. This is more commonly found in manuscript rather than in cursive writing by children and in typewriting rather than in handwriting by adults. The problem with orientation and sequencing, especially left-right and mirror image alternatives, seems to depend on how our environment and how we ourselves are constructed (4). There is a wide range of differences in the signals and consequences provided by our environment. Gravity, for example, signals up and down but not left and right. Two-dimensional pictures cannot be turned around or looked at from behind as three-dimensional objects can. Our body has bilateral symmetry. We have two cerebral hemispheres in our brain with similar, differing, and complementary capabilities. By the nature of our environment and ourselves, some things are easier to learn than others.

Even if we examine some of the simpler letter forms that children are not likely to reverse, the complexities are surprising. Even more surprising, perhaps, are the different strategies that children use to cope with this complexity. Take a "T" form, for example. The task of copying such a form and the strategies used by children to construct it have been analyzed in the following manner. The "T" form is composed of two line segments in specific directions, one common point bisecting one of the lines, and a 90 degree angle between the two lines. When both direction and order of movements are taken into account, there are 48 different ways to draw a T-form. The strategies used by 30 nursery school children to copy an inverted "T" fell into categories which differed in their degree of complexity:

> The modal strategy of the youngest group was to draw the inverted T with three separate movements, starting with the vertical and drawing the two horizontal sections as departures from the common junction. The medium age group selected a modal strategy of starting with the horizontal line and drawing the vertical from the junction up. Only in the oldest age group did some children evince the "adult" pattern, namely not starting the second line from the junction. These three strategies form a scale of amount of stored information required for the selection of the starting point (zero, one, and two stored dimensions). (5)

A second study with 173 children from kindergarten through sixth grade further supported the finding that, with increased age, children prefer increasingly complex combinational structures. This is consistent with the view that, when a skill is initially brought under control, there is a tendency to minimize the degrees of freedom controlled at a given instant (6). Mastery of a skill is characterized by simultaneous control over increasing degrees of freedom, dimensions, or alternatives.

There are definite implications here for the development of children's skills in forming letters. The easiest method for a beginner to use may not be the most attractive method for an expert who has mastered the skill. If we, as adults who have mastered skills in letter formation, seek to have children duplicate the strategies that we ourselves follow in performing the task, we may be making the task unnecessarily complex for the inexperienced child. Furthermore, no one strategy may be the best strategy for all children. The complexity of the task (the conscious alternatives that need to be kept in mind) depends upon the development of the child and the skills the child has already learned. The individual differences may be considerable.

Problems in Following the One Best Sequence

Many guides to handwriting recommend that all the parts of a letter be formed in the same sequence and that all the parts of letters be formed by strokes that move in the same direction. The usual recommendation for lines is to make strokes that move from top to bottom and left to right: "As children transfer this activity to paper, some supervision is necessary to establish certain habits. All lines are made from top to bottom and left to right. All circles are started at the two o'clock position or where one would start to make the letter *c* and move toward the left" (7). This is not necessarily the easiest way for any particular child to form any particular letter.

Consider the letter *N*. If the downstroke is consistently followed, the pencil must be lifted from the paper in order to produce the letter. The decision of where to lift the pencil from the paper and where to put it down again adds more complexity to the task than there would be if the pencil could remain on the paper. Reversals of the letter *N* are common when the letter is formed by downstroking the first line. It is often easier then to move diagonally up to the right and then down again, thus forming a reversal (as lettered signs all over the country can show). If all the strokes must move from top to bottom and left to right, then the child must lift his or her pencil twice and decide where to put it down before deciding which direction to go. These decisions can be removed from the process of forming the letter *N* if the child begins the first line with an upward stroke, then a diagonal downward to the right, and then upward again. The child must decide where to stop and which direction to go, but the child does not have to decide where to replace the pencil, since the child does not need to remove it from the paper. Indeed, beginning the *N* with an upstroke is a recommended procedure for reducing the reversal of the letter *N* (8). Consistency in downstroking thus comes at the cost of increasing complexity for some letter formations.

Requiring invariant consistency suggests that the determination of sequences may depend more on what seems easier for the teacher to do than on what is easier for the children. Group-paced directions that are given to all children at the same time will be simpler if all the children are to form the letters in the same way and if the directions are similar for all the letters. This may make the initial giving of directions easier, but it is hardly a saving in the long run if it leads to more time and effort by both child and teacher to assure that a child forms legible letters easily.

At one time, some handwriting rules may have had a more practical reason than they do now. For example, recommending downstroking makes sense with copperplate pens that were dipped in inkwells because they were likely to catch on the paper and splatter ink on the upstroke. But when was the last time you saw a child write with a copperplate pen that the child dipped into an inkwell? The handwriting rules have not changed even though the children's writing instruments have. This is one of the problems to expect when all the attention is focused on simply following the rules of handwriting. These rules become increasingly inappropriate as environmental conditions change.

Even if a sound rationale should be developed for recommending a new set of handwriting rules today, children should still be allowed flexibility over time to follow this sequence in full or in part. If you examine the variety of handwriting techniques used by adults who were presumably taught a uniform method as children, you might wonder whether it is possible to prevent natural variations from occurring anyway. In the final analysis, it is the final handwritten product that matters rather than the sequence in which the handwriting is produced. The natural consequences of ease, legibility, and attractiveness can determine the letter structure and the sequence in which that letter structure is formed.

APPLICATION

Some Variations of Handwriting Responses

Most children in schools today first learn to write in manuscript letters, and then learn to write in cursive in the second or third grades. Early studies that supported the use of manuscript writing for beginning letter formation found that children learned to read print more effectively if they learned to write print-like letters. Children who were taught to print showed greater advancement in reading and printed language skills than children who were taught in cursive (9). Several studies have also found that children and adults write about as fast in manuscript as their peers do in cursive and that it does not seem to make much difference when the transition is made (10). Some people have questioned then whether there is any need to make the transition at all and have recommended teaching children to write only in manuscript. Other people, however, believe that the continuous and rhythmical movements of cursive writing have inherent advantages, such as making it easier to avoid reversals, and recommend that children be taught only to write in cursive.

D'Nealian handwriting. Some lettering experts in England have called for a new method of handwriting that fits modern pens, suggesting that both the way in which letters are formed and the way in which the pen is gripped should be modified (11). A recent innovation in handwriting in the United States, called D'Nealian Handwriting, addresses itself to some of these concerns with the problems of traditional handwriting. D'Nealian reduces the gap between manuscript and cursive writing by making the formation of letters in both scripts more similar. The most striking change is in the formation of manuscript letters. The directions for forming these letters are designed to reduce the need for children to lift their writing instruments from the paper and to decide where to start again. It is also designed so that the stroke which completes

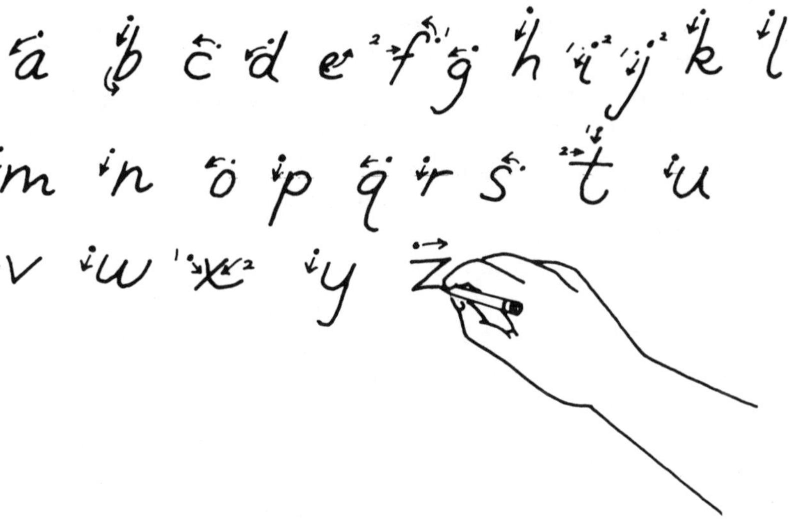

Figure 16. D'Nealian letter forms for manuscript reduce the number of separate strokes for handwriting.

one letter can be easily connected to the stroke that begins another letter when the time comes for children to write in cursive (see Figure 16). The D'Nealian method also encourages a flexible evaluation of handwriting: "Since handwriting develops into such a mark of individuality, it is fruitless for teachers and children to spend endless hours trying to emulate a machine-perfect handwriting model. A child's self-image can suffer when his or her handwriting—however legible—is criticized for minor deviation from a perfect model. How much more encouraging for children to be praised for fine efforts within a wider range of legibility" (12). In these and other ways, the D'Nealian approach appears more adapted to modern pens and the needs of children than traditional handwriting programs.

Teachers who have used the D'Nealian method have reported a surprising lack of reversals in the children's manuscript writing. This lack of reversals holds true even for the confusing letters *b* and *d*, which are formed with dramatically different motor movements in D'Nealian. The *b* begins with a downstroke and then a circular upward movement to the right and down again. The *d* begins with a downward circular movement to the left that turns into an upstroke and then a downstroke with a "tail" at the end. In this way, the beginning, middle, and ending differences in making *b* and *d* in D'Nealian are much greater than the differences in making a "stick" and "ball" to one side or the other.

Letter parts. A strikingly different approach, which replaces "handwriting" in forming letters, is one used by Renee Fuller, who by her own account did not learn to read until she was 12 years old. In developing a reading program for children classified as retarded, she used basic elements of letters with which children could build letters themselves: "Using three basic forms—a line, a circle, and an angle—one can make all the letters of the alphabet. Even a two-year-old can build letters this way. To make the figures stand out clearly, I gave each a different color; to make them amusing, I gave them fun names. The circle became a ball, the line a stick, and the angle a bird. With these three basic forms children can build letters themselves. Thus, the student has tactile and kinesthetic feedback as he [or she] learns" (13). Different lengths of lines and sizes of "oblong" circles are used, with U-shaped parts of circles for open curves. Another way to do this is to use solid shapes of squares, triangles, and circles with borders highlighted so that they can be fitted together to form letters. In using such a method, the basic forms may be constructed for the child out of any convenient material: wooden blocks, cardboard, vinyl, etc.

A child can "trace" a letter simply by covering the pattern of a letter with the letter parts that will "match" it. The child can "copy" a letter by placing a similar combination alongside. Later, the child might do this from memory in response to hearing the letter name or sound. The child could even vocalize the distinctive features of the letter parts as he or she placed them together to form a letter.

Invented handwriting. A study by McCarthy (14) illustrates what happens when a young child learns to write letters outside the classroom. Sarah began to teach herself at the age of two and one-half years. Assistance given Sarah included writing the letter she requested so she could copy it and later giving her oral cues on the distinctive features of the letter, i.e., circle, line, loop, and angle.

The first letter that Sarah wrote was *Q*, which she requested that someone draw for her after viewing the presentation of the letter *Q* on *Sesame Street.* The letter *O* developed from the letter *Q* when she discovered the similarity after writing hundreds of *Q* letters. She then created notes and letters consisting of a series of *O*'s and *Q*'s which were read as words. A month later she became interested in *A* which she made with an open curve bisected in the middle. All these beginning shapes contained a circle with a line distinguishing one circle from another.

Three months after she learned the letter *O*, Sarah learned *T, H, I, E, L*, and *i*, all composed of straight and vertical lines. The letter *E*, which was made with one vertical line and two to seven horizontal lines was the only one that continuously varied in shape. The next group she learned was *R, B, P, D, m*, and *n*, which all contained a loop and a straight line. Angle letters, *K, W, X, M, N, A*, and *V*, were the last to be learned. The letter *A* was then formed with two diagonal lines and a horizontal. The incorporation of angle lines as a distinctive feature resulted in some confusion with writing *U*, which was sometimes written as *V*.

The letter *S* in Sarah's name was also difficult for her, although she was highly motivated to write it. Since she would make straight or backward starts herself, she asked someone to start it for her. While a tracing session helped her to do the letter on her own, within a few weeks she was unable to write it as well as she had after the tracing activity and eventually returned to backward starts.

Tracing and copying aids to handwriting. The research is somewhat ambiguous on the independent benefits of tracing and copying. Even though the research fails to show there are advantages to spending time in tracing before copying, it is hard to tell how much a particular child would have benefited if that child had more experience or a different kind of experience in one method rather than another. Although direct copying methods are often fairly similar, tracing methods may vary considerably, especially tracing methods that lead to direct copying by gradually fading out stimulus support. This makes it difficult to generalize across all types of tracing methods. Tracing is generally easier than copying. Most children can do a tracing task before they can do a copying task. The decision of when and how to use tracing or copying can be left to the child or to the teacher or to a combination of interactive decision-making. It is common for programs in developing letter or symbol formation with young children to use some sequenced combination of tracing and copying, with relatively more or less emphasis on one aspect or the other.

Hertzberg (15) compared four methods of learning to write: (1) groove tracing, sandpaper outline tracing, and finger tracing; (2) tracing over transparent paper; (3) copying directly from a model; and (4) a combination of the above. The first method using tactile groove stimulus support was least effective. The third method using direct copying was most effective, even though many children showed considerable difficulty with their first efforts and were not as initially interested as those using tracing paper. The tracing method with transparent paper seemed to produce an irregular series of short "shaky" strokes. Hertzberg suggested that children might more profitably begin to learn writing skills by direct copying of simple shapes.

However, there are many other ways of providing stimulus support cues or prompts for aiding children. And some methods of using cues in providing a matrix grid or a fading out of a dotted outline seem to be more confusing than others. The children may respond to the cues in ways that the designers of the method had not foreseen, showing that they were not able to make use of the cues as the designers intended. The extent to which some arrangements of stimulus cues may assist children in their handwriting still remains to be determined.

Tracing over an underlying form has an advantage in that the child can quickly see how well he or she is covering it and can modify his or her movements according to the feedback; however, the child is dependent on seeing the stimulus support to which the child responds. Another way of providing immediate feedback to the child on his or her movements uses specially treated paper with latent images. The images and feedback are invisible until the child touches the "special" pen or crayon to the surface. The child can thus be given quick feedback on deviations in his or her drawing (16). Unless the images fade entirely away, however, the specially treated paper may not be suitable for reuse. The option of the child to erase and redo the formations is thus limited.

Using highly erasable material reduces costs and permits children to redo their formations, which they are often likely to do in the beginning. Much use can be made of a clear plastic cover under which models to trace or copy can be slipped, or the cover can be removed and placed on another sheet of paper. There are a variety of possible sequences that the child might choose to follow with any particular symbol: e.g., (1) finger tracing on the plastic cover over the model underneath, (2) grease pencil tracing on the cover over the model, and (3) the child copies alongside the model, first big copies then little ones. The underlying sheets can provide different degrees of stimulus support cues, and the child may select which ones to use and which to ignore (17).

Any tracing and copying task can be broken down into an indefinite number of small steps for children by providing stimulus support which is later removed: (1) A child might walk along the outline of a symbol drawn on the floor, with more or less prompts or cues to guide changes in direction. (2) The child can trace over symbols that are raised and covered with sandpaper, to get strong tactile feedback for stimulus support. (3) Letters can be "sculptured" in clay, sand, cookies, or even telephone wire, which is quite flexible and can be hung like a mobile. The child might even glue dot-to-dot models on a sheet of paper by placing Cheerios at suitable points. (4) Shiny black tape in the form of the letter symbols can be placed on the bottom of a tray and covered with a layer of sand or salt (thin to begin with so the tape shows through, then thicker later on to fade out the visual cues underneath). The child can trace over the tape with his or her finger, moving away the salt to reveal the accuracy of his or her performance. (5) Tracing can also be done at the chalkboard with finger and water over letters taped on the board. Later, the child can move to a paintbrush and water at the chalkboard (18). (6) Plastic folders with taped edges can be used with symbols underneath for tracing or copying with crayons or grease pencils. (7) Construction paper can be used that is unlined but folded in rows for a guide. (8) Lined paper can be used with a heavy marginal border line, running vertically from top to bottom on the left side to provide an environmental cue for orientation (19). (9) Lined paper can be used with colors or distinctive spacing for the top and bottom lines. (10) A middle line can be used with wide dashes that provide distinctive visual points for the child to guide the child's strokes (20). (11) An underlying "grid" can be made as detailed as desired and then faded out (21).

Initially, the problem may be to find some point at which the child can be successful and make progress in a task the child finds meaningful and at a rate that is challenging, neither boring nor frustrating. The problem then becomes one of adapting each new change to the child's level of progress. All this is possible with evidence from records that show how well the instruction worked. Without flexible instruction and systematic assessment, however, the subskills of handwriting may become tasks for "busy work" instead of tasks for learning. There is no point in forcing children to go through steps they do not need.

Consequences

In tracing and copying tasks, teachers have many opportunities to provide feedback on the smaller and larger units of performance. For example, many tracing tasks require children to follow along a dotted outline. Movement in a continuous straight line or arc between the dots is normally an improvement over movements with crooks, angles, false starts, or hesitations. Children may be informed of their improvements in moving from a crooked arc to a smooth one by circling the improvement or commenting upon it. A larger unit of feedback may simply be to circle the best complete symbol drawn by the child that day. Decisions on the size of the unit of feedback can be adapted to the child's progress.

A variety of scales and legibility criteria are available for use in evaluating progress in forming the letter structures (22), although they are typically not used or consistently applied by classroom teachers. There may be inconsistencies in the standards set between schools, between teachers, and within teachers. The child may wonder when another more or less rigid set of structural requirements will be presented as if it were the one and only "correct" method.

A more effective arrangement of consequences gives priority to the function of handwriting: to be legible. In natural settings, this can be determined through frequent writing and exchanges of writing, e.g., encouraging notes to be written and exchanged in class. High productivity and display of meaningful writing, e.g., for signatures, labels, notes, letters, stories, and reports, tend to have the natural consequences of ease, legibility, and attractiveness built into them.

These natural consequences may be augmented by collections and records. See Figure 17. By collecting their own best productions of their letters, children may produce their own alphabet book as a record of their progress. Charts may also record the letter mastered by having that letter written down by the child, even in an early childhood report to be taken home (23). A simple checklist can tabulate all the children's handwriting skills, indicating what they have achieved and what they need to work on next. See Figure 17.

The visible display of these records, particularly the actual letters that children produced, permits additional responses and comments to be made. Talking about these letters and making comments about them provide additional information about how the letter looks, how a particular part looks, and how it was made. The child can compare and discuss the way he or she produced the letters with the way others did them. These are further consequences that children can use for improving their handwriting.

Occasions for Handwriting

In a broad sense, any use of pens and pencils by children to leave traces will involve them with handwriting skills. Any drawing activity will involve the child in forming lines that could be used as

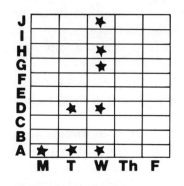

Stickers for letters written

Alphabet book of letters written by child

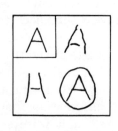

Circle the better letter

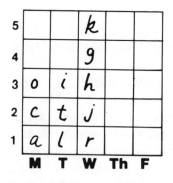

Actual letters written on a chart

Figure 17. Some handwriting records.

parts of letters. Cutting out, rearranging, and repasting together the parts of a child's scribble could even result in a recognizable letter. The child can draw a story or include details in his or her drawings that are composed of letter parts. Short vertical lines, for example, can represent boys or girls, long vertical lines can represent soldiers or big people. Diagonal lines (//////////) can represent rain. Diagonal crosses (XXXXXXXXXX) can represent Indian tents. Circles (OOOOOOOOOO) can represent stones, clouds, balls, or coins. Drawing a house with a square bottom and a triangle top and a round sun outside also combines most of these letter parts. Any drawings with lines, circles, and arcs allow children to draw more steady and more confident lines and curves that form the parts of letters; e.g., in animals, faces, people, houses, cars, etc.

The occasions for handwriting are increased when writing instruments and writing surfaces are made more available to children and when frequent opportunities for using these writing materials are provided for children with stimulus supports for getting them started and helping them along. It is not as difficult to do this as it might first seem. A big increase in writing occasions may occur simply by removing current restrictions on the use of writing materials and helping aids. Teachers may be concerned about children leaving "marks" or "messes," and this is especially understandable in the old pen and inkwell days. But it should not be forgotten that children learn handwriting and all the writing skills they will ever learn through the marks that they make.

Tools that leave a mark. Hands and the tools they control leave marks. While working with two hands, one hand typically employs a power grip to hold or position the object while the other hand uses a precision grip to make a more specific movement. It is this more specific movement of the precision grip which tends to characterize the marks that are left behind. People are called right-handed when they use that hand to do the precision work.

Fingers leave marks. The pointing index finger is often used to leave marks, e.g., traces on a frost-covered pane, a dust-covered table, or a dirt-covered car. A wet finger can also be used to leave a trace on a chalkboard. Children soon learn they can use their fingers to draw on frosted or fogged windows. But since their fingers also leave a trail of "grease" marks, they are often discouraged from touching their hands or fingers to windows. Some children even take a while to readjust to the idea that it is all right to leave marks with their fingers in fingerpainting.

Sticks leave marks. Any handy stick can be used to make marks in the sand or the dirt on the ground, perhaps while sitting around a campfire. Sticks can also be shaped to perform their task more effectively. A stylus can be shaped for easy marking on clay, a wax tablet, or a plastic cover that picks up a trace of the markings from the material underneath.

Sticks or stick-shaped instruments can be designed to hold a material that leaves a trace. Hair can be fixed to the end of a stick to make a brush that will hold paint or water. A hollow reed or feather quill can be slit at the point so that it will hold the fluid it is dipped into long enough to leave a trace which can be very delicate. The "stick" itself may be made of material that leaves a part of itself as a trace, e.g., chalk, a crayon, and a lead or grease pencil. Some markers have replaceable fluid containers, like ballpoint pens, while others do not.

Anything that leaves a trace can serve as a writing instrument. And it seems reasonable to assume that, given the opportunity, virtually anything that leaves a trace will be used to do so. The immediate feedback which traces provide for our actions is a powerful attraction. At an early age, a child or infant will be fascinated with an object he or she can make a trace with, losing interest when that same object leaves no traces (24). Much to the consternation of many a parent, children are fascinated with what they spill and the traces it leaves, delighting in the "mess" they make. Much parental and teacher effort goes into restricting and controlling the traces which children leave behind them. The solution, however, is not to control for "messes" by indiscriminately suppressing the traces a child may leave. Rather, the solution is to provide the child with frequent opportunities for discriminating the occasions when it is proper to leave traces.

It is common to observe how happy children can be while leaving traces behind them. The "mess" they make with the traces left upon themselves as well may put them in utter delight. The child who is being "too quiet" is often found completely enthralled with the traces he or she is making. There need be no recognizable image or product produced. It is the sheer exhilaration of making a mark in the world. Put a writing instrument in the child's hand, give the child a surface to write on, and the child will produce marks. Give the child frequent access to alternative writing instruments, alternative surfaces, and alternative helping aids, and the child will learn to do this easily.

Materials that receive a mark. The wind can leave its trace on hard rock, and the hardest diamond can be marked. But some materials are just much easier to work with for different purposes than others. Sometimes it depends on whether the mark is to be made into or left on top of the material. It is easier to carve straight lines into wood than it is to carve curved lines. It is easier to leave a trace on top of a smooth surface than a rough surface.

Sometimes it is an advantage for material to retain a mark fairly permanently, like stone, wood, or paper. At other times, it is an advantage for the markings to be easily erased. It is easier to erase pencil markings that stay on top of the paper than ink markings which penetrate further into the material of the paper. Markings in clay take a little more time to erase than markings in sand. An advantage of the chalkboard is that it is easy to erase chalk marks or water marks. A similar advantage applies to clear plastic covers of acetate or vinyl. Marks left on them with a grease pencil—in tracing, copying, or drawing a figure underneath or alongside—can be wiped off with a cloth. Marks from the impressions made by special material underneath a plastic cover can be erased by simply lifting up the cover.

It is always an advantage for materials to be readily accessible, both for marking and for later viewing. Walls are very convenient for this purpose, having an advantage shared by chalkboards. Even walls that were not consciously designed for writing will be used for this purpose, as witnessed by the extensive grafitti to be found on buildings, fences, and the walls of restrooms. Why not then make deliberate use of the classroom walls for grafitti? (25) The surface of classroom walls could be designed, as are chalkboards, so that markings on the surface could be easily removed. Wallpaper with a plastic coating could be used which is resistant to receiving a permanent mark. Writing instruments could be used which do not leave a permanent mark. Replaceable paper could cover the walls. The paper might ring the room like an extensive mural, or it might be confined to a particular section of the wall. The paper might be very large or no bigger than standard 8 1/2" by 11". Work could be done at the walls or at a desk first and then placed on the walls. The practice of writing on standard size paper and then putting it up on the wall is a frequently followed and commendable procedure, although it is only one of many ways.

Even the ground or floor that children walk on is a potential writing surface. It is said that the Greeks covered their palace floors with fine sand in Plato's time so that they could write and work on problems in mathematics right at their feet (26).

The child's desk is another convenient place to mark, and it is often difficult to preserve desks and tables from being carved or marked upon. Although desks are often designed so that they are resistant to permanent markings, they can be covered with paper. While desks and table tops are more convenient for the production of writing, they are less accessible than walls for the display of writing. Desk tops get covered with other things, and whatever lies on those surfaces is not easily seen by other children, who must crowd up close to get a good look. See Figure 18.

Any way of increasing the square footage of writing surfaces available to children would provide an advantage in giving children occasions for writing. This includes every surface in every room the child is in, from bedroom to classroom. For many purposes, e.g., murals on tables or walls or drawings on easels or large clip boards, large sheets of paper are well suited. A major advantage of smaller sheets of paper is that the individual drawings and writings can be compactly collected into folders, booklets, and books. These can then be made accessible for display as newspapers, magazines, or books. When there are restrictions in making paper available to children because they will use so much of it, relatively inexpensive paper like newsprint may be used to lower the cost of materials. And more priority may be given to reusable surfaces that can be wiped clean.

Writing Surfaces a Child Can Use a Finger On

Tray with salt

Blackboard

Water

Writing Surfaces a Child Can Use Various Writing Instruments On

Airplane

HAPPY BIRTHDAY

Writing with pen and pencil on large sheets of paper taped to table

Writing with chalk on blackboard

Spring

Figure 18. Some writing surfaces.

Cues for reducing reversals. The history of writing over the centuries shows a wide variety of sequences, from circular spirals to alternating lines from left to right and right to left, to writing from the top down on one side and from the bottom up on the other so that the end of the writing is underneath the beginning. It should not be surprising then if children take awhile to acquire a preference for writing left to right and top to bottom.

Even after a child has learned to form firm, steady, highly legible symbols, the child may still have a problem producing them in the standard orientation. Children may need to learn to attend to critical cues before they tend to draw vertical lines from top to bottom and horizontal lines from left to right (27). The starting point, for example, may shift from the lower right-hand corner with children two to three years of age, to the center with children three to four years of age, to the top center with children who are five to six years old, and finally starting at the top left with children seven years of age and older (28). Learning the cues to begin at the top left, of course, increases the likelihood that lines will be formed from top to bottom and left to right. Our bilateral midline body orientation also plays a role in motor responses. A reversal on the right side by the right hand may be corrected if done on the left side of the body (29). The motor pattern now becomes a mirror image of the reversal pattern in the normal position. Children may be given practice in a midline crossover technique that helps them to retain the proper orientation as they cross their body midline, gradually shifting the relationship of what they are drawing from one side of their midline to the other.

Given appropriately designed instructional conditions, children can learn to become aware of the signals in their environment for determining direction (30). Some environmental orientation cue is often helpful for indicating left and right. The vertical line on the left-hand margin of the paper is helpful because our environment does not normally provide us with signals for left and right. Curiously enough, we may supply older children and adults with paper that has ruled left-hand margins (e.g., yellow legal pads with three red lines to signal the margin), but the paper we give young children to use often has no margin signal. The vertical line provides a distinctive spatial cue between the edge of the letter and the vertical line, which is particularly helpful for reducing left/right reversals. The vertical line also permits directions to be given to the child to move "toward the line" and "away from the line."

Enstrom and Enstrom (31) have provided a list of aids and guides for alleviating reversals: model one stroke at a time; imitate first in air writing ("sky writing"); separate the teaching of *b* and *d*; call attention to the parts of the letter formation (e.g., *c + 1 = d*); use verbal maps and guides (*C* and the "*c* backwards" to describe the parts of the "seven *c*'s" family, *c, p, d, q, g, a, b*; "*b* right," "little brother *b*"); and other suggestions. There are a wide variety of memory devices in terms of visual images and stories about them which appeal to the imagination of young children and which can help them to recall appropriate letter orientation and production.

Some aids and reminders may simply be taped to the child's desk. For example, the child might simply have a model of the way D'Nealian letters are formed taped to his or her desk, which the child could consult when necessary. As soon as the child could form the letter properly without referring to the model, the child would save himself or herself the time and effort to look at the model. There may be no need to remember an elaborate system of cues.

Adaptations for left-handers and other individual differences. The case for adapting different conditions for different children can be made through the example of left-handers. Each child differs in the skills that child possesses. The left-hander makes this difference conspicuously obvious and forces some recognition of the limitations for the one best way. Earlier efforts to convert left-handers into right-handers may be seen as an ill-advised attempt to enforce the one-best-way method.

Since traditional handwriting standards have typically been set for uniformity and for right-handers, they are not well suited to left-handers. With appropriate adjustments, however, left-handers can write as rapidly and as legibly as right-handers. But they need some guidance that is adapted to their abilities, e.g., in positioning the paper, in being allowed to have a vertical or back slant, a writing grip further from the point, and perhaps even cards with models of left-handed cursive writing (32). One special way to help the left-hander is to have him or her learn to type: "Here the left-handed have an advantage over right-handed people: the standard typewriter keyboard was designed by a left-handed person" (33).

In general, much of the recommended assistance for left-handers comes in the form of adapting the learning conditions to their individual capabilities. The insistence on uniformity is suspended somewhat for left-handers. The criteria for the left-handed are oriented toward more ease and legibility in writing. Left-handers are even encouraged to find the alternatives that work best for them. If individualization and alternatives are good for left-handers, why not for right-handers as well? Every child could be encouraged to develop that child's own particular style of handwriting, evaluated according to that child's personal growth and improvement, with a resulting performance through individualized methods that surpasses formal group methods. How can handwriting be learned easily when ritualistic practices are simply required for everyone without supporting evidence: e.g., in demanding downstrokes for manuscript letters, prescribing large "primary" pencils for all children (34), insisting on extra-wide writing spaces between the lines for beginners (35), and supplying paper without a vertical marginal line?

SUMMARY

The "one best way" to write letters has typically resulted in setting restrictions on how a child writes. Letters are to be formed in the same direction and in the same sequence of strokes, according to the regulations for a standard form and slant. Other restrictions have included the writing instrument and the writing surface. Many of these restrictions have been rather arbitrary with little supporting evidence, relying more on a belief that the one best way had been discovered once and for all.

The practical consequences of much of this have been to

unnecessarily limit the child's production of letters. When we consider the additional attention to and punishment for the "errors" of handwriting, it is not difficult to see how handwriting may be more inhibited than facilitated. Furthermore, when children must devote all their concentration to correctly forming standardized letters, their responsiveness to spelling and word formation as well as to sentences and meaning must necessarily be restricted.

If we replace the structural goal of the "one best way" to produce a letter with the functional goal of "high productivity of legible letters," we are free of many of these constraints. We can then work directly to increase children's access to writing instruments and surfaces with and without aids, allowing children to explore alternative ways for producing letters, and providing them with conspicuous consequences for this.

REFERENCES

1. Addy, P., and Wylie, R.E. The "right" way to write. *Childhood Education*, February 1973, *49*(5), p. 253.

2. Watt, W.C. What is the proper characterization of the alphabet? I. Desiderata. *Visible Language*, Autumn 1975, *9*(4), p. 301.

3. Hildreth, G. The success of young children in number and letter construction. *Child Development*, March 1932, *3*(1), pp. 1-14.

4. Corballis, M.C., and Beale, I.L. On telling left from right. *Scientific American*, March 1971, *224*(3), pp. 96-104. Staller, J., and Sekuler, R. Mirror-image confusions in adults and children: A nonperceptual explanation. *American Journal of Psychology*, June 1976, *89*(2), pp. 253-268.

5. Ninio, A., and Lieblich, A. The grammar of action: "Phrase structure" in children's copying. *Child Development*, September 1976, *47*(3), p. 849.

6. Bruner, J.S. The growth and structure of skill. In K. Connolly (Ed.), *Mechanisms of motor development*. New York: Academic Press, 1970, pp. 63-94.

7. Anderson, P.S. *Language skills in elementary education* (2nd ed.). New York: Macmillan, 1972, p. 179.

8. Enstrom, E.A., and Enstrom, D.C. In print handwriting: Preventing and solving reversal problems. *Elementary English*, October 1969, *46*(6), pp. 759-764.

9. Cutright, P. Script-print and beginning reading and spelling. *Elementary English*, April 1936, *13*(4), pp. 139-141, 160. Long, H.H., and Mayer, W.C. Printing versus cursive writing in beginning reading instruction. *Journal of Educational Research*, December 1931, *24*(5), pp. 350-355. Voorhis, T.G. *Merits of cursive and manuscript writing*. New York: Lincoln School Research Studies, Teachers College, Columbia University, 1931.

10. Huitt, R. Handwriting: The state of the craft. *Childhood Education*, January 1972, *48*(4), pp. 219-222.

11. Breim, G. Wanted: Handwriting that fits modern pens. *Visible Language*, 1979, *13*(1), pp. 50-62. Gray, N. Toward a new handwriting adapted to the ballpoint pen. *Visible Language*, 1979, *13*(1), pp. 63-69.

12. Thurber, D.N. *D'Nealian handwriting* (Teacher's Edition). Glenview, Ill.: Scott, Foresman and Co., 1978, p. 10.

13. Fuller, R. Breaking down the I.Q. walls: Severely retarded people can learn to read. *Psychology Today*, March 1946, *68*(1), p. 97.

14. McCarthy, L. A child learns the alphabet. *Visible Language*, Summer 1977, *11*(3), pp. 271-284.

15. Hertzberg, O.E. *A comparative study of different methods used in teaching beginners to write*. New York: Teachers College, Columbia University, Contributions to Education, No. 214, 1926. (AMS reprinted edition, 1972)

16. Skinner, B.F., and Krakower, E. *Handwriting with write and see* (Teacher's Edition). Chicago: Lyons and Carnahan, 1968.

17. Scott, B. Personal communication, 1975.

18. Bauman, T., and Horton, L. Is teaching handwriting really important? *Instructor*, January 1973, *82*(5), pp. 68-69.

19. Smith, D.E.P., and Smith, J.M. *The Michigan language program*. New York: Random House, 1975.

20. Squires, C. Personal communication, 1976.

21. Rosner, J. *Perceptual skills curriculum: Introductory guide.* New York: Walker Educational Book Corp., 1973. Smith, D.E.P., and Smith, J.M. *The Michigan language program.* New York: Random House, 1975.

22. Enstrom, E.A., and Enstrom, D.C. In print handwriting: Preventing and solving reversal problems. *Elementary English*, October 1969, *46*(6), pp. 759-764. Horton, L. Illegibilities in the cursive handwriting of sixth-graders. *Elementary School Journal*, May 1970, *70*(8), pp. 446-450. Huitt, R. Handwriting: The state of the craft. *Childhood Education*, January 1972, *48*(4), pp. 219-222. Lehman, C.L. Handwriting legibility: A method of objective evaluation. *Visible Language*, Autumn 1973, 7(4), pp. 325-344.

23. Rupich, E. *Early childhood record.* Wheeling, WV: 51 Haddale Lane, 1978.

24. Gibson, E.J., and Levin, H. *The psychology of reading.* Cambridge, Mass.: The MIT Press, 1975.

25. Kohl, H. The writing's on the wall—use it. *Learning*, May/June 1974, *2*(9), pp. 10-15.

26. Ravosa, C., and Huttar, E. With a stick on the ground . . . *Early Years*, November 1979, *10*(3), pp. 38-40, 67.

27. Gesell, A., and Ames, L.B. The development of directionality in drawing. *Journal of Genetic Psychology*, March 1946, *68*(1), pp. 45-61.

28. Ames, L.B. Postural and placement orientation in writing and block behavior: Developmental trends from infancy to age ten. *Journal of Genetic Psychology*, September 1948, *73*(1), pp. 45-52.

29. Zaslow, R.W. Reversals in children as a function of midline body orientation. *Journal of Educational Psychology*, June 1966, *57*(3), pp. 133-139.

30. Moxley, R.A. A program for reducing reversals of digits and symbols produced by kindergarten children (Doctoral dissertation, University of Michigan, 1970). *Dissertation Abstracts International*, 1970, *31*(5), 2192A-2193A (University Microfilms No. 70-21741). Sidman, M., and Kirk, B. Letter reversals in naming, writing, and matching to sample. *Child Development*, September 1974, *45*(3), pp. 616-625. Stromer, R. Modifying letter and

number reversals in elementary school children. *Journal of Applied Behavior Analysis*, Summer 1975, *8*(2), p. 211.

31. Enstrom, E.A., and Enstrom, D.C. In print handwriting: Preventing and solving reversal problems. *Elementary English*, October 1969, *46*(6), pp. 759-764.

32. Anderson, P.S. *Language skills in elementary education* (2nd ed.). New York: Macmillan, 1972. Burns, P.C. *Improving handwriting instruction in elementary schools* (2nd ed.). Minneapolis, Minn.: Burgess, 1968.

33. Anderson, P.S. *Language skills in elementary education* (2nd ed.). New York: Macmillan, 1972, p. 205.

34. Krzseni, J.S. Effect of different writing tools and paper on performance of the third grader. *Elementary English*, November 1971, *38*(7), pp. 821-824. Otto, W., and Andersen, D.W. Handwriting. In R.L. Ebel (Ed.), *Encyclopedia of Educational Research* (4th ed.). New York: Macmillan, 1969, pp. 570-579. Wiles, M.E. Effect of different size tools on the handwriting of beginners. *Elementary School Journal*, March 1943, *43*(7), pp. 412-413.

35. Halpin, G., and Halpin, G. Special paper for beginning handwriting: An unjustified practice? *The Journal of Educational Research*, March 1976, *69*(7), pp. 267-269.

Chapter VI

Increasing Reading Responses

Reading is often considered as though it were an activity confined to just one kind of behavior, The Act of Reading. This has placed unnecessary constraints on the way children have been taught to read. In reality, reading consists of a wide variety of behaviors with a wide range of purposes, performed on a number of diverse occasions. Instead of there being just a few signs of successful reading, there are many. The different kinds of things we do in reading, and knowing that reading has occurred, are similar to the different kinds of things we do in "seeing" and "listening" and knowing what kind of seeing and listening has occurred. We would not consider the mere evidence that someone is not blind or deaf to tell us much about his or her seeing or listening. Similarly, the mere evidence that someone is not oblivious to a text does not tell us much about his or her reading. Yet, on the basis of a rather curiously selected and narrow sample of reading behavior, inferences are made as if these indicators of reading actually demonstrated the existence of a much more extensive set of reading skills, presumably comprised within The Act of Reading. This resembles the idea that I.Q. tests show evidence for a general intelligence that can perform all sorts of other tasks beyond the similarly curious and narrowly selected items on an I.Q. test. This resemblance may not be so surprising when we consider that I.Q. tests and standardized, normal-curve-referenced reading tests are based on the same psychometrics and questionable assumptions. To make matters worse, reading instruction is then often organized to directly teach those curious skills so selectively sampled as if this were sufficient for teaching a general Act of Reading ability.

This is foolish. Unfortunately, much of this foolishness has acquired a kind of respectability by simply having survived so long in theories and practices of reading. It might help to step back a little to gain a broader perspective that avoids disabling preconceptions about reading.

BACKGROUND

By "seeing," we often mean what someone does when he or she is looking in the direction of something. By "listening," we often mean what someone does when he or she hears sounds. We regard seeing and the thing seen, listening and the thing listened to as occurring simultaneously. We infer by attending responses, an eye movement, a turn of the head, that seeing and listening are occurring. But that does not take us as far as we would like to go in determining the nature of seeing and listening.

We must look to what a person does *after* seeing and *after* listening to infer any details about his or her seeing or listening. The traffic signal changes to "Walk," and then the person walks across the street. The person's name is called, and then the person stands up. Sometimes the sequences occur quickly in a continuous cycle of seeing and doing or listening and doing. We maneuver a car in traffic or read a text aloud. We dance to music or nod in agreement to what is being said. Sometimes the sequence is more delayed. We avoid a street where we have seen heavy traffic. We rehearse a movement to the tune we have heard. We ask or answer a question about something we have read or heard sometime before. In these and other ways we show a wide range of responses to seeing and hearing things. These range from immediate attending responses that seem close to being instantaneous with the stimuli to delayed responses that show what we "got" from it. We typically refer to the more delayed responses for indicating what we remembered or what we learned.

If we assume that the best indicators must occur at, or very near to, the moment of attending to the sights and sounds, it might seem logical then to focus our attention on increasing these near indicators of attention, e.g., reading aloud or eye contact with the speaker. We might then talk louder to assure eye contact or teach rules for sounding out letters and words in order to assure reading aloud. But this would grossly oversimplify the range of useful indicators.

If we looked only to the immediate indicators, we would be neglecting delayed behaviors that provide us with indications of comprehension. Eye contact or reading aloud have not turned out to be reliable indicators that comprehension occurs. In our daily lives, we do not limit ourselves to immediate indicators. We examine delayed indicators of comprehension: What the person does after he or she "has read" or "has listened." We look for indicators that someone *had* listened, *had* read, *had* understood, *had* comprehended.

Even if we consider that the real Act of Reading or listening co-occurs with the attention to the stimulus, it does not follow that the best instructional indicators must also co-occur. Nor does it follow that the best instructional indicators should bear a close correspondence or resemblance to the stimulus. Imagine, for example, if a child were taught to see by teaching the child to draw a reproduction of what the child saw. The child could be shown photographs or pictures of various levels of difficulty in composition and asked to draw what he or she saw. The child's performance could then be scored on the basis of the accuracy of his or her reproductions in comparison to other children of similar age. Would we conclude that children who score well must see well and that children who score poorly must see poorly? Would we use increased skills in copying to infer that there has been an increase in the child's comprehension of what the child has seen? Imagine if children were taught to hear by having them imitate or echo the sounds of what they heard. Or, imagine if children had to learn to listen by writing down what they heard in some kind of transcription. We would protest that these are absurd constraints to impose on learning. Such a protest would also apply to reading instruction that confines itself to having children speak aloud what they read.

Let us examine listening to verbal behavior more closely. How do we tell if a child is listening? Is eye contact sufficient? Nodding? Repeating back what we have said? Notice we always have to observe what the child does. How much of what the child hears can we infer the child understands? We observe if the child follows directions, if the child expands on what we said, if the child answers in a similar theme. By the variety of such responses, we determine the extent of the child's understanding. We make further inquiries. We look for evidence of understanding in all the things the child says and does in response to our speech. We assume the child understands when the child responds in ways relevant to what we said and in ways that the child would not otherwise have acted. Or, to put it another way, we infer understanding by those responses we infer are controlled by our speech.

The nature of this control by speech is one where what we say to the child may be continuously modified by the subsequent responses of the child. In turn, the responses of the child may be continuously modified by what we say to the child. In the typical context of talking to a child, the child can ask for help at any point. The child can ask us what we mean. If we detect a misunderstanding or a lack of responding, we can supplement our speech with additional clarification or by showing what we mean. We may point to something in the immediate context that we are referring to. We observe further "listening responses" and provide further clarification to those responses. We can watch what the child does later. We infer the understanding of verbal stimuli by a wide variety of responses to those stimuli. Accordingly, we could define a listening response to speech as any response under the control of speech, both during and after the speech.

In contrast, The Act of Reading is often viewed within an assessment tradition that focuses on a relatively narrow range of behavior. In standardized assessment tests, the child may make token responses with paper and pencil to multiple choices of text related to other texts (and/or pictures). The correct choice is often one with a close structural correspondence, and it must be made quickly. The reading performance in the standardized, normal-curve-referenced test-setting is one in which tasks are to be performed as if the child were isolated in a chamber with pencil, directions, and answer sheet. The task demands are a series of immediate responses under limited time constraints to items selected because they provide a distribution between individuals. It is difficult to imagine a more minimal, overt response (a token pencil mark) in a more minimal environment (a token exposure to a set of verbal directions) for providing an enduring record of evaluation.

In the classroom, children's reading ability is often determined on the basis of their reading a text aloud. Round-robin oral reading, for example, may be performed under conditions that serve as constraints and barriers to responsiveness within a larger context: without rehearsal, without guessing or skipping, insisting on sounding out; in a story selected by the teacher; with the same book used by other students who follow at the same pace; with feedback and penalty for mistakes, including dialect variants and immediate correction of omissions and errors; when called upon by surprise to stand up, hold the book in a certain way, with a certain posture, etc.; following one method, one set of rules and procedures for reading; when students are ranked and compared (1). Calling out words shown on flashcards and saying the "sounds of letters" may also be done in order to teach the component parts of reading aloud. Presumably, skills in attaching sounds to isolated parts will lead to skills in attaching sounds to recombinations of these sounds.

A sequenced plan of instruction may then be organized for building the parts of texts and words into larger units to develop increasing skills in reading aloud, e.g., from saying letters, to saying blends, to saying words. Many of these classroom responses may also be required to be practiced under test-like conditions of unfamiliar material, limited time, one opportunity, and a penalty for error.

This kind of testing and instruction can easily be used to differentiate students. It is relatively easy to administer. It is easy to get a score or a relative impression of performance and to compare one child's performance with another. Such convenience is supported if it is believed that there are only a few good indicators of reading needed and that these indicators are well represented by standardized tests and similar test-like instruction. If the child fails to learn to read effectively under these conditions, that is unfortunate. "The child wasn't ready," "the child is slow," "the child is underprivileged," "the child didn't have it in him or her," or "the child has a learning disability" explains the failure away.

Standing back a little to take a broader view of this standardized test-like instruction reveals that isolation from a naturalistic environment is one of its most striking features. The standardized-normal-curve-referenced test setting is a kind of microscopic model for an expendable environment. There is only a need for directions, paper and pencil instruments, and a brief time for immediate, minimal responses. In this and in classroom activities that are variations of this model, students are to behave as though they were alone in some kind of invisible cell. Students learn and perform as if they were in isolation from an unneeded and unwanted environment. They follow directions. They memorize and copy. They recite when called upon. Responsiveness to the environment beyond immediate responses to verbal directions is incidental if not punishable. Instructional attention to consequences beyond the response is negligible. Assessment needs only token indication for the skill taking place within the child's "mind." The natural, rich context in which the child learns to speak and listen has been "peeled away."

However, peeling away the layers of the natural environment, like peeling away the layers of an onion, may leave virtually nothing, at least nothing to do with instruction and learning. Something may be left in patience for following rules. And something may be left in a sorting system that breaks out along social class lines. In peeling away the layers of the environment, the functions of reading have also been peeled away. Only the structures remain—the text and its parts, the word, the letter—and immediate responses to them.

APPLICATION
The Variety of Reading Behaviors

Instead of limiting our attention to selective, immediate indicators of reading behavior and looking inward to what is happening inside the child for explanations of reading failures, we can embrace all the indicators of reading behavior and look outward to the natural environment in which children have learned to speak and listen easily. An approach to reading that looks to the environment takes on quite a different look. It looks outward instead of inward.

Instead of a shrinking and confining attention to inner events, there is an expanding attention to what happens, as Skinner puts it, when a child "shows that he [or she] knows how to read":

> Traditional characterizations of verbal behavior raise almost insuperable problems for a teacher, and a more rigorous analysis suggests another possibility. We can define terms like "information," "knowledge," and "verbal ability" by reference to the behavior from which we infer their presence. *We may then teach the behavior directly....* Instead of teaching "an ability to read," we may set up the behavioral repertoire which distinguishes the child who knows how to read from one who does not.
>
> To take the last example, a child reads or "shows that he knows how to read" by exhibiting a behavioral repertoire of great complexity. He finds a letter or word in a list on demand; he reads aloud; he finds or identifies objects described in a text; he rephrases sentences; he obeys written instructions; he behaves appropriately to described situations; he reacts emotionally to described events; and so on, in a long list. He does none of this before learning to read and all of it afterwards. To bring about such a change is an extensive assignment, and it is tempting to try to circumvent it by teaching something called "an ability to read" from which all these specific behaviors will flow. But this has never actually been done. "Teaching reading" is always directed toward setting up specific items in such a repertoire.... In the long run, all parts of the repertoire tend to be filled in, not because the student is rounding out an ability to read, but because all parts are in their several ways useful. They all continue to be reinforced by the world at large after the explicit teaching of reading has ceased. (2)

The parts of the student's reading repertoire may not be very well filled in, however, when the gap between the student's world at large and the artificial setting of reading in the classroom is excessive. The child may then be left to adventitious events such as parents who read to him or her if the child has that good fortune.

The above account suggests that the problem of teaching reading can be resolved by enlarging the consideration of reading responses. As we enlarge our consideration of responses, we also enlarge our consideration of the conditions surrounding a reading response. It all seems simple enough. But if we pursue this direction, we arrive at a striking, if not startling, contrast to traditional perspectives of reading and its instruction. See Figure 19.

We simply replace the peeled back layers of the environment to include a fuller account of the behavior by which a child "shows that he [or she] knows how to read." This expansion into the environment includes legitimate consideration of any behavior (and its context) from which we infer the occurrence of reading. We do not need to confine ourselves to overt responses that are in close temporal proximity to covert responses we feel must be occurring within the child when the child examines a text. Control by a text, not temporal proximity, is decisive for selecting reading behaviors. If attention is directed simply to increasing overt responses (both immediate and remote) that are controlled by texts, there is then a much vaster domain of accessible behaviors for reading improvement than is generally considered in theories of reading and their applications. In contrast to the artificiality of many formal reading settings, such an increased domain may be described as belonging within a *natural setting* for everyday reading.

A reading response defined as any response under the control of a text opens up a variety of reading responses to be used in testing and teaching. It includes responses made in the presence of the text and after the text is no longer available: e.g., reading aloud and commenting on yesterday's headlines. It includes responses more or less under control of the text, e.g., writing a reading critique or filing a book among other books on a shelf. It includes overt and covert responses, e.g., discussing a story and fantasizing or daydreaming about it. It also includes responses in different modes, e.g., speaking, writing, drawing, pointing, and acting. These are all reading responses when they are controlled by a text.

Whether all of these responses are actually called reading responses or indicators of reading responses is not critical as long as we do not narrow the range of responses that we can use to

Figure 19. Some extended consequences for reading.
(Figure continued on p. 162.)

Figure 19 (continued)

Discussing it

Writing about it

increase reading. What is wanted in teaching is access to behaviors that can be improved, easily, with motivating consequences, tangible evidence of progress, and strong inferences for increased skill toward what is wanted.

Consequences for Variety and Frequency of Reading Behaviors

If we want a variety of reading responses, then we should also have a variety of consequences that these responses produce. This variety applies both in the sense of different consequences for different responses and in the sense of a variety of extended consequences for any particular reading response. When these consequences are reinforcing, they will increase the probability or the rate at which a particular reading response occurs. Charts are a convenient way for making consequences conspicuous and effective. Recommendations for using rate charts to increase reading speed are not new. As previously mentioned, the *Maryland School Bulletin* on silent reading in 1924 stated: "Each pupil should keep an account of the number of lines and pages he [or she] reads each day. By knowing the average number of words per line and dividing by the total number of minutes used in reading, a pupil may get his [or her] score in number of words read per minute. If these scores are kept on individual class charts, the children will be stimulated to beat their own records and to raise their class score" (3). Recording a score is a consequence of the child's reading. It also provides the occasion for comments, discussion, and other consequences. If reinforcing consequences follow from increasing his or her rate, then the child will learn to increase his or her reading rate further. This procedure can be applied not only to silent reading but to any kind of reading and any kind of reading purpose, e.g., reading to discuss, reading to find the answer to a question, reading to write a summary, etc. Attention to the different reading behaviors for different reading purposes often becomes noticeable only when rate becomes important. Children often learn just one all-purpose reading rate, which may be little faster than they can read aloud. As a result, they fail to learn which reading behaviors are important for the different purposes of reading. They may even perform The Act of Reading as if it had no purpose.

In traditional approaches to reading, reinforcing consequences are usually not systematically arranged and are often incidental. The consequent events that are arranged are more likely to be punishers for "reading failures" than rewards for "reading successes." Giving attention to errors and introducing punishing events lead more to cautious slowness than confident speed (4). And, of course, if you read slow enough, you will not be able to comprehend anything. What is done to increase the rate of reading responses in schools is often rather crude. If a child's oral reading, for example, is slow enough to be frustrating to listen to (and perhaps even more frustrating to the child), the teacher may say "next." Subsequent readers may then read more quickly to prolong the terminating "next," if they find it aversive. A college student once informed me of a personal experience she had in reading in elementary school. The readers were called upon to come to the front of the class and to read aloud while standing in front of the teacher, who would then prod them by poking a finger in their back whenever they were to read faster. The student added, parenthetically, that she had hated reading.

An increased rate of reading may be discouraged in the classroom in many ways. If one child reads ahead in the basal reader faster than the child who is reading aloud, that child may be punished when called upon because that child has "lost the place" where the next reader is to continue. Children may be punished in other ways as well. If one child reads ahead to the next section, that child may then be bored when that next section is considered. Teachers may even find that they themselves are actually encouraged to slow down the rate at which children read rather than to speed it up. Teachers are sometimes directed by principals or other teachers in the next grades to prevent children from reading ahead in material that will be covered in the next class or the next year. Individual rates of responding must make way for the inexorable constraints of group-pacing.

Instead of preventing the occurrence of reinforcing consequences to reading responses, positive consequences can be systematically increased. This will increase the likelihood and rate of reading responses. Children can be allowed, for example, to choose stories that have reinforcing consequences for them. They can be allowed to put their reading to direct use in class plays, group discussions, scientific experiments, and other activities with reinforcing consequences of their own. They can be given the opportunity to select their own goals and the points at which they wish to display their progress to receive attention and reinforcement. They can be directly encouraged to increase their reading responses, to continually read as fast as they can to achieve the goals at hand without the penalties that are imposed from the constraints of group-pacing.

Rate of responding is often very sensitive to any changes. Because of this sensitivity, rate often will fluctuate when progress is recorded and the consequences of behavior are arranged so as to make a change. Advantage can be taken of this in designing reading instruction. A first step in increasing any response rate is to identify the intentions, objectives, goals, and indicators for the response. A second step is to derive a convenient method for recording progress. Examples of recordings that could be used include the following:

a. Simple collections of what the child has actually produced in a reading-related activity. This may be a collection of stories written or dictated; a collection of vocabulary cards a child can identify, piled in a word bank or pasted on a chart; or an alphabet book of letters a child has written with key words for their sounds.

b. Attractive tokens in the form of stamps and stickers can be used to represent the number of stories or words read and which letter and letter sounds in key words that the child knows.

c. Abstract marks are convenient to use. Simple checklists can be used to mark off a "grocery list" of reading tasks accomplished. Bar graphs and point-to-point charts (for recording either a daily frequency score or a cumulative score) can be adapted to reading related activities throughout the curriculum, e.g., the daily plotting of questions asked during or after a science activity, the number of pages read in different subject areas, or the number of questions answered.

A third step is to ensure naturally reinforcing consequences by making reading behaviors accessible to interaction, feedback, and follow-up. This means making the child's reading accomplishments and the records for them prominent and visible. See Figure 20.

Children's progress records should show when increases in their reading responses occurred. The conditions that existed at the times of increased performance can then be identified. As the facilitating conditions for improvement in reading are identified, they can be increasingly incorporated into the classroom environment. If, for example, a child discovers he or she can locate the correct answer more quickly by surveying and scanning the reading material, the child can then be provided with the opportunity to quickly familiarize himself or herself with a variety of reading resources in the classroom. If the child finds that he or she retains more comprehension of a text when there is an opportunity to discuss it afterwards with classmates, then opportunities for small-group discussion can be increased.

A classroom environment designed to increase reading responses could be expected to result in the following: (1) establishing a learning rather than a "test-hurdle" condition for instruction by allowing for more flexibility and openness in times and occasions for reading, (2) establishing far more useful record-keeping than what is provided by standardized tests or merely incidental reading activities (where the record-keeping is anecdotal at best) by having children develop and maintain their own progress records, (3) increasing the automatic reading responses and the ability to shift attention elsewhere, e.g., to the next level of reading complexity, (4) increasing skills in separating the relevant from the irrelevant for accomplishing the reading purpose at hand, and (5) increasing differentiation of sophisticated reading skills as one reading response after the other gets filled in.

Occasions for Increasing Reading

The variety and frequency of reading responses have a parallel

Figure 20. *Increasing some consequences for reading.*

in the variety and frequency of listening responses. What can be done with listening might then be done with reading.

Listening events. There are a variety of speech *stimuli* to which a child can respond. This variety ranges from exclamations, commands, and requests to descriptions of personal experiences, fanciful stories, and events in the child's own world.

Some of the variety of *responses* to speech include repeating or echoing what was said, word for word; fulfilling requests; answering questions; following directions; asking questions; writing down what was said; displaying attending responses to what was said, e.g., eye contact, reactions of wonder, surprise, laughter, nodding, etc.; making comments afterwards; making up a story about the story listened to; and completing the sentence of the story that was started. For example, one of the best learning experiences for a young child is to be read to while sitting on your lap (5). What signs do we have that the child is listening and learning from this experience? Is the child sitting still? Is the child looking at the page? Does the child ask questions? Does the child ask you to read the story again? Does the child ask you what a word means? Does the child tell you that you skipped a page? Does the child bring you another book to read later? All of these are examples of the child's responses to what the child hears you say.

These responses in listening to a story or to other spoken words include both verbal expressions and nonverbal movements. The movements may be in following directions or requests, dancing to a song, or looking for something that was mentioned. The responses may be during the presence of the continued speech or after the speech is over, but they are to some extent influenced or controlled by the speech.

These responses are considerably more than the limited responses that are often considered in listening: sitting still, eye contact, recall of what was said, and obedience to commands and directions. In some restricted listening situations in the classroom, the teacher is the speaker while the children are to attend quietly, perhaps with folded hands and eyes facing the front of the room. If the speech is a direction, the children are to quietly follow that direction. The practice and learning of many listening responses are omitted under these conditions. There are constraints here on responses initiated by the child in asking questions or in initiating actions to some description in the speech and doing something about the events described.

The *consequences* for following requests and directions may be the approval of the speaker who made them or the removal of a threat for not following them. They may also be in the speaker's feedback to the listener's comments. Reinforcing consequences also lie in the particular contacts that hearing a description gives to the child; for example, experiencing scary stories in a safe environment. Either commands or descriptions may result in the child directly contacting subsequent events. For example, the child may play on the "swing" that was named in the direction, "Go play on the swing," or the description, "There are swings in the park." The child is then exposed to the consequences of that "swinging" experience.

Providing for on-going listening activities. Providing occasions for increasing listening responses in the classroom requires selecting on-going activities that allow for varied cycles of antecedent stimuli, student responses, and following consequences. If children are encouraged to ask questions and perform actions in a variety of responses to a variety of speech stimuli under various conditions, they will learn many kinds of listening responses.

Large-group circle times: Large-group circle times, with informal discussions, show-and-tell, and questions and answers by both the teacher and children, provide occasions for a variety of listening responses. In regulating these activities, taking turns, expressing approval with soft clapping, and other methods may be used to assure that a variety of responses can occur.

Small groups: Small groups provide more opportunities for each child to make responses and to receive feedback on those responses. Children discussing, working on projects, or playing games in small groups or in tutoring relationships expose themselves to a variety of interactions among and between themselves where they can enjoy reinforcing consequences to the variety of responses to speech. If a child asks a question about something that was said, other children can answer. If a child makes a comment about something that was said, other children can make comments to what that child said. In turn, the child can comment on their comments to his or her comment, and so on. A reciprocal chain of interacting responses, listening then speaking then listening then speaking can be shaped as what the children do acquires meaning, becomes clarified, and is modified. With small groups of two, three, or four, there is opportunity for a rich in-depth interacting chain of consequences to each child's "acts" of listening.

Independent work: Relatively independent individual listening skills can be encouraged by simply encouraging children to ask questions, even listing them, and allowing them to make "free responses" to whatever was described with an opportunity to compare their responses with others. Children can respond to a "manageable part" of what they hear, live or on tape. Children may listen to a story of a gingerbread man from a tape at a listening post or from TV. Some may then make a gingerbread man. Some may act out the story. Some may make up a parallel story of their own. All of these responses can be considered as listening responses.

Reading events. Reading is distinguished from listening by a couple of dramatically different features. First, all of the written text to which reading responses occur are a visible record. The parts of a text are, as it were, simultaneously available. This increases the opportunity for selective responding and returning again for more selective responding to the same stimuli. New relationships can be seen and viewed again in one way then another in an evolving pattern of organization. Second, there is much more limited access to the author and the conditions under which the author wrote. In listening to a speaker, it is much easier to obtain access to supplementary information provided by the situation, the speaker's responses to comments and questions by the listener, and the reinforcing consequences that the speaker can arrange right then and there. Speaking and listening lend themselves to immediate shaping. Writing and reading lend themselves to future plans and actions.

The type of text *stimuli* range from written commands and directions, e.g., "stop," "go," and "exit" signs, to descriptive labels on cereal, "Grape-nuts," "Cheerios," "Corn Flakes," and signs on stores, "Tires," "Gas," "McDonald's," to books of children's stories, cooking recipes, and science experiment directions.

The *responses* to a text include copying, answering questions, following directions, asking questions about the text, discussing it, displaying attending responses, eye movements, lip movements, calling out words, making comments afterwards, making up a story about the story read, imagining the scene described, completing sentences that were started, analyzing and critiquing the text, creative writing in response to two or more texts, connecting different sections of texts or different texts together by finding a common word or theme, cooking from a recipe, predicting results from the directions of a science experiment, locating a town on a map, finding a word in a dictionary, editing, proofreading, revising personal writing, outlining the chapter of a book, writing notes in the margin, underlining sections of a book or a sentence, acting out a charade in response to what is written on a slip of paper, singing a song from a song book, answering a note, making a collage of letters or words, cutting sentences into their constituent parts, and any other response in writing, speech, or movement that is dependent upon a text.

The primary, natural *consequences* of responding to a text give a child contact with experiences beyond the child's immediate surroundings. The reader is able to extend himself or herself to events, roles, and situations that would otherwise be inaccessible to him or her. The child may bring back what he or she learns and apply it in everyday living. The child may learn about boats, cars, animals, food, vegetation, clothing, astronomy, etc. And the child may then do something about it, e.g., keep a pet, sail a boat, look at the stars. Responding to labels on a cereal box brings a child his or her favorite food. Following the signs for entrance and exit on doors avoids collisions and brings a child to where the child wants to go. Following street signs brings the child home. The natural consequences may be augmented by activities such as small-group discussions which a teacher arranges to follow children's reading responses. And they may be augmented through the use of conspicuous record-keeping on the children's progress in making reading responses.

Providing for on-going reading activities. Providing occasions for reading, as in listening, can proceed under the three conditions of (1) large-group circle activities in classrooms and at learning centers; (2) small-group or peer-tutoring activities at learning centers and stations, and in kits and packet activities; and (3) independent skills at stations, and in kits and packet activities for reading. The three response modes of (a) writing, (b) speech, and (c) nonverbal action can be used with each of these conditions. This modal classification refers to the structure rather than the function of the response. In a functional sense, all responses controlled by a verbal stimulus are verbal responses.

Written responses to a text: (1) The large-group circle activities can include group composition and editing, e.g., writing a newspaper or anthology or a class play in response to texts. (2) In small-group or peer-tutoring conditions, there may be letter/word matching games, exchanging notes, or co-authoring responses to texts. (3) Independent activities may include copying; selecting some word(s) to fit or match a word or phrase in a text, e.g., finding a synonym printed on a card; editing, revising, or finishing a note, letter, or story; writing an outline, analysis, summary, or paraphrase of a text; or writing creatively in response to two or more texts as Coleridge evidently did in writing "Kubla Kahn" and "Rime of the Ancient Mariner" (6).

Spoken responses to a text: (1) In large-group circle activities, there are opportunities for questions, comments, and oral interpretation of texts read by volunteers. Encouraging flexibility in conditions for oral reading has several advantages. When children are allowed to rehearse the readings they volunteer to give, they are allowed to improve their oral expression under conditions that make it easier for them to be successful. When they can choose their own reading selection, they can select a passage that is appropriate to their own individual reading level. And when they volunteer, they are learning to actively initiate reading responses instead of being passively dependent on another's initiative. (2) In small-group or peer-tutoring activities, children may dictate their spoken responses to a text. Children may guess and interpolate out loud what the text is saying, and they may ask questions of a "talking dictionary" (7). Children can also play "say the sound" games, e.g., saying a rhyme to a printed word. Small groups are excellent for discussing a text, since they provide each child with an opportunity for a high rate of interaction. (3) In independent skill work, children may practice oral interpretation in rehearsing a poem out loud. And they may say other responses to a text aloud to themselves depending on how useful they may find that. Even adults are likely to pronounce aloud words that are faintly written. It gives them something stronger to respond to.

"Nonverbal" responses to a text: (1) In large-group circle activities, children may produce a mural, act out a play, cook, or do science experiments in response to texts. (2) In small-group or peer-tutoring activities, children can follow the directions of a text in turning to the pages indicated or mixing a recipe while being monitored by a peer. They can also play games like "Charades" and act out what was written or follow the rules in "Monopoly" (e.g., "Go to Jail"). (3) Independently, children can respond to signs, labels, and flashcards by doing what they direct. Children can also draw pictures and maps in response to texts. And they can be helped to imagine and create fantasies about what they read. Examples of guided fantasies can be given to children from books like *Put Your Mother on the Ceiling.* There may be an indefinite number of shadings in progressing from nonverbal to verbal responses to texts, from the scribble writing of children to more and more realistic presentations to more and more schematic conventions and diagrams with many of the features of our writing system, all of which may be in response to texts.

Figure 21 summarizes the above domain of reading responses in different response modes and learning conditions. It is an outline sketch of examples which are representative of any responses to texts, whether in writing, speech, or nonverbal acting, whether in large group, small group, or alone. This also includes those responses to texts that are the focus of traditional reading instruction as well.

Response Mode

	Writing	Speaking	Nonverbal Acting
Large-small group circle activities	group composition and editing, e.g., writing newspaper, anthology, or play in response to texts	questions; comments; answers; oral interpretation in response to a text	cooking; science experiments; play acting; attending to story being read
Small-group/ peer-tutoring activities	letter-word matching games; exchanging notes; co-authoring correspondence	"say the sound" games; rhyme matching; dictating a response to texts; "talking dictionary"	following directions; games like "Charades" or "Monopoly" (e.g., "Go to Jail.")
Independent skills in stations and packet activities	copy; selecting some word(s) to fit or match a word or phrase; write note, letter; create analysis, summary, paraphrase	use a word from a text in speaking; rehearsal for recital of poem	responding to signs, labels, flashcards by performing an action, e.g., reaching for the box of cereal; drawing pictures and maps

Learning Conditions

Figure 21. Reading responses to a text.

Implications of a Functional Approach to Reading

The above approach to reading would have a dramatic effect on increasing the reading behaviors learned by children as well as in reorganizing and integrating the school curriculum. The narrow, isolated set of structures for The Act of Reading would be replaced by a broad range of functions for acts of reading within naturalistic settings. Children would receive far greater feedback on their reading progress than what is made available from incidental reading experiences or standardized tests. And there would be continuous occasions for success in reading with a variety of resources. The following indicates some of these changes in more detail.

1. Integrated connections to all language arts activities are strengthened. Responses to reading may focus on either writing or speech. And a listening response that is a written response to speech and a reading response that is a spoken response to texts can be closely interrelated. For example, (1) a written response to speech, e.g., "Put *i* or *e* between *p_n* depending on the word I say," is in close parallel to (2) a spoken response to text, e.g., the child is to say the word /pin/, which has the /i/ sound, or the word /pen/, which has the /e/ sound, depending upon whether the word the child sees is *pin* or *pen*. After learning tasks (1) and (2), the child may be able to put in the letter from a printed word as in (1) and pronounce the word correctly as in (2): i.e., if given the task "Fill in this word *p_n* and then say it," the child would be able to do so. There is some research which suggests once some connections are made by children as in tasks (1) and (2), they will make other connections automatically under the right conditions, as in the third task (8). The expressive and receptive relationships between spoken and printed media would be tightened in many more ways than "reading as speech written down," which is a misleading as well as limiting oversimplification.

2. The overt to covert relationships between writing and reading, speaking and listening, and cross modal relationships between writing and listening and speaking and reading are allowed much more freedom to develop at many points in a variety of strengths and extents. Increases in variety, frequency,

and occasions for responding to texts can contribute to the internalization of what is useful from external responding. It would be expected, for example, that the more a child discusses a book with others in public, the more the child might think about it in private.

3. Skills are included that might otherwise be left out through neglect. Not all students will automatically increase their reading efficiency when left on their own after acquiring skills that represent The Act of Reading. Many adults respond to different texts in different contexts in much the same way as they responded to basal readers in elementary school. They respond to words in the text in the same order as reading aloud, and they read at about the same rate as they would read aloud. They do not know how or when to survey, skip, scan, focus on titles, headings, summaries, and other organizational structures or to take notes, make outlines, or write an abstract in order to find out just what they need to know. They do not know how to bring useful questions to a text or how to take the answers they need away from it.

4. It permits more flexibility for individualizing, self-pacing, and peer-tutoring activities. This takes an organizational burden from the teacher and allows for new kinds of learning for the students, which would be impossible with exclusively group-pacing constraints.

5. Whole-to-part as well as part-to-whole activities can be included. Reading progress is not made dependent upon a serial buildup of small atomic parts of letter sounds, to blends, to syllables, to words, to phrases, etc. Progress can also be made from larger, less differentiated responses to texts, e.g., from acting out the story, to dictating supplementary dialogue, to editing phrases, words, and spellings; from general and vague responses to texts, e.g., like "Wow!," to specific acts such as pouring one-half cup of milk according to the directions of a recipe, to asking for the sound of a letter in a particular word.

6. A much denser and richer range of activities can take place which allows children to see their progress and to experience naturally reinforcing consequences in some reading activities.

Somewhere, somehow, all of the children can more easily experience success and reward in a reading response when there are so many more things a child can do which are considered reading responses. And these successes can be built upon.

7. The accessibility of reading responses is increased. Once accessible, many more things can be done to increase different behaviors related to reading improvement. It makes it easier for the child, with the help of teachers, parents, and other children, to have an opportunity for increasing reading skills.

SUMMARY

The traditional, formal treatment of reading responses has been handicapped by a restricted consideration of The Act of Reading. There is test-like inflexibility and isolation in this instruction. While this view may be convenient for the administration of standardized tests and for group-paced methods of classroom control, it does not make it very easy for the child to learn to read. It inadequately samples reading responses and leaves the child too few stepping points to develop reading skills. An alternative that encourages children to learn to read through informal, incidental reading experiences may be feasible for children who have the support of a rich, naturalistic setting in their homes for learning to read. But it is hardly a reliable method for assuring a wide range of reading skills for all children.

In contrast, the functional approach to reading suggested here focuses simply on increasing reading responses by (1) increasing the variety and frequency of responses to texts, (2) increasing the rates of these responses with an increase in the consequences for these responses, and (3) increasing the occasions upon which these responses occur. This functional view of reading allows for flexibility in reading purposes, creative alternatives in achieving these purposes, and a step-by-step individualization of the reading curriculum. Not only would the responses of the children be different, but so would the classroom environment.

REFERENCES

1. Moxley, R.A. The world's worst reading objective. *Educational Technology*, August 1974, *14*(8), pp. 20-26.

2. Skinner, B.F. Why we need teaching machines. In his *Cumulative Record* (3rd ed.). New York: Appleton-Century-Crofts, 1972, pp. 177-178.

3. Smith, N.B. *American reading instruction* (1934). Newark, Delaware: International Reading Association, 1965, p. 189.

4. Smith, F. *Understanding reading.* New York: Holt, Rinehart, and Winston, 1971.

5. Bullock, Sir A. *A language for life.* Report for the British Government, 1975.

6. Goldiamond, I. Literary behavior analysis. *Journal of Applied Behavior Analysis*, Fall 1977, *10*(3), pp. 527-529.

7. Wilhelm, R. Improving writing with a talking dictionary. *The Reading Specialist*, Fall 1977, *10*(3), pp. 527-529.

8. Sidman, M., Cresson, O., and Willson-Morris, M. Acquisition of matching-to-sample via mediated transfer. *Journal of the Experimental Analysis of Behavior*, September 1974, *22*(2), pp. 161-273.

Chapter VII

Comprehending Words

We are often given the impression that we can determine the meaning of a word through its structure. After all, we use the structure of a word to locate it in the dictionary, and then we read its meaning. We observe the structural composition of a word, its prefixes, its suffixes, and may have learned those parts with Greek and Latin roots. This provides us with a lot of information. However, it is the function of a word and its uses in contexts which determine its meaning. Even dictionary definitions are determined by examining the functional uses of words in context. The definitions written in a dictionary are simply a summary of different uses in different contexts. And the current structures of the words themselves have been determined by their previous uses, new instructional components like adjectival or adverbial endings being acquired with new uses. The structure of a word gives us access to the past history of its uses. This, together with the current use of a word, gives us its meaning. Functional uses have, and have always had, priority in determining the meaning of words. Unfortunately, some approaches to reading comprehension have tended to rely on the structural qualities of words, neglecting the functions of words in contexts. This has been a characteristic of both standardized reading tests and formal reading instruction.

BACKGROUND

Conflict over the meaning of words is not new. Many people at many times have wanted to have a simple, single meaning attached to the structure of a word, and they have argued over how that is to happen. Plato's *Cratylus* raised the issue between *physis* (nature) and *nomos* (law or custom), and the dissension between those who see the meanings of words rooted in the nature of things and those who see them as a simple product of human choice and convention has continued.

It would be an extreme position to hold that there is only one true meaning for a word whenever it is used, one that is unalterably fixed in the nature of things, once and for all. The meaning of a word is then always the same, no matter who uses it or how it is used, independent of the user and the context in which it has been used. When we hear or read words, we simply match them to their true meaning, like matching a word to a single dictionary definition. If our assumptions as to the true meanings of words are firmly fixed, it is then a simple matter to judge whether what is said is true or false, correct or incorrect. Comprehension then resembles an exercise in formal logic where the meanings of word symbols have been predetermined in simple, single correspondences. We agree with people when what they say is right, we correct them when what they say is wrong.

Many of us, however, rebel when we feel that the meaning of our words has been somewhat arbitrarily restricted by others in this fashion. We know what we mean. But it would be an equally extreme position to hold that words mean whatever we arbitrarily choose to make them mean. In Lewis Carroll's *Through the Looking Glass*, Humpty Dumpty asserts that he himself will arbitrarily determine what his words mean:

> 'I don't know what you mean by "glory,"' Alice said.
>
> Humpty Dumpty smiled contemptuously. 'Of course you don't—till I tell you. I mean "there's a nice knock-down argument for you!"'
>
> 'But "glory" doesn't mean "a nice knock-down argument,"' Alice objected.
>
> 'When *I* use a word,' Humpty Dumpty said in rather a scornful tone, 'it means just what I choose it to mean—neither more nor less.'
>
> 'The question is,' said Alice, 'whether you *can* make words mean different things.'
>
> 'The question is,' said Humpty Dumpty, 'which is to be master—that's all.'
>
> Alice was too much puzzled to say anything . . . (1)

By asserting that the meaning of "glory" was entirely his own arbitrary decision, Humpty Dumpty was denying any source of control for the meaning of the word beyond a private act of choice whose causes were hidden from Alice. There would be no way for Alice to understand what Humpty Dumpty meant by "glory," if she could not determine the sources for its meaning. She had to wait for Humpty Dumpty to explain what he meant in words whose meaning she could determine.

Fortunately, Humpty Dumpty did not keep all the sources of meaning for the words he used a secret. As it turned out, what Humpty Dumpty said was determined by more than just arbitrary whim. He even helped Alice out by pointing to some sources of meaning for words in the first verse of the poem "Jabberwocky":

> Twas brillig, and the slithy toves
> Did gyre and gimble in the wabe:
> All mimsy were the borogroves,
> All the mome raths outgrabe.

Humpty Dumpty tells Alice that "slithy" is a "portmanteau" word composed of two meanings packed into one word—from "lithe" and "slimy." Here, knowing "lithe" and "slimy" are sources of meaning for "slithy" provides Alice with access to some of the meaning of the word "slithy." Another internal (or structural) source of control in the word is the /-y/ ending, a common inflection for adjectives.

There are other sources of control not mentioned by Humpty Dumpty. "Slithy" follows a determiner ("the") and precedes a noun headword ("toves") that comes before the auxiliary ("Did"). This is the position for a modifying adjective, a source of control that is external to the structure of the word. In addition to syntactic sources of control, there are other semantic constraints (determined, for example, by the lively "toves" who "gyre and gimble in the wabe").

In everyday usage, the actual meanings of words are not confined to either a single fixed meaning or a single arbitrary meaning. And when we encounter unfamiliar words and words used in different ways than we have seen before, we can still gain an understanding of what that word means. We can examine its structure. What do we associate with /sl-/? Is it a noun or a verb? We can examine its functions. What is its syntactic relationship? Is it controlled by a determiner or an auxiliary word? We can examine the semantic context. How is the word related to the topic or theme? Is it frequently reoccurring? We can examine the context outside of the text. What do we already know about what is being said? What association do we have in our personal history that the author may also have? What do we know about the author's previous use of words? What do we know of the current and previous use of the word in our culture?

We can explicate the meaning of a word like a critic who explicates the meaning of a word in a poem, searching for relationships that we may infer were controlling the author's usage. The literary critic, for example, may allude to sources of control outside the poem itself in the author's personal history or the cultural events of that time as well as to sources within the poem. The sources for the meaning of a word turn out to be far more multiple and varied than a simple permanent fixation or Humpty Dumpty's assertion would have it.

When we are comprehending, we may not be consciously doing all of these things. But we still act to bring ourselves in contact with the sources that controlled the verbal behavior of the author. While we are never completely under the same sources of control as those which controlled the author and our responses are not exactly the same, we try to get close enough. We may seek to approximate the author's meaning by putting ourselves "in his or her shoes" and adopting the author's viewpoint. Even young children can participate in the vicarious experience of a well-told story. When we are responding to the more subtle controls for a word, we may refer to "connotations" or "shadings" of meaning.

The instruction and assessment of reading comprehension in schools, however, have often relied on rather isolated sources of control for the understanding of words. Words are often taught and tested in isolation from a context, without a function. For example, shown the word *dog*, the child may be asked to say the word aloud, indicate the appropriate picture, or find a synonym for it. Any one of these responses may pass for comprehension.

The child is left to depend upon the structure of the word itself for a source of control along with selective criteria for an acceptable answer. This is an exceedingly limited sampling of the sources for meaning. Anyone who tried to follow this approach literally in reading would have great difficulty with comprehension.

Relying on any one kind of connection, even if that connection is to spoken language, is not going to be a reliable source of meaning. What does the ability of children to produce oral sound structures when they are shown visible print structures tell you about their comprehension? Presumably, once the written form is linked to the spoken form in the reader's repertoire, the reader can then rely on the ability to comprehend speech in order to comprehend writing. But is this assumption warranted? The comprehension of words in speech is under different sources of control than the comprehension of words in writing. In speech, the speaker and the listener are often under the control of the same situation, the one they are experiencing at that moment. The listener may need little effort to make contact with the sources of meaning for the speech he or she hears. Many are there before the listener. They are there controlling the listener. The listener may, and often does, interrupt to obtain further clarification of meaning whenever the listener needs it. The listener may ask questions or use the speaker's own words as a check in restating what the listener heard. The speaker can supplement his or her words with intonation and gesture to ensure the listener gets the speaker's meaning (guided by immediate feedback from the listener's reactions). In speech, access to the sources of control is often a cinch. We typically do not bother to use formal training to teach listening comprehension to school children. We normally worry only if children do not listen because they are not motivated to listen. We rarely worry if a child does not comprehend a spoken word—we use another word, explain it, or wait until the child is more "mature." In reading, similar sources of control are often not available. And we do not risk assuming that every child will discover access to them without help, although some children may do well with little if any formal training. In particular, children need help in gaining access to the sources of meaning beyond the structure of words. They need to understand the relationships of words in a written context. They need to integrate relationships more than they need to match structures.

As illustrated in the following studies, the skill required to synthesize or integrate the relationships between words is strikingly different from the skill required to match one structural unit with another structural unit. Denner, building on a study by Farnham-Diggory and later elaborated upon by Keeton (2), found that first-grade and third- to fifth-grade children classified as problem readers by their teacher performed as well as first-grade average readers on simple representational tasks, whether in enactive (acting out), pictograph (word picture), or logograph (abstract symbol) tasks, but they could not synthesize as well. For example, none of the groups had a great problem in showing their understanding of the following italicized words: (1) obeying the spoken commands, "Now show me a *walk*," "Walk *around* the block," and "Shake hands with the *teacher*; (2) saying the names of "pictures" that represent *walk* (a stick figure), *around* (a snake coiled on a stick), and *teacher* (a simple drawing), after training in saying the names to the pictures; or (3) saying the names of logographs of simple line drawings (e.g., *teacher* was represented by an oval circle) for *walk*, *around*, and *teacher*. It was in the fourth task of synthesizing or putting these together that the problem readers were differentiated from the average readers.

In this task, a sentence was constructed from the logograph cards and the child was asked to read it. After the sentence was read, the child was asked to do it. Some children performed the sentence meaning by performing each word as a separate meaning, one at a time. For example, in response to being shown the logographs, "*Walk-around-teacher*," a child might first walk, then go up to the teacher and ask, "How do you do around?" These tended to be the children identified as problem readers. Other children read the sentence and then walked around the teacher. First-grade average readers were more likely to do this integrating synthesis than any other group. The first-grade problem readers were the least likely to do this. Even though the problem readers could syntactically integrate words in spoken sentences, they had difficulty integrating words in print.

This distinction between the functional use of the word in a text and a standard reference for the structure of a word is reflected in other studies. Guthrie, Seifert, Burnham, and Caplan (3) examined oral reading in comparison to comprehension in normal and poor readers. They found that normal children understood the sentences they read very nearly to the extent that they could read them orally. However, many of the disabled readers had very deficient comprehension in comparison to their oral reading level. It was comprehension rather than oral reading scores that distinguished good from poor readers.

This evidence fails to support a simple link between visual form and spoken form as a reliable indicator that reading comprehension has developed or will develop. In particular, "isolated word practice does not generalize to reading in context" (4). And why should it? We can imagine an actor or a student with the help of some coaching who might read fluently from a text in a foreign language without understanding what he or she has read. There are many responses to words. Some are to the structure or form of the word in isolation or under a limited influence of context, e.g., word calling or saying the spoken sounds to letters. Other responses are to the word as it relates to other words in a sentence. Responses to syntactic arrangements of texts of more than one word seem to involve a different class of responses. There are responses not only to word structures but also to the functional relationships between words.

To many people, it may seem obvious that the everyday use of the term "reading comprehension" must include responses to the "network" of relationships between words. The assessment of comprehension, however, is often inadequate in this respect. For example, items on a Gates-MacGinitie reading comprehension subtask have been found to predict performance more accurately in a reading-words-aloud (word calling) task than in an integration task (5). One explanation is that there are items on this test which may be solved simply by connecting the spoken responses that have been linked to a written word with the spoken responses that have been linked to a picture. For example, if the sounds a child has learned to say in response to a written word are not the same sounds the child has learned to say in response to a picture, the child may then simply eliminate this alternative as a possible answer. Test-wise children may soon learn the game is to match structures in one passage with the same or similar structures in another. Consider a comprehension example in the Stanford Diagnostic Reading Test (6):

> The mouse ran away from the cat.
> The cat ran after the . . .
>
> dog   boy   mouse   horse

When the child inspects the four choices from which the child is to select the word to complete the sentence, the child can eliminate those structures that do not appear in either sentence. The child may have little idea of what the word means in a text in order to get the correct answer. Many methods of assessing comprehension have been used which also seem to require skills other than an understanding of the functional relationships between words. They seem to require more skills in memory, verbatim recall, and insight into testing riddles than in a comprehension of what words mean when they are written down.

The following list, which is modified from one by Guthrie and Tyler (7), presents several operational definitions of comprehension as it is assessed in reading. The different operational definitions illustrate some of the many different responses to a written word. Some of these responses seem to sample a rather limited aspect of what we might want to call comprehension. Others sample a comparatively broader range of comprehension, which may include fairly sophisticated skills in understanding the relationships between words. It should not be surprising then to find that limiting reading instruction and assessment to just one or a few of these responses to the written word will result in a rather questionable interpretation of the child's ability to understand what he or she reads.

1. Comprehension may be determined by how adequately the subject can judge the equivalence of a written message with another representation, e.g., a picture. A sentence is presented,

and the child selects the appropriate picture from an array of several pictures. This method relies less on memory, prior knowledge, or inference than some other measures of comprehension; but the set of written messages that may be conveyed in pictures is restricted, and a child may eliminate some foils by simply saying aloud words in the sentence as well as events in the pictures, eliminating those without a match.

2. A nonverbal response to a message may be used. Following directions such as "mark all the numbers except the two" and physical execution of commands such as "place the pin under the square" exemplify this technique. This can be a realistic and functional task; however, the messages which can be used are limited, and in a lengthy message performance may be reduced by memory limitations.

3. The cloze technique, in which the subject fills in words that are missing from a written text, can assess a variety of functional relationships; however, some of the relationships may be rather trivial, as when an earlier phrase in the text is repeated but with a word missing, requiring only a word-for-word matching skill. One of the variations of the cloze technique is the "opin" cloze (8), which may allow several alternative fits, all of which could make good sense: The boy climbed up the ladder _____, showing he was nervous. *Quickly, hesitantly, shakily*, etc., could fit in here. Discussion on which is the better word follows. This discussion helps to reveal the various sources of control that those who chose a particular word were responding to. Very subtle differences may be considered, such as which word fits best in a poem.

4. The subject may read a message, then try to detect a subsequent message with modifications from the original. This performance can reflect comprehension of functional relations, but is limited by memory of the original.

5. The subject reproduces the message either verbatim or in paraphrase form. However, it is often difficult to score this reproduction, particularly in the paraphrase form.

6. A verbatim question is formed from a statement taken from the text. From the textual statement, "The miner found the cabin," one may form the question, "Who found the cabin?" The

child may answer on the basis of orthographic or phonological matching between the sentence and the question, a rather limited demonstration of word relationships.

7. A transformed verbatim question consists of a logical and/or syntactic transformation of a verbatim statement. From the textual statement, "The miner found the cabin," one may form the question, "What was found by the miner?" The answer depends on the child's ability to infer the syntactic relationship between the expression of a given set of words and their transformation, which may be largely accomplished here by matching and elimination.

8. Paraphrase questions can be constructed from words that are different in form, but equivalent in meaning to the words of the original sentence. From the textual statement, "The miner found the cabin," one may ask, "Who located the small house?" The answer is made on the basis of the child's ability to infer a correspondence between the string of new words and the string of old words. This may be accomplished largely by matching words by position rather than by their structure.

9. The latter two question types may be combined to generate transformed paraphrase questions, such as "What was located by the man who digs coal?" The answer here may depend on the child's ability to infer the transformation, e.g., cueing off of "by" and matching by position.

10. Another method of questioning is the substitution of particular terms for general terms and vice versa. For instance, "The terrier broke his toe," may be examined by asking "What did the dog hurt?" While this may be solved by transforming and matching, the questions become more difficult as the inferences of control become more difficult. From "Chickadees eat suet, Grosbeaks prefer fruit, Oven birds feast on insects," one may ask what principle is represented? "Birds have different diets," could suffice. Children may be asked to progress from a general statement of a principle to an instance of the principle. From "Boiling removes water from fluids," an instance could be "Boiling sap from maple trees makes syrup." The difficulty of questions appears to increase directly with the semantic distance

between the questions and the examples. If the principle of predation is taught (or read) with an example of wasps that kill bees, test questions involving two types of fish will be easier than questions relating hawks and mice (9).

11. In the maze procedure, approximately every fifth word in a passage is replaced by three alternatives in the following manner:

hillside
The groundhog walked up the apple and sat down.
near

One alternative (hillside) is the original word from the text. A second alternative (apple) is the same form class as the original word, but is semantically incompatible with the context. In this example, it is difficult to imagine how these events could have occurred and be a source of control for the author when another alternative seems much more likely. However, a large context with tiny creatures in Alice's Wonderland playing in an apple orchard would have substantially increased the semantic compatibility. The third alternative (near) is a different form class from the original word and is syntactically incompatible. Any passage in a text may be converted into this format. The child may then be asked to read it silently and to circle the word believed appropriate at each "maze." Guthrie and Tyler commend this method for its reliability, correlation with standardized reading comprehension test performance, and efficiency.

The above measures show various emphases on word structures and on word relationships. Paraphrases and transformations obviously rely heavily on relationships, as do clozes and mazes. The cloze is interesting in that, since the word is missing, everything is left to context. The maze approach may be regarded as a modified cloze with a periodic forced choice from three alternatives within an extended text. When it is considered that the maze technique can be applied to any passage at any level of difficulty, this method shows promise for conveniently assessing much of what is meant by reading comprehension. See Figure 22.

On the other hand, it is difficult to imagine how reading instruction through the use of mazes could adequately represent the practical tasks for which a child needs comprehension. The

Figure 22. Word comprehension.

child wants to acquire that particular comprehension which meets his or her particular purpose in reading. In many practical instances, this means beginning with a particular question (or set of questions) and then reading to find the answer. Although test administrators may try to prohibit it, many test-wise people recommend looking at the questions first and then reading the previous passages to find the answer. This kind of skill could be more openly and directly pursued in both reading instruction and assessment.

APPLICATION

As the above illustrates, the ability to infer the sources of control for the author's use of a word depends on being responsive to many different sources: the structure of the word, its syntactic inflection, its stem, its position, its frequency in a text (where other uses supply additional information), the other words in the sentence and their correspondence to another sentence, the likelihood of events that may have controlled the selection of a word, etc. The overall fit for the best inference may be dependent on any or all of these sources. In general, when we encounter an unknown word, the richer the context, then the more the sources of inference, and the more confident our ability to identify the sources of control for the author.

Rather than limit the child's responsiveness to only a few of these inferences (whether for assessment or instruction), the child could be exposed to many different textual and extratextual sources of meaning and allowed a variety of inferential responses. The variety of these tasks, their consequences, and the occasions for them could be increased in the classroom. Instead of depending upon the one or two best links to reading comprehension, the student could be brought to depend on an interconnecting web of sources for comprehension. Instead of teaching children to look for a particular narrow source of control, we could teach them to respond to broad sources of control. By doing so, we could provide them with a reading flexibility that is suited to reading comprehension in natural settings outside the classroom. We would then make reading comprehension a more natural task, such as listening comprehension has been.

The Variety of Comprehending Behaviors

There are many responses to words from which we infer comprehension. In isolation, a word may be acted to nonverbally. It may be obeyed as a direction (e.g., "Exit"). It may be classified, sorted, or listed. It may be responded to orally. It may be spoken aloud. It may be questioned and commented upon, "What a silly word." It may be rhymed. It may be alliterated. It may be repeated. It may be matched with another printed word. It may be talked about in a variety of ways, now and later.

In relationship to other words, a word may be acted on, as in following directions that require syntactic integration, e.g., "Walk around the teacher." It may be responded to orally with questions, comments, and discussion. It may be responded to in print with transformations, questions, answers, summaries, paraphrases, and outlines. And it may be inserted within other printed words, like a cloze, or substituted for an existing word.

If we infer comprehension from any of these responses, then the reader has been brought into contact with one or more of the sources for the meanings of words. To the extent that different responses indicate a responsiveness to different sources of meaning, then increasing the variety of comprehending responses increases the reader's responsiveness to different sources of control.

Consequences for Comprehension

Many of the consequences for comprehension will be natural ones. The child's questions will be answered. The child will be able to follow the story. The child will be able to follow the directions and solve the problem. Some readings will provide the child with more tangible consequences in comprehending words than others. In reading the directions for a science experiment, for example, the child will often have the opportunity to check his or her comprehension directly against the concrete events that the child arranges after the child reads the text. The child will often have evidence as the child goes along step-by-step, as well as from the conclusion of the experiment. Davidson and Steely have used a modified rebus approach in giving directions at learning centers for "not-yet readers," using self-correcting and self-recording techniques (10). In this context, the directions help children learn to comprehend written words.

Other consequences may need to be arranged for children. An extended sequence of succeeding effects can be built in to follow children's responses to words at different points afterwards. Discussions of children's interpretation of meaning can be arranged, from supplying the missing word in "opin" cloze sentences to explicating the multiple levels of meaning of a word in a poem. They can be asked and they can ask others, "Why do you think this is a better word?" They may be asked to find support for their interpretation in an example from another passage. They may be asked to summarize the arguments for and against a particular interpretation. Disputes over the meanings of words can also provide informative consequences. The resolution of these disputes provides even more information. The frequency with which philosophers and other people engage in arguments over words suggests not only that they enjoy doing this but that they are continuing to learn something from it. Such "philosophical inquiry" could be encouraged in early readers.

Charting a child's responses and progress in making these responses will further augment the consequences for comprehension. The sheer number of questions answered may be recorded as well as any other indicator for comprehension. The rate of doing these things may also be recorded. Rate is particularly appropriate for comprehension, since it puts a priority on the child's selecting the relevant from the irrelevant sources of control. Yet, rate is singularly neglected in reading instruction in elementary schools. Rate of answering questions is especially appropriate for developing comprehension (11). Short selections from publishers of reading materials, such as provided in SRA kits, lend themselves to charting progress in answering questions with an answer key for checking accuracy. Julie Vargas' *Something to Think About* does this with a maze approach and latent images for immediate feedback (12). Eventually, of course, we would want children to be able to construct their own questions and confirm their answers without the need for an answer key. They might even check their ability to construct and answer good questions as well as the teacher does before their next test. This, by the way, is a highly recommended procedure to prepare for any test you might take. See if you can make up the questions and find the answers which you predict will be on the test. Charts on other rates might include rate of outlining, rate of defining, rate of indexing key words to a text, rate of using a word in a sentence, rate of collecting words, as well as rate of reading aloud and rate of word identification. See Figure 23.

Occasions for Increasing Comprehension

We can increase the variety and frequency of comprehending responses by increasing the occasions in which these responses can occur. These occasions include the antecedent conditions to a response and its consequences. A parallel for illustrating what the occasions for responses to the written word may be can be found in the occasions for responses to the spoken word.

Listening events. The spoken word may be presented as a *stimulus* in the form of a command, request, question, or statement. Its syntactic relationship may designate it as the subject, verb, object, etc. It may be accompanied by a clarifying or defining context such as pointing to the object identified by the word.

The *responses* to the spoken word may be to simply repeat aloud the word that was said, to echo it. There may be a questioning intonation in the repetition, or there may be a request for more information, "What does that mean?" Another spoken response may be to repeat the word in another syntactic structure, e.g., "Where is my cap?" "Your cap is on the chair." Or, a pronoun reference could be used, "It is on the chair." The request for more information may refer to a property of the reference, e.g., "What color is your cap?" Or, it may be put under an umbrella term, e.g., "Is a cap something that you wear?" The word may be responded to by placing it in a variety of other syntactic and semantic relationships.

In a written response to a spoken word, the word may be spelled out and written down. It may be put into a new written

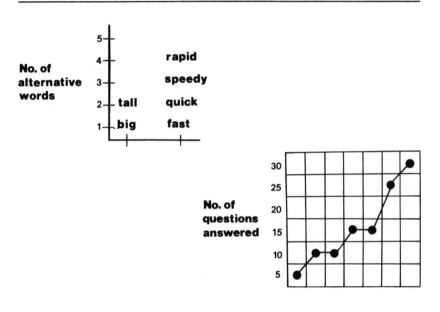

Figure 23. Records of comprehension.

context. It may be tried out by the child in systematic variations within a text the child writes. It is common to observe when children have acquired a new word: they try it out in so many ways.

In a nonverbal response, there may be a series of trial-and-error actions like playing a game of "hot and cold." In response to "Bring me something to eat," a variety of different foods may be brought until one is accepted. In response to any word identifying an object or action to be performed, the listener may run through a series of alternative actions or objects, noticing the consequences to his or her actions, e.g., the comments of the speaker. Parents are often seen doing this with their children.

As a *consequence* to the listener's response, the speaker may indicate explicit or tacit acceptance of the listener's comprehension of a word. The speaker may supply the feedback requested or add additional supplementary clarification. The speaker may give additional illustrations of how the speaker means the word to be used, e.g., "A cap is something you wear on your head, like a hat." The speaker may provide additional details, "It's black with a red band."

Much of the determination of what a spoken word means is taken care of informally in person-to-person or small-group interactions that also model for the observing child how word comprehension is clarified in spoken discourse. The child can often obtain a series of clarifying feedback exchanges on the meaning of a word from the speaker who is immediately present. The consequences following each of the child's responses to a word can guide the child closer to an adequate comprehension of the word within what is often a clarifying setting with physical references present for the meaning of the word.

Reading events. Since the written word often exists outside the context of the physical events it refers to and the author may not be immediately present to provide feedback, the child responds to the written word in a state of comparative stimulus deprivation. The child may still make a variety of responses to a particular word, but the child may not be able to obtain clarifying feedback on what the word means. Readily available feedback is a crucial consideration in designing instruction for increasing the comprehension of written words. The following describes some of the variety of occasions for comprehension responses within the three-term contingency of antecedent stimulus, behavioral response, and consequence.

As a *stimulus*, the written word may be in the form of a pictogram or rebus, a logogram symbol unit (e.g., Chinese ideograms or our numbers like six, seven, eight, etc.), or composed of units from a syllabary or alphabet. The written word may exist by itself, as a sign or a label, or be in the context of one or more other words. These verbal contexts may be lists or syntactic organizations of sentences, paragraphs, chapters, stories, or other complete texts. In addition to any interverbal contexts, there are the accompanying nonverbal conditions which may be more or less relevant to the written word. A sign that says "Exit" will typically be accompanied by the physical doorway and passage to which it refers. A story about the "Grinch," however, may have nothing in the immediate physical environment that can be matched up with a "Grinch." Instead, the story may have illustrations that provide a context. These illustrations may provide occasional background or continuously support the story line. Using controlled levels of reading difficulty in a comic-book format is one way of providing a rich background of context (13).

The *responses* to written words include attending responses and eye movements, copying words, talking about them, asking about them, trying to sound them out, using the word in a spoken or a written sentence, rhyming the word, looking the word up in the dictionary, editing and rewriting the word, inspecting the textual references of the word, and examining other textual relationships of a word. In responding to interverbal relationships, the child may look for the previous reference of the pronoun, the use of the same word again in another sentence, or the child may try to determine if the word used in one context has about the same meaning as another word used in a similar context. In responding to relationships outside the text, the child may examine objects that the word refers to or perform the action that the word indicates. The child may try to see how well the word fits physical events.

Among the *consequences* of the child's responses to written words, the child may find he or she can increase match-ups between physical events and written words. Like deciphering a cryptogram, one word may be the key to the text when that word is "understood." The directions, requests, descriptions, or story may now make sense. Responding to a word within a text may produce immediate consequences, e.g., the excitement of discovering it was "Fred" who did it, or delayed consequences, e.g., going out and playing tennis after reading a book on how to play tennis. The child's response to an isolated word may also produce direct consequences from others like "Good!" and "That's correct" from the teacher as well as more delayed comments later.

Occasions for on-going comprehension activities. Occasions for responses to a written word may be designed for large groups, small groups, or individual conditions of learning. These responses may be written; spoken, or nonverbal.

Written responses provide the reader with access to the same sources of control as the author when reader and author are one and the same. When you read your own writing, you are literally "in the shoes" of the author. As the author responds to diverse sources of control in producing the words the author writes, the author can become sensitive to their sources of meaning. This becomes particularly evident in rewriting or when an author is debating over which word or phrase to use. In editing his or her own writing, the child can respond again to the context in which the child has earlier produced a word. The child can then see if another word or phrase would be better. This can be an individual activity for whenever children write, or it can be a group activity as in jointly editing a poem, a newspaper, or a story.

Written responses also include the following: given a sentence frame with an open slot to fill, i.e., a sentence with a word left out as in programmed instruction or in cloze assessments of comprehension, the child is to point out or write in the correct word. This can be done as part of a programmed text procedure or a maze procedure that provides alternatives at every fifth word. The child may make generic matches of words, connecting the word with those that the child supplies or brings from another text. These lists of thematic or syntactic matches can be sorted and classified. In syntactic matches, for example, the child may determine all the words that fit a slot in a model sentence, e.g., "That food tastes very ___." The child may then supply a list of *sweet, sour, nice, yucky,* etc. After forming such word classes, the child can generate sentences by selecting a word from the pile of words like *That,* followed by a word from the pile of words like *food,* and so on. This can be done in small-group format with feedback from other children. Popular variations of fill-in-the-word methods include crossword puzzles, which depend on comprehension and context sensitivity as well as spelling skills.

Spoken responses to words are often easy to produce. Discussions about written words can generate feedback and clarify sources of meaning in a manner that takes advantage of listening comprehension and the natural way in which it is acquired. Occasions that encourage children to talk about words in print give them access to many sources of meanings through spoken language skills that they have already acquired.

Spoken responses to a written word within a text include asking questions about that written word as in a "talking dictionary" activity where the child receives information about a word whenever the child requests it (14). This activity needs a tutor or someone else in the role of helper. Children can also practice predicting or guessing what a word means or how the word will be used again in the text. At first, children may be asked to guess aloud with questions and prompts from the teacher. Later, children can be encouraged to generate alternatives on their own for predicting what the word means. For example, a child might be shown a word and two alternative objects to which it might refer (e.g., the word *cup* and an actual cup and an actual fork); the child can be encouraged to say the alternative the child thinks is a match. More alternatives, including more similar alternatives, can be added indefinitely into the situation, and the child can be encouraged to generate more than one alternative verbal match. Skill in suggesting (speaking aloud) alternative meanings for a word can be expanded from simple contexts to complex contexts in different texts. Generating alternative meanings for words and selecting the more meaningful alternative may eventually approximate an automatic habit that no longer needs to depend on making overt responses. Children can also practice strengthening their responses to words by saying them aloud when they have difficulty (15). This would be a cross modal equivalent to writing over a word that is faintly written. Making a stronger, more salient stimulus can make other responses easier.

In her observation of classrooms, Casteel (16) found that students often had little opportunity to generate questions of their own in response to a written text. Her study showed that providing children with the opportunity to ask questions resulted in a change in the kinds of questions that they asked. Over time, the children began to ask more evaluative questions in contrast to literal questions. They did this with and without the presence of the teacher, but their rate of increase in asking evaluative questions was higher without the teacher's presence. This suggests that children's sensitivity to more complex sources of control can be enhanced through informal discussions of their reading.

There are also many *nonverbal* responses to written words. Following the directions to a cooking recipe or a scientific experiment provides a very clear indication of comprehension. Nonverbal responses to writing can indicate both simple and complex comprehension skills.

Given a word in isolation or targeted in a sentence, the child can go and hunt for a match-up. Many verbal games could be adapted to this, e.g., instead of saying, "I spy something green," a sign may be held up saying, "I spy a . . .," or "Bring me a . . .," with different words (e.g., *pencil, big book, drawing that has blue and green in it*) placed in the slot. The child may then hunt, locate, and bring back the object spied or requested. If it is an action to be performed, as in "Charades," children may try alternative behaviors (as they tried other objects) until one that results in a correct identification is made. Children might even practice acting out various words so as to build a "nonverbal vocabulary" for "Charades." Children may also do experiments with concepts. Given lists of words, in a packet or at a station, like *hard, rough, heavy*, etc., they may check the supplied objects and determine, say, the rank order of their hardness. They can also determine the properties of various content words by listing the properties of various objects, e.g., hard, black, heavy, rough, etc., for a piece of coal. They can do similar activities with function words like *in, on, over* in terms of matching the word to the operation and generating alternative operations with physical objects (17).

Responding to symbols on maps or charts shows a comprehension of sources of meaning that are similar to the sources of meaning for words. The symbolic and pictorial representations on a map can provide a natural context for revealing a child's sensitivity to various sources of control. Checks on these sources of control can be made by giving children specific directions for responding to maps. The ability to read maps and graphs is highly practical, and it is easy to check on a child's comprehension of them.

Figure 24 summarizes some of the responses to a written word,

Response Mode

Learning Conditions	*Writing*	*Speaking*	*Acting*
Interverbal Functions	editing; write down a synonym from another section of the text; write a paraphrase of section; supply the missing word in a cloze; supply alternative words for a cloze	ask for antecedent; discuss relationships to other words in the text; suggest another word for the context; discuss reasons for selecting a word for a cloze frame	search, locate, and point to antecedent of pronoun; circle syntactic cues; perform action indicated by the integrated relationship between words, e.g., "Walk around teacher"
Structural Isolation	copying; use word in a written sentence; write down synonyms from memory; write a definition of the word; retype it	talk about the word; ask questions about it; sound it out; say a rhyme	eye movements; locating word in a dictionary; examining object referred to; performing act referred to

Figure 24. Reading responses to written words.

primarily in terms of its function to others within the text and to conditions outside of the text.

SUMMARY

The sources of meaning for words lie within the text (intratextual) and outside the text (extratextual). Responses to words in their relation to other words within the text are responses to functional relationships, i.e., syntactic and semantic organizational relationships with other words. This relationship is illustrated by the programmed frame, the cloze procedure in reading, or a slot-and-filler grammar in linguistics. All present a text with a vacant place for a word. Responses to extratextual functions refer to previous uses of the word and to the objects and events that the word refers to in the physical world. Word calling is a response to the isolated structure of a word, but this is often an overused and misleading focus for determining comprehension. Responses to the structure of a word, in particular its sound correspondence in spoken language, comprise a narrow domain of all the responses to a word. Word calling responses actually reveal more about the relationships of letters to sound than the relationships of words to other words or to physical events. These functional relationships of letters are more properly dealt with at the level of letters, their structure and functions with other letters.

Any response controlled by a word may be considered as a comprehending response to the extent that it makes contact with the sources that controlled the author's use of the word. The means for increasing comprehension lie in increasing the variety of comprehending responses (spoken, written, and nonverbal), their consequences, and the occasions in which they occur. Traditional reading instruction and assessment often rely on relatively narrow and isolated sources of meaning for reading comprehension. A more natural approach to reading comprehension gives children access to broader and fuller sources of control for words. With instruction that assures this access is provided, reading comprehension can become as natural as listening comprehension.

REFERENCES

1. Heath, P. *The philosopher's Alice.* New York: St. Martin's Press, 1974, p. 193.

2. Denner, B. Representational and syntactic competence of problem readers. *Child Development*, September 1970, *41*(3), pp. 881-887. Farnham-Diggory, S. Symbol and synthesis in experimental reading. *Child Development*, March 1967, *38*(1), pp. 223-231. Keeton, A. *Word decoding skills related to semantic integration of sentences in early reading.* Toronto, Ontario: Ontario Institute for Studies in Education, 1977.

3. Guthrie, J.T., Seifert, M., Burnham, N., and Caplan, R.T. The maze technique to assess, monitor reading comprehension. *The Reading Teacher*, November 1974, *28*(2), pp. 160-168.

4. Fleisher, L.S., Jenkins, J.R., and Pany, D. Effects on poor readers' comprehension of training in rapid decoding. *Reading Research Quarterly*, 1979, *15*(1), p. 47.

5. Keeton, A. *Word decoding skills related to semantic integration of sentences in early reading.* Toronto, Ontario: Ontario Institute for Studies in Education, 1977.

6. Allen, V.F. Riddle: What does a reading test test? *Learning*, November 1978, pp. 87-89.

7. Guthrie, J.T., and Tyler, J. Operational definitions of reading. In T.A. Brigham, R. Hawkins, J.W. Scott, and T.F. McLaughlin (Eds.), *Behavior analysis in education: Self-control and reading.* Dubuque, Iowa: Kendall/Hunt, 1976, pp. 174-182.

8. Greene, F. An opin and cloze case. Paper presented at the meeting of the North Central Reading Association Nineteenth Annual Conference, Ann Arbor, Michigan, October 1976.

9. Markle, S.M., and Tiemann, P.W. *Really understanding concepts.* Champaign, Ill.: Stipes, 1970.

10. Davidson, T., and Steely, J. *Using learning centers with not-yet readers.* Santa Monica, Calif.: Goodyear Publishing Co., 1978.

11. Moxley, R.A. Specifying behavioral objectives. *Educational Technology*, June 1972, *12*(6), pp. 30-35.

12. Vargas, J.S. *Something to think about.* Piscataway, N.J.: New Century Corp., 1981.

13. Oliphant, D. *Solarman.* West Haven, Conn.: Pendulum Press, 1979.

14. Wilhelm, R. Improving writing with a talking dictionary. *The Reading Specialist,* Summer 1972, *9*(6), pp. 12-16.

15. McGuigan, F.J. Electrical measurement of covert processes as an explication of "higher mental events." In F.J. McGuigan and R.A. Schoonover (Eds.), *The psychophysiology of thinking: Studies of covert processes.* New York: Academic Press, 1973, pp. 343-385.

16. Casteel, C.P. The effect of peer-participation upon the oral question-generation ability of third-grade learners. Unpublished doctoral dissertation, West Virginia University, 1978.

17. Richards, I.A. *Design for escape: World education through modern media.* New York: Harcourt, Brace, and World, 1968.

Chapter VIII

Responding to Letters

A long-standing, but not well-defined, issue in reading has been whether it should be taught through a linkage to sounds or through a context of meaning. And if through a linkage to sounds, should the letters be taught as isolated parts or as related in a context, e.g., as a letter in a key word? Should reading be taught as a decoding of letters to the sounds of speech in a simple, direct transformation of text into speech? Or, should reading be taught as a meaningful activity that is responsive to a rich and varied context of words and events over time? One of the distinguishing features of this contrast lies in the relative difference between single (or simple) and multiple (or complex) sources of stimulus control. Sounding out letters is a relatively more simple process (if not exactly a series of single one-to-one correspondences). And meaning is a relatively more complex process (there are a wide variety of sources for meaning). When this distinguishing feature is applied at each level of task analysis in reading, the issue is then seen to extend beyond being merely one of sounding out versus comprehension—even though the contrast appears most sharply joined in this opposition. Sounding out may be attributed to narrow or broad sources of control, and comprehension may be attributed to narrow or broad sources of control. Since there are only 26 letters in our alphabet, the issue at the letter level seems to provide more support for a narrow source of stimulus control. But since there are a multitude of words and a multitude of meanings for those words, multiple sources of stimulus control may seem more obvious at the comprehension level. This issue becomes critical when beginning reading is treated as basically a problem of decoding print into sound in which letter-sounds must be mastered before meaning can be obtained. The trouble is that a focus on narrow sources of control in the beginning may, in effect, drive out the opportunity for children to learn to respond to multiple sources of control when they read for meaning later.

The extensive literature on "decoding" at the "elementary" level of reading in letter-sound relationships reveals persistent "links-of-a-chain" approaches to reading theory and practice, even though these approaches have not been particularly effective. This is, perhaps, a curious testimony to the desire for simple structural rules to solve problems. When reading is explained in terms of linear sequences of atomic units that are organized into larger units, attention is directed to structural components and structural relationships. This stands opposed to functional explanations, which are relatively rare in the literature on reading. Although the literature has described many reading activities that are functionally oriented, functional explanations in terms of consequences and their conditions have been lacking.

BACKGROUND

The structural links-of-a-chain approach has been called a part-to-whole method. More descriptively, it is the linking of one part to another part until a whole is attained, i.e., part-to-part-to-whole. Functional approaches are reflected in whole-to-part methods. More descriptively, a whole context is used for relating the part to a whole, i.e., whole-to-part-to-whole. In sequencing instruction at the letter level, this is sometimes presented as a contrast between synthetic phonics (part-to-whole) and analytic phonics (whole-to-part). Other contrasting terms are an alphabetic or a word approach, a subskills or a holistic approach. Unfortunately, there is a rather high degree of inconsistency in the way these terms have been used in the literature. Even analysis and synthesis seem to mean quite different things to different people (1). Unless the usage is examined in detail, it is hazardous to assume what these terms mean in the reading literature. The following describes a links-of-a-chain approach in part-to-whole sequencing, after which functional approaches to multiple sources in whole-to-part sequencing are presented.

The Links-of-a-Chain Approach

Following methods imported from Great Britain, the English-speaking Colonists in America used instruction that proceeded from small to large units in the following manner:

> The following sequence, apparently growing from a simplistic notion that instruction proceeds from small to large units, seemed to be the customary methodology.
>
> 1. Learn the alphabet by rote, forward and backward.
> 2. Point out the individual letters, in the alphabet and as they appear in words. (There appears to have been some use of squares of ivory with pictures and letters on them.)
> 3. After mastering all the letters, proceed to the syllabarium (organized groups of consonant-vowel clusters) and learn them by rote: *ba, be, bi, bo, bu,* and so on.
> 4. Then, using the ability to name the letters, spell out lists of short words—using this [magical] means of pronouncing the words.
> 5. Proceed to memorization of sentences and selections.
> 6. In some cases, answer general questions about selections.
>
> In all cases, content was considered more important than any methodology directed toward developing independent readers. Oral reading was promoted as *the* reading procedure for social and religious needs. *The* reader in the family read to other family members from what was probably the one piece of reading material in the home—the Bible. (2)

The rationale for this part-to-whole buildup may be seen perhaps in the analogy of crystal formation. A couple of "atomic" units (molecules or letters) come together and stick. Tiny parts of a liquid crystallize. They become larger as more molecules are added. They accumulate to become a solid crystalline structure. To wait for the entire mass to solidify at once would be an unlikely chance. There is no effective way to begin the whole in any fashion, outline or otherwise, and proceed to differentiation of the parts. This crystalline formation is distinguished by the simplicity of its organization. While there is a somewhat arbitrary randomness in the sequence of crystalline formation, some part-to-whole approaches in reading seem to prefer invariant to incidental accumulations.

Alternative structural explanations of reading today propose competing linear sequences which can be represented in a flow-chart diagram and described with metaphors from computer models. One prominent part-to-whole approach is represented by a position which holds that the child must first master phonic-graphic elements of letter and word units before integrating higher-order meaning units. Samuels is fairly explicit about the sequence in which the smaller units are first learned, then combined into larger units, which are in turn combined into ever larger units:

> Leaving the psychomotor domain, one can find examples from perception and reading to illustrate the principle that smaller units are mastered prior to mastering the larger units. The model of perceptual learning developed by LaBerge and Samuels (1974) is a hierarchical model and shows the sequence and progression of learning from distinctive features, to letters, to letter clusters, and on to words. In the process of learning to recognize a letter, the student must first identify the features that comprise the letter. For the lower-case letters b, d, p, and q, the features are vertical line and circle in a particular relationship to each other; that is, the circle may be high or low and to the left or right side of the vertical line. Having identified the parts and after an extended series of exposures to the letters, the learner sees it as a unit. (3)

The ultimate atomic units are fairly small, straight, and curved lines. How they are linked together determines a letter. How the letters are linked determines a letter cluster, and so on. Presumably this logical chain eventually makes contact with meaningful reality in a full context.

Samuels provides some illuminating examples from the psychomotor domain. One is learning to ride a bike. "Would it be preferable simply to place the child on a two-wheeler or to allow the child to gather experience on a graded series of activities, each somewhat more difficult, before encountering the two-wheel bicycle?" The graded series is one in which "They frequently practice first on a tricycle, then graduate to a two-wheeler with a small frame, and practice getting their balance on the small-frame bike before they use the pedals on the two-wheeler" (4). It is interesting to note that Samuels did not suggest breaking up the learning of riding a two-wheeler into the following parts: identifying the pedals, wheels, handle bars, etc.; turning the handle bars, sitting on the seat, etc.; then on to the next larger unit and so on. Rather, he suggested beginning with a whole, complete, and meaningful task in itself, i.e., riding a tricycle, and then moving on to tasks that are wholes with increasingly differentiated complexity requiring finer and finer motor coordination.

Samuels also refers to the graduated length method (GLM) of learning to ski as another example of building more complex skills upon simpler skills. Here also, however, he is not suggesting that the skier begin by first learning to perform the parts of the terminal skiing skill, i.e., first identifying the boots, the poles, the skis, putting on the boots, sticking the poles in the ground, practice in turning one of the big skis while standing still, then the other, etc.; then combining turning the skis while holding the poles, etc.; then skiing down the first part of an advanced hill; etc. Rather, he is suggesting that the skier begin with the whole performance of skiing, using shorter skis that require less differentiation of fine motor movement before moving on to whole tasks that require finer and more differentiated motor skills.

What would the GLM approach be in reading? Would that be to start with a small, easy, and complete text and then gradually increase the length and complexity of complete texts? Would that be considered a part-to-whole approach or a progressive differentiation of a whole-to-part approach?

It seems that Samuels is opposing his part-to-whole approach to a rather limited concept of a whole-to-part model. The whole-to-part approach that he seems to oppose is one that requires coping with all of the finer differentiations of a complex text at once. This, of course, is not the only way to consider beginning with a whole and moving on to a part.

In other instances, Samuels more clearly follows a links-of-a-chain argumentation. His language often echoes that of Noam Chomsky and other "rationalists" who pursue a logical, chain-of-being causality. One similarity is an appeal to innate or inaccessible sources of causality: "A number of arguments support the belief that the child's learning a language involves innate, genetically determined mechanisms operating on information about the structure of language that a child acquires from listening to the speech of adults" (5). This directs attention along the line of reasoning to sources that we can do little about instead of to the many things in the environment that we can do something about. Another similarity is a reliance on a priori assumptions for generating the "train" of reasoning: "Even when the teacher is able to diagnose accurately the cause of the problem, the managerial problems of providing individual help are so large as to make the system difficult to operate, if not unworkable. It would seem more manageable to assume on a priori grounds that beginning readers require subskills, which would be taught routinely to students" (6). Again, our attention is directed away from the environment and the opportunity for children to respond to multiple sources of control. We are given the assembly-line managerial solution for making mechanisms work routinely. Behind it all is a rather restrictive cognitive model that the reader is supposed to follow. Typically, these models are like descriptions for computers and other machines with a high degree of internal (logical) consistency and little sensitivity to environmental (empirical) sources of control.

As the above suggests, there are a variety of perspectives for a part-to-whole approach. For example, instead of the letter level, the word level may be taken as the building unit. Reading then builds on responses to words, then to phrases, etc. Such a position has been called a sight word approach. Although the starting unit of a word is larger than a letter, subsequent progression may rely on a part-to-whole sequence, matching "names" to words until a sentence can be called out. In principle, any level—sentence, phrase, word, syllable, letter, distinctive feature, angle and extension of traces, etc.—could be the starting point for a part-to-whole (or a whole-to-part) approach. Knowing the actual beginning unit does not tell us about the method of approach. Likewise, as we have seen, the fact that an approach has been labeled as part-to-whole or whole-to-part is not very informative unless we know more about it.

Responsiveness to Multiple Sources of Control
for Learning Letter Values

One might wonder how children do learn to read "naturally"

without the aid of formal instruction which gives children a priori rules to connect elementary subskills. Information about this has been obtained from studies of children who have learned to read at home before they went to school:

> For more than half of the early readers in California, and again in New York, interest in learning to print developed prior to, or simultaneously with, an interest in learning to read. In fact, for some early readers, ability to read seemed almost like a by-product of ability to print and to spell. For these "pencil and paper kids," the learning sequence moved from (a) scribbling and drawing, to (b) copying objects and letters of the alphabet, to (c) questions about spelling, to (d) ability to read . . . . when help with letter sounds was given, it was usually directed toward independence in spelling rather than reading . . . . Repeatedly the children were described as having had interests which were indulged in for long periods of time, then suddenly discarded. In one case, a mother said her daughter had gone through a stage in which she did nothing but copy people's names and addresses. In another home, an early reader had spent weeks making and remaking calendars . . . . One frequent source of interest in whole words was the experience of being read to by a parent or an older sibling. Stories which were read and reread were generally the ones that led to such questions as "Where does it say that?" or "What's that word?" Other important sources of interest in whole words were television programs—especially commercials, quiz programs, and weather reports. Important, too, were the words found on such places as outdoor signs, food packages, menus, phonograph records, and cars and trucks. (7)

This approach to reading by preschoolers resembles what might be called a language arts approach, a holistic involvement with several related language activities. These children were responding to a variety of stimuli and pursuing a variety of interests related to language arts, some of them special projects over time of their own choosing. They were learning to read from multiple sources of control.

Price (8) gathered data on children selected for the exceptional child program in Palm Beach, Florida (who read at least two years above grade level and ranged in I.Q. from 125 to 155) from mothers of fourth, fifth, and sixth graders. Twenty-eight of the 37 children were reading when they entered first grade. Of the nine reported to have learned at home (without the.aid of nursery school or kindergarten), the six who learned incidentally (without systematic efforts by the parent to teach the child) were reported to be very persistent in asking names of letters and words, e.g., magnetic letters, words on books at home, and words on packages in stores. Being read to was a common experience for most of the children from birth, or when they were able to sit up. One of the children who was not read to very often learned the letters from alphabet blocks before he could talk. A member of the family would name a letter and the child would get the block with that letter on it. The general pattern that emerges is one with a variety of exposures to printed language. Sometimes the parents made the access to print easy for the child. Sometimes the child's persistence and questions gave the child that access. Reliance on a links-of-a-chain approach for decoding sounds is conspicuously missing.

It may be argued that "precocious" children have an "innate mechanism" that gives them an advantage over other children. And we may wish to examine the strategies that more typical children use when they try to read in school. Francis examined children in their first year of school, between five and six years of age, when they read in a booklet and from word lists that were composed of words from the book of the reading series they were using in school. The children were from two schools who used the *Gay Way* series of reading books. One school also encouraged a phonics approach, and the other school encouraged a word recognition and flashcard technique to introduce the words of the book. The similar patterns of their errors, however they were instructed, revealed the sources of control to which the children were responding:

> 1. Some of the reading was based on only a fraction of the actual text, and each individual word was not necessarily read. "An extreme example was the reading of an entirely different sentence from the one given, when *Down the hill went the hen, Meg* was read as *Meg the hen had no house to live in.* The cue seemed to be the preceding familiar sentence which also preceded the mistaken version in the Red Book itself."

2. When incorrect substitutions occurred for both 'content' and 'frame' words, they were derived from the book vocabulary and yielded both grammatical and sensible sentences.

3. Many misreadings showed some graphic similarity with the correct version. "A special case of similarity was the capital letter, since the form of print seemed to remind children of other words in the book beginning with capitals whether there was any letter similarity or not."

4. Sometimes an adjacent word was substituted. "It seemed possible that in reading their book children had not always clearly distinguished each word, and that while, for example, *fell down* was read aloud correctly in a familiar sentence, it was not clear to the child that *fell* was *fell* and *down* was *down*." (9)

The mistakes were strongly controlled by the text. There was no tendency to fill in words from everyday speech. A word known in one context was not necessarily known in another. And none of the children appeared to 'sound' a word they could not recognize on sight. The children were apparently responding to a variety of sources of control from the whole text and their previous exposures to texts.

Another illustration of how children begin with wholes can be found in the way that children learn to segment language. Fox and Routh (10) found that three-year-olds can segment most sentences into words and most words into syllables, in an oral response to a spoken request. By age five or six, the ability to segment at word or subword boundaries is virtually errorless. Conventional syllable segmentation, however, was still developing (and may be influenced by exposure to print). Segmenting syllables into phonemes was still developing even by age seven, e.g., segmenting /w/ from /i/ in *win* was difficult. To teach children of ages five and six to segment the phonemic sound values of letters before they learn to segment syllables or words is to reverse this natural process.

In modern approaches to reading, a whole-to-part approach holds that skills in handling the semantic, syntactic, and contextual cues of larger units like sentences assist in the identification of smaller units like single words and letters (11). This position implies that lack of mastery of skills in the smaller units, e.g., decoding words in isolation, will not necessarily prevent the child from learning larger meaning units, e.g., obtaining meaning, or performing useful responses, from a sentence that has a word the child could not decode in isolation. Over time, children will fill in, or induct, responses to smaller units from responses to larger contexts. Such induction, however, may not occur easily without directed training (12). Although the one level may facilitate the other, competence in the "higher" level is not dependent upon competence in the "lower" levels as implied by advocates of part-to-whole approaches.

As a general principle, as long as the conditions or elements of language have an organized relationship to one another, it seems worthwhile to expose the child to tasks in which these relationships occur. In training a response to a visual display, which varied in terms of type or stimulus—aircraft, carrier, or submarine; location—left, center, right; and number—one, two, or three objects of the same type, Naylor and Briggs (13) found evidence to suggest that a whole-task training method should be superior to a part schedule at all levels of task complexity for a highly organized (integrated) task. However, for a relatively unorganized task (all task dimensions independent), an increase in task complexity will result in a part-task training schedule becoming superior to a whole-task training method. We should consider then whether we wish to teach reading as an organized or an unorganized task.

It also seems to be an advantage to provide reading situations with an opportunity for a high degree of interaction. Surveys of successful reading programs have pointed to small-group or individualized instruction, parental involvement, satisfactory pupil-teacher or pupil-personnel ratios, continuous assessment, frequent positive reinforcement, and time spent on reading as components in producing successful readers (14). This is further supported by the evidence that early readers enjoyed early interaction with their parents. Seen as a general enrichment of the environment over time, frequent interaction provides opportunities for the child to respond to multiple sources of stimuli.

Another approach to providing multiple sources of control is to enrich the environment in which the response is to occur.

Coleman and Morton (15) discussed the effects of restricted, intermediate, and enriched environments. They then suggested some approaches for mastering graphic-phonic units that incorporated mnemonic devices that integrated the part within an "enriched" whole. For example, the letter *o* in *ghost* goes "oo-oo." Three overlapping images were tied into a coherent story about this letter and its sound: an owl, a ghost, and a train that made the sound and were drawn to emphasize the visual printed form of *o* in eyes and wheels. A similar approach is to use a vivid picture of an animal with the visual shape of the letter imposed on its form and a short statement containing the animal's name, the letter, and its sound in alliterative fashion: "Amy ape ate apples" or "Sammy snake says sssssss" (16). We can imagine an indefinite elaboration of context with inflatable "Mr. M's," stuffed animals, or puppets named after letters, which may be accompanied by stories, songs, dramatic play, and discussions with the animals and their sounds.

APPLICATION
By responding to a variety of stimuli in rich contexts, children learn naturally. Children's responses to texts illustrate how they learn a variety of responses. They learn to respond to a variety of different stimuli, especially in comprehending words. But even at the level of letters and more restrictive contexts, reading instruction may develop responsiveness to multiple sources of control by increasing the variety of responses to different sources of control, increasing their consequences, and increasing the occasions on which they occur.

Variety of Responses to Letters
In one way or another, different responses depend on different sources of control. Increasing the variety of reader responses means an increase in the sources of control to which the reader is responding. Some of these sources may prove to be trivial and later abandoned, although (as with the child who spent weeks making and remaking calendars) it may be difficult to predict which stimuli will be insignificant and which will be significant for

the child. Meanwhile, the child is learning by responding to multiple sources of control, hopefully with an opportunity to respond to new sources of control as he or she needs them.

Responses may be to isolated letters or to their functions within a context of other letters. Flashcards may have an isolated letter or a word written on them. The child may say a letter sound, name a letter, say a word, or do what is indicated by the flashcard, e.g., "jump," all of which depends upon some response to letters and their distinctive features. Individual letters may also be discussed and talked about, as in mnemonic aids, or simply considered in terms of their shape and general resemblances. Letters may be traced, copied, or written from memory, all in response to a present or previous letter stimulus. In an art activity, letters may be formed out of a variety of materials from clay to paint to magic markers. This may be in response to a current model of a letter or from memory. And one pre-formed letter may be matched to another pre-formed letter, using individual letter tiles or typing one letter beneath another. To bring out responses to relationships between letters, a cloze procedure can be used on flashcards with the letter of a word left out. Alternative letters might also be suggested, as with the maze procedure with words. The child may then supply the missing letter by putting in a letter form, e.g., on a card, a tile, or a block, to complete the word. This might also be done with a "bingo" card on which the child places a small letter tile. Or, the child might respond by holding up a large card with the letter on it when the teacher presents the stimulus. The teacher can then see all the children's responses at a glance. Depending on the task, children may supply the written form and/or say the name or sound of it aloud. They may be encouraged to generate as many plausible alternatives as they can. Letters in a word may also be changed in order to obtain a different reaction from the child to the new letter, e.g., "Pick up the pin/pen." The child might respond with the appropriate action, with the appropriate diacritical marking, or with the example of another word with that sound. In short, any response that can be inferred to depend upon a letter may be considered as a response to the letter. See Figure 25.

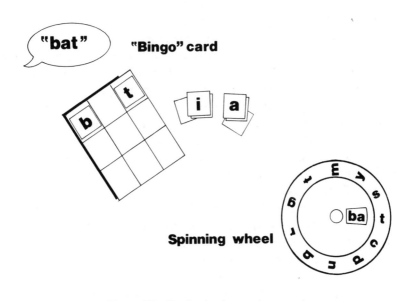

Figure 25. Producing letters in a word.

Consequences for Responses to Letters

Rate of responding to letters is often examined only in test-like conditions, e.g., speed of word identification from flashcards or slides. Rate can also be applied to blending, word sounding, letters said, words read aloud, supplying letters for spelling, responding with actions to flashcards, etc. Using time, games could be played that assigned different "weights" (or points) for different levels of difficulty. Existing differences between children's skill levels could be compensated for by focusing on each child's rate of increase from whatever the child's initial baseline condition. Simply recording rate of performance over time, so the child has it available for display and reaction, will provide for more effective consequences. The feedback on progress, in itself, may be sufficient to be reinforcing to the child. One practical consequence should result in the child's performance becoming more automatic, which will allow the child to turn his or her attention elsewhere. Such a result, however, will have little further benefit to the child unless the child can apply his or her "attention elsewhere" to deriving meaning from a reading context.

In addition to the frequency of consequences, the variety of consequences may also be increased. A variety of events may follow a child's response to a letter. The child may do something. Someone else may comment. The result may be put on display. It may be discussed. Something else may be done with it later. And so on. Some of these consequences will follow by the nature of the activity. Some may need to be arranged. Some may need to be made more conspicuous. Some will occur soon after the response, some later. Any consequences that may be inferred to depend on the child's response may be reinforcing for the child, in one way or another, if the child is aware of them. Increasing feedback that is positively reinforcing, both in frequency and variety, will increase the child's responses to letters. See Figure 26.

While many consequences may follow responding to letters within a limited context, it should be kept in mind that broader contexts always contribute as well if not better. Any increase in the higher levels of word comprehension skills will facilitate the letter skills that are the natural parts of these "wholes." And much can be done to develop comprehension without waiting for any particular letter skill to develop.

Occasions for Responses to Letters

The responses to written letters also have a parallel in the responses to spoken sounds. There is a three-term contingency of stimulus, response, and consequence that has application in the classroom.

Listening events. As a *stimulus,* letters may be said aloud individually or in clusters that may represent a word. They may be named one at a time in a series of spoken letters as in the spelling of a word. Or, sound values may be given for the letters.

In *response* to a spoken letter (its name or sound), the letter may be written down. In response to a series of spoken letters ("c-o-w"), the word spelled may be written down. The word spelled aloud may also be responded to by saying the word aloud.

"I can point them
out when someone
else says their name."

"I can say the name
when someone else
points them out."

Figure 26.   Records of letter identification.

Or, the object indicated by the word that is spelled may be retrieved.

As a *consequence*, the child may receive approval for a correct response from an adult, feedback from the comments of peers or a score of the performance, and natural consequences.

Applications may occur in the form of games played by the child with a tutor who spelled out words for the child to respond to. In informal interactions, many a parent has done this in the presence of a child in order to keep the communication a secret from the child. And many a child has found that when he or she can say the word spelled, e.g., "i-c-e c-r-e-a-m," there are reinforcing consequences.

Reading events. As a *stimulus,* letters may be written in manuscript, cursive, or other varieties of letterforms. They may also be written with diacritical notation for their sound value, as in a dictionary key. The i.t.a. alphabet and the DISTAR alphabet are examples of letter modifications that serve the function of diacritical markings to give a distinct sound to distinct forms. Rebus forms can also be used to indicate a meaning and/or a sound value, e.g., the picture of an eye can represent the sound and hence the letter *I.*

The *responses* to isolate written letters include naming; saying the sound; copying; matching one form of the written letter to another, e.g., a capital letter to a lower-case letter; matching the sound of the letter to the printed form; giving feasible alternatives for the way that letter sounds in different words, e.g., gh*o*st, t*o*, t*o*p, w*o*men; matching the name of the letter to the written form, e.g., "Bee" to *b;* and turning to a page in the dictionary that has words beginning with the letter shown. Responses to letters (or letter positions) in a context of other letters include the substitution of other letters that would make sense, i.e., still make a word, still sound the same; supplying clarifying diacritical marking for the sound value; and saying the word aloud. Responses also include generating alternative letters or diacritical marks for a letter position or a letter within a word, making a selection from those alternatives, and responding to this construction in some way, e.g., saying the word or using it in a sentence.

The *consequences* in many games and small-group or peer-tutoring interactions are often in terms of corrective feedback that allows or disallows the match or the suggested alternative. Natural consequences for correctly saying a word aloud on the basis of appropriate letter-sound matchings follow from being able to request or do something about what was named, e.g., "Pass the *Cheerios.*"

Occasions for on-going activities in responding to letters. Implementing occasions for responses to letters may be introduced through game-like activities and convenient aids for making practice in reading letters easily available to the child.

In a *written* response to an isolated letter, the child may try to construct the letter out of pre-formed parts, e.g., straight lines, and open and closed curves. In a written response to a word with a letter missing, the child can supply the missing letter. The child may also supply a diacritical marking to a letter within a word. All of this may be applied to a game like "Bingo" or to the use of an aid like a child's dictionary.

In a *spoken* response to a written letter, the child can name the letter or say a word with the letter in it. This could be done on a board game with the letters and examples in words written in the spaces. In spoken responses to letters within a word, the child can say the word on the card, say alternatives for alliteration, rhyming, blend letters, say syllables, or repeat a mnemonic aid. This may be done at first with known words in a systematic order, i.e., alphabetical, then later in a random order. Afterwards, "regularly" spelled unknown words and nonsense words that follow regular English orthography could be used. Finally, the child might try "irregular" words within his or her spoken vocabulary and then words outside of his or her spoken vocabulary.

Various letter features in form and sound value are more or less critical in distinguishing words from other words and in producing one letter rather than another (or something illegible). Most of us learn to make these distinctions without being taught rules for doing so. The sound value of a letter, for example, varies with its environment within a word, e.g., *p*ut, to*p*, co*pp*er. The first *p* in *put* may blow out a match when it is said too close, while the *pp* in *copper* may produce hardly a quiver. The child is unlikely to obtain much benefit from learning rules for assigning different sound values to the same letter in different contexts. While a few rules may be helpful, it is more practical for the child to develop a sensitivity to contexts in general. In order to develop skills in giving the proper sound value for various positions and contexts, responses to words can be designed to help induce the appropriate sound value. In combinations of responses, given "I saw a big black _at" in writing, the child may be asked to place the missing letter and then say the word. The connection between the printed letter and its sound value can be emphasized by asking for both types of responses, placing the letter and saying the word. Both the missing letter and its environment in a word can be varied to increase the child's sensitivity to different sound values in different contexts. A simple way to direct the child's attention to the sound values of different letters and different letter clusters in words is to cover some letters of a word with a card, revealing only that letter or letters to which the child is to respond. For example, by moving a card across the word *cat,* the teacher can reveal first the *c,* ask for its sound, then the *ca,* and ask for its sound, and then the *cat* and ask for its sound, with prompting and feedback as needed. In this way, the child can see the relationships of sounds and letters as they are revealed within a natural context of other letters.

The child may develop skills in producing sound values for letters more naturally when the child reads a complete text aloud. A teacher, aide, or peer may provide help upon request. In a repeated readings approach, the child's progress in giving spoken sounds to interrelated letters can be recorded and followed quite closely. In readings of the same text, the child's spoken responses to letters are gradually filled in over time. See Figure 27.

In *nonverbal* reactions, the child might perform the action indicated by the flashcard in competition with other children to see who can make the designated action first. For example, if the flashcard says "Sit," who will be the first one to sit? This would place a priority on responding to just the minimal critical features of letters in a word which are needed to make the designated

Figure 27. Giving sound values for letters in repeated readings of a complete text. (Figure continued on p. 224.)

Figure 27 (continued)

Third Week

Fourth Week

response. With an emphasis on positive consequences for being successful, children can learn to make better "guesses" on less information. Children might also present alternative objects that are available which begin with the same letter sound or have the same rhyming sound as the word on the flashcard. Much of this could be done in game-like activities modeled after card games. Practice in distinguishing one letter from another could occur as a variation of card games like "Fish." Speed in making a discrimination can be encouraged in games like "Slapjack" where points go to the one who first slaps the card that belongs to the designated category.

Some children may benefit more from certain subskill activities than other children. There is an advantage then to allowing the children to choose the activity on which they would like to work, individually or in small groups. The record-keeping should confirm what the child is learning from the activity and whether it is helping the child to acquire global comprehension skills as well. There is little point in the teacher taking time and effort away from higher-level writing and reading activities by requiring all of the children to go through all of the subskill activities available. Priority should always be given to filling in the more valuable writing and reading behaviors for each particular child. Completing a workbook in a skill area just because the book is there may not be the best choice for each child.

SUMMARY

The above argues against exclusive reliance on narrow sources of control in teaching reading even at its most elementary level. It is an argument to deliberately expand the sources of control that are made available to the child, both at one time and over time, by increasing the variety, consequences, and occasions of the child's reading responses at every level of consideration. For various reasons, some of the alternatives will be preferred to others. But this should never lead to a dependency on narrow part-to-whole approaches, whether modeled after a "look-and-say" buildup of sight words or after letter-by-letter linkages of letter sounds.

The fundamental problem with the part-to-whole approach is

that it may place so much time and emphasis on the separate, lower-level parts that the search for meaning is abandoned: "While taken for granted by effective readers, this demand for meaning seems to be the basic ingredient absent from the ineffective reader's approach to print. Well-intentioned traditional instruction, rather than emphasizing a commitment to understanding, has distracted the reader by paying undue attention to the mechanics of the process (decoding, pronunciation, intonation, etc.). The ineffective reader, as indicated above, has no focus or goal beyond attempting to figure out the parts. There is a lack of awareness that the parts add up to a whole with potential meaning" (17). The child may even find he or she is punished rather than rewarded for efforts to make sense of what he or she reads aloud if this takes more time, adds to the complexity of the task, and still results in punished errors when the child substitutes a relevant meaning but not the right sounds for a word. The child may find that the better classroom payoff is to forget about the meaning and attend only to saying the sounds of letters. Given the sentence in writing, "She stopped to pick a flower," the child may be led to say, "She stopped to pick a *flowed*." The child may find little encouragement in searching for meaning that leads to "errors" like "She stopped to pick a *daisy*."

At the level of text or word comprehension, it seems obvious that effective comprehending responses depend on multiple sources for meaning. At the letter level, the need for multiple sources of control may not seem so obvious. Simple decoding linkages seem a plausible alternative to many investigators of reading. Yet, even at the level of responding to letters, there are a variety of ways in which multiple sources of control can and do operate. See Figure 28. The whole-to-part approach is as persuasive at the letter level as it is at the levels of word and text comprehension.

In practice, this means that the development of children's responses to sources of word meanings and complete texts should *not* wait until after the children have mastered letter-sound correspondences. Rather, children should be given the opportunity for simultaneous (or closely followed) responses to texts, words,

Response Mode

	Writing	Speaking	Acting
Interletter Functions	spelling alternatives or inventions to written words; supply diacritical markings; supply written missing letter; supply alternatives to written missing letter	spelling aloud; saying missing letter name; saying the sound of the missing letter within the context of the word; saying the separate sound as it sounds within the word; blending aloud; saying alliteration examples aloud; rhyming aloud	matching alternative sounds of images and physical objects that rhyme with letter clusters in words
Structural Isolation	copy letter; supply diacritical alternatives for a letter; write and draw the mnemonic aid	name letter; say typical sound of letter; give example of typical sound in a word; give alternative sounds with examples in words; say the mnemonic aid	match letter to shapes; find sounds from physical objects and pictures that are similar to the typical letter sound

Learning Conditions

Figure 28. Reading responses to written letters.

and letters. If any sequence has priority, it is a whole-to-part progression in successive stages of development, cyclical and interactive.

REFERENCES

1. Roberts, T. Skills of analysis and synthesis in the early stages of reading. *British Journal of Educational Psychology*, February 1975, *45*(1), pp. 3-9.

2. Robinson, H.A. Reading instruction and research: In historical perspective. In H.A. Robinson (Ed.), *Reading and writing instruction in the United States.* Newark, Delaware: International Reading Association, 1977, p. 46.

3. Samuels, S.J. Hierarchical subskills in the reading acquisition process. In J.T. Guthrie (Ed.), *Aspects of reading acquisition.* Baltimore: The Johns Hopkins University Press, 1976, p. 170.

4. Samuels, S.J. Hierarchical subskills in the reading acquisition process. In J.T. Guthrie (Ed.), *Aspects of reading acquisition.* Baltimore: The Johns Hopkins University Press, 1976, p. 169.

5. Samuels, S.J., and Schachter, S.W. Controversial issues in beginning reading instruction: Meaning versus subskill emphasis. In S. Pflaum-Connor (Ed.), *Aspects of reading education.* Berkeley, Calif.: McCutchan, 1978, p. 49.

6. Samuels, S.J., and Schachter, S.W. Controversial issues in beginning reading instruction: Meaning versus subskill emphasis. In S. Pflaum-Connor (Ed.), *Aspects of reading education.* Berkeley, Calif.: McCutchan, 1978, p. 59.

7. Durkin, D. *Children who read early: Two longitudinal studies.* New York: Teachers College Press, 1966, p. 137.

8. Price, E.H. How thirty-seven gifted children learned to read. *The Reading Teacher,* October 1976, *30*(1), pp. 44-48.

9. Francis, H. Children's strategies in learning to read. *The British Journal of Educational Psychology,* February 1976, *68*(1), pp. 122-123.

10. Fox, B., and Routh, D.K. Analyzing spoken language into words, syllables, and phonemes: A developmental study. *Journal of Psycholinguistic Research*, October 1975, *4*(4), pp. 331-342.

11. Goodman, K.S. Reading: A psycholinguistic guessing game. In L.A. Harris and C.B. Smith (Eds.), *Individualizing reading instruction: A reader.* New York: Holt, Rinehart, and Winston, 1972, pp. 15-26.

12. Elkonin, D.B. Development of speech. In A.V. Zaporozhets and D.B. Elkonin (Eds.), *The psychology of pre-school children.* Cambridge, Mass.: MIT Press, 1971, pp. 111-185. Fox, B., and Routh, D.K. Phonemic analysis and synthesis as word-attack skills. *Journal of Educational Psychology,* February 1976, *68*(1), pp. 70-74. Gibson, E.J., and Levin, H. *The psychology of reading.* Cambridge, Mass.: The MIT Press, 1975.

13. Naylor, J.C., and Briggs, G.E. Effects of task complexity and task organization on the relative efficiency of part and whole training methods. *Journal of Experimental Psychology,* March 1963, *65*(3), pp. 217-224.

14. Samuels, S.J., and Schachter, S.W. Controversial issues in beginning reading instruction: Meaning versus subskill emphasis. In S. Pflaum-Connor (Ed.), *Aspects of reading education.* Berkeley, Calif.: McCutchan, 1978, pp. 44-62.

15. Coleman, E.B., and Morton, C.E. A modest plan to raise the national intelligence. *Educational Technology,* September 1976, *16*(9), pp. 7-17.

16. Hitchcock, F. Amy ape ate apples. *Grade Teacher,* October 1971, *89*(2), pp. 61-63.

17. Taylor, J. Making sense: The basic skill in reading. *Language Arts,* September 1977, *54*(6), pp. 68-69.

Chapter IX

Managing the Learning Environment
for Writing and Reading

We can distinguish between the ways that teachers respond to present, past, and future events in arranging learning environments for writing and reading. One group of teachers gives priority to present inner feelings, another gives priority to past antecedent structures, and the other gives priority to future functional consequences. While it would be unlikely that any one teacher would always and everywhere rely on any one of these sources to the exclusion of the others, it would also be rare for teachers to be able to achieve an even balance and integration of these sources of control. Most teachers probably fall somewhere in between the following descriptions for these teaching styles.

Teachers who give priority to their present feelings about how children are doing tend to focus on immediate learning experiences. They want to expose children to many different learning experiences. However, there is often little organization or follow-up to these experiences. These teachers will jump from one activity to another, arranging things in ways they feel will help the children. Their decisions are strongly colored by their own personal feelings, doing what they like to do and what they feel the children like to do. They want children to have happy learning experiences, and this is often accompanied by approving acceptance of whatever it is the children are doing. The problem with this approach is that children may actually learn little that is useful to them. Like play, school may be fun, but the children's learning experiences are rather haphazard and unpredictable. The obligation to teach children what they really need to learn is put off for another time. They will learn what they need to know outside of school or later in life. Now they will learn to express their present feelings toward immediate experiences. Some people, carrying this position to its extreme, have wondered whether we need schools for this.

Teachers who give priority to antecedent structures typically want to know beforehand how everything is supposed to turn out before they do it. The teacher prepares the lesson plans, gives the directions, and sees that the children follow the rules under the threat of punishment for deviations. Since everything is to be done by following formal guidelines, children are often given low-level tasks that are easily described by rules for imitating a model, e.g., a lot of memorization and copying tasks in handwriting, spelling, and math. Children are then compared with one another on how well they have succeeded. If something unanticipated happens, if the structural models are not followed very well, efforts to see that the structural models are followed are likely to be redoubled. The assumption is that by learning to follow models and rules which represent successful achievements in the past, the students will be learning what they need to know later in life, easily and safely. However, these rules are often followed so intently for so long that sooner or later they become separated from the useful things for children to learn. What is learned in school is then regarded as not being at all practical for life later on.

Teachers who give priority to functional consequences assure that children will benefit from their immediate experiences and that the structures children follow will be useful. Attention is directed to the natural consequences of what children do. These and other arranged consequences are augmented with records for making the consequences more conspicuous. Instead of depending on personal feelings for providing immediate experiences from which the children can learn, the consequences determine the next learning activity. Instead of following structural models, no matter what the consequences, the consequences determine changes in the structural plans for the next learning occasion. Over time, both the teacher and the children become increasingly aware of what indeed is gained from a particular model or learning experience.

Those experiences and models which prove beneficial are kept, and those without benefit are replaced. Ultimately, it is the future functional consequences which determine whether present learning experiences and past structural guidelines are worthwhile. A full implementation of this approach integrates all three learning considerations of present, past, and future in terms of the child's behavior, the antecedent conditions for learning, and its consequences.

WRITING AND READING ACTIVITIES

The teacher or parent who would use a functional approach for managing the child's learning begins by considering the behaviors to be encouraged. These are behaviors that reflect the child's present level of development and lead to the development of other valued behaviors in writing and reading. In particular, they should lead to the development of self-management skills in writing and reading.

Beginning with Behavior

To begin with, you want responses from the child that you can observe. In writing, you want any mark the child can place, e.g., making a scribble, a drawing, a letter, or moving an alphabet block, a letter tile, a word card. And you want an extended sequence of responses following other responses whenever feasible, e.g., discussions and comments by the child on his or her own markings, drawing and writing in response to a story listened to. When the child responds to a written text, you want the child to ask questions, e.g., Where does it say that? What does that word mean? Why did he or she do that? You want the child to make comments, to react, e.g., to come closer when you read, to ask for another story, to bring you a book. The beginning responses may show no more than that the child can make marks on paper or enjoys being read to. Richer and more conspicuous writing and reading responses are to be encouraged later.

By and large, it will be the written responses of the child which will provide the most detail and visibility over time, and it will be these responses that provide the greatest insight into writing and reading skills. Accordingly, writing activities should be placed at the center of the curriculum. Use writing activities for the development of reading and other curriculum areas. Use writing activities in math, science, social studies, and expressive arts. As the British Infant School has shown, it is more practical to integrate the areas of the curriculum around writing than it may first appear.

Beginning with the Ability Level of the Child

The child's level of development is indicated by what the child does and what the child is interested in doing. At an early stage, children may engage in play and random-like organization of materials, as in playing with blocks or making scribbles. Later, children may become interested in seeing how well they can reproduce a resemblance in the pattern of a picture, an arrangement of letter blocks, or in copying their name. Still later, children may wish to recombine established patterns in novel arrangements.

The level of complexity of the task confronted by the child should be suited to the child's current level of development. Too much complexity can lead to frustration, too little can lead to boredom. Generally, the complexity of the task depends upon the number of alternatives the child needs to consider. Early activities may be designed to limit the alternatives in some areas while gradually opening them up in others. Writing by hand in the beginning may involve only a wet finger on the chalkboard. Alternative choices with writing instruments, different media, e.g., ink colors and writing surfaces, can be added later. Alternatives may be adjusted for any level of development. In the beginning, the child may need to choose only between reproducing X's and O's in playing tic-tac-toe. Later, more letters can be included for reproduction until the child can handle likely mirror-image confusions like b and d.

Children continually need to move on to confront tasks of greater complexity. When their approach to a new problem is not working, children should be encouraged to try another way. As children progress, tasks that were once complex and consciously time-consuming for them will become more spontaneous and automatic. The complex problem of how to put the parts of the letter together becomes more of a copying task of recall and finally an automatic task without conscious reflection. Much of the development of memorization and automatic responses can then be left to run their natural course in a "push-down" effect from higher-level learning. The child's attention is then drawn to a new task of greater complexity until that uncertainty too is reduced.

No matter how complex a task may appear, there are ways to reduce its complexity until it engages the ability level and interests of the child. It is neither necessary nor wise, for example, to delay a child's encounter with complete texts before the child tackles problems with individual words and letters. Tasks with complete texts can be simplified for the child, and the child's progress in these tasks leads naturally to the development of related skills within the whole task of constructing and responding to complete texts.

Procedures with complete texts. Children who cannot produce their own texts by handwriting or typing can have them produced by dictating to those who can take down and collect their dictations in a booklet. Such early texts will generally be brief, one page or less, but they can easily grow into illustrated booklets. They may include a story narrative, a brief description of an observation, or a recording of a conversation. When adults read a text to a child, whether a story book from a publisher or one produced by the child, they model the reading of a text by reading it through aloud. During and after each reading, the child should be encouraged to ask questions and to discuss the contents of the text. Teachers and parents can model questions to ask about the story and encourage children to ask these questions as well. Children should also be encouraged to ask and answer questions about particular words, e.g., What does this word mean? Where does it say that? What is another word that might go here? What is another word that sounds like this? What word would this be if you replaced this letter? When the text is reread, the child should be allowed to say the words that he or she knows. Eventually, the child should be allowed to read the text as much as the child can on his or her own with assistance from others when the child indicates it is needed.

Procedures focusing on words. Children should be encouraged to produce words, and to "try another word" that would fit in a sentence, either by writing it, typing it, or dictating it. Children should also collect words of their own choosing for their word bank, including words that they produce and those that are produced by others. They should be asked to show they can identify the word on sight, especially within context, to suggest other words that could be used in place of it, and to select the best words for a context from among the alternatives. Discussions of reasons should also be encouraged.

Procedures focusing on letters. Given a blank space for a letter in a word, children can produce letters by handwriting, letter tiles, or dictation to fill it in. They might do this within the context of a complete text, with vowel and consonant wheels which can be turned to form a word with other letters on another wheel around it, or with "bingo" cards that are set up like little "cross-letter puzzles." Children can also show how well they can find words in a child's dictionary. The child may be shown a word and then asked to find it. Later, the child may listen to the word being said before trying to find where it is listed.

Self-Management by the Children Themselves

The eventual goal of educational experiences should be to produce children who will continue to learn on their own without the presence of the teacher. Toward this end, it is helpful to have children responsible for projects in writing and reading which they can work on at their own pace, without being rushed and without being forced to abandon them before they are completed. Children need some projects that they can set aside and pick up during selected periods of time, in which they can manage their own progress in producing a resolution to a problem of their own choosing.

In helping children to select realistic and useful goals for themselves, the teacher can introduce them to the kinds of writing that people prefer to read. Much of adult reading, for example, is of writing in the form of newspapers, magazines, books, mail, labels, notices, signs, memos, notes, manuals, written instructions, forms, schedules, lists, telephone or address books, reports, pamphlets, catalogs, brochures, printed advertising, legal documents, etc. (1) Children can begin early to produce some of them, e.g., labels, signs, notes, names, and addresses. They can soon choose their goals from items on useful lists of objectives. And then they can construct lists that include their own objectives.

All of the higher-level activities that some adults learn to manage can be managed in some form by children early in their school experiences. Children can monitor and manage their own writing output as adults do in college newspapers, poetry journals, yearbooks, original works, etc. The children's tasks may be smaller, their booklets and newspapers may be briefer, but they can learn to manage it themselves. Wherever the children are, they can begin on some level of self-management and build upon it, even if it is simply picking up and putting away their writing and reading materials when they are finished.

Many classroom organization problems can be resolved when children are self-organizing. It may be a long way to that goal, but the steps can be made one by one as the children learn to evaluate their improvements. Children can make progress along this path as they become aware of and learn to manage the alternatives in writing and reading and their related skills. Ideals of independence, self-determination, responsibility, and participation in decision-making have been values in our society for a long time. Children who have the power to organize their environment so that it helps them to acquire self-improvement through self-evaluation have the power to acquire these ideals.

Children who can adapt the environment to fit their goals have the power to accomplish whatever is in the curriculum. For writing and reading, this would mean adapting an environment to increase the writing skills of all the children. Not only does the child need to adapt an environment which can increase his or her own writing and reading abilities, but the child should also adapt an environment which will increase the writing and reading abilities of others. It is an advantage when what each child does results in supporting each of the other children.

Activities for cooperative interaction. Cooperative interaction between children is needed for group writing and for assisting one another in his or her individual work. Authors and readers need feedback. They need other readers and critics. They need people who can act as resources for some of their requests. Any development of a peer-tutoring relationship, for example, is an advantage in fostering cooperative relationships. Group participation in dictating stories, composing interviews, constructing a mural, putting on a puppet show, etc., also encourages cooperative efforts where success for one means success for the other. Any activities leading to the reciprocal exchange of positive reinforcements should be encouraged. When children share or exchange valued consequences with one another, this helps bind their relationship.

Children can learn how to reinforce one another. They can be told about *warm fuzzies* in books, articles, slides, or a record (2). Whether the term is warm fuzzy, stroke, or positive reinforcement, the principle is the same. Children can learn appropriate ways to give them out, e.g., as soon as feasible with clear identification of the behavior it is for. And they can learn that the stickers on charts can function much as warm fuzzies do. Children can also learn how to reward each other with preferred activities that follow less preferred activities. In the beginning, the teacher may choose which activity is to precede while the children may choose which activity is to follow. Later, children can assist each other in arranging for the "more fun" activities to follow after the "more hard work" activities. Positive reinforcement, from and to each other, not only supports cooperative interactions, it also facilitates successive approximations to both self-selected and mutually selected goals. This is the most reliable and effective means for increasing the probability of a response (3).

Activities for self-recording. Records of the child's progress in all related areas of writing and reading are highly desirable. They show the teacher, the parents, and the child how the child is doing and when (under what conditions) the child does better. The more the child is involved in his or her own record-keeping, the more sensitive and aware the child can be of how he or she is doing.

Simply collecting and keeping visible the written products of a child provides frequent opportunities for comments and interactions with others. In themselves, collections of actual accomplishments like these are highly concrete records of progress. Charts are convenient for making progress conspicuous in selected features of the child's performance. All of these records can be assembled, constructed, and managed by the child. All of this aids the child in that child's own self-improvement through that child's own self-evaluation.

Children have achieved considerable independence in self-management when they can manage their own feedback for what they write. It is important for them to learn what kind of feedback helps them to learn so that they can seek this out and put it to work for them. One of the most difficult problems for children to overcome occurs when they have learned to avoid feedback because it has been useless or punishing to them. The beginner, for example, needs to know what he or she has done successfully. This is the most informative feedback for him or her. Being told what was not done, was not accomplished, or was not improved upon has far less informational value for a beginner. There are simply so many more ways of not being or not doing something than there are of being or doing something. On the other hand, information on what the child has achieved or improved upon gives the child a clear picture of what to keep and build upon. After all, the child has just produced it. The child can see what is being referred to. If the consequences of feedback make it easier for the child to be successful in attaining valued goals, if they make it easier for the child to see how he or she is doing and to make improvements, then the child will seek and use those consequences. Evaluation can take a favorable and sought for connotation when it is linked to positive consequences. It is a decided advantage then for children to learn how to produce such evaluation for themselves.

Learning to keep records and to chart are valuable skills for children to learn. Children can benefit from counting and recording anything that interests them, e.g., height, weight, the length of the room, their table, their chair, the number of children in the room, the number of letters in their name, the number of words they have written, etc. They can be challenged to find other ways to measure the same thing, e.g., height, weight, texture, etc. They can be challenged to find other ways of displaying this information, e.g., in tables, charts, bar graphs, point-to-point charts, frequency counts, cumulative records, logarithmic scales, etc. In so doing, the children can learn valuable concepts about matching groups of events, counting, and arithmetic computation. Mathematics and virtually all the other basic skill areas are involved in record-keeping: the computation of scores, the writing of labels and descriptions on the chart, the reading and understanding of the results, and the oral discussion and interpretation of progress. See Figures 29-31.

In fact, there is no area in the school curriculum which does not have component skills that are contained in self-recording. Making records of observation and interpreting these records lie at the very heart of science. Sensitivity to human behavior and what contributes to that behavior lies at the very core of the social sciences, and records for understanding personal and interpersonal behaviors are essential for meaningful social studies activities (4). And the ability to design an attractive display of records that integrates diverse information with striking clarity is fundamental to expressive arts. The time that the child spends in record-keeping should not be considered as adding to the response cost or as replacing the learning of curriculum goals. Record-keeping by the child, of which writing is one form, lies at the center of curriculum skills. Activity in learning record-keeping skills *is* activity in learning curriculum skills.

Children can begin to learn about record-keeping by collecting actual events in ways that are easy to refer to. See Figure 32. All children love to collect. The child's work provides a record in itself. A note indicating the number accomplished or the percent correct can be added to the work and kept with other works in a cumulative folder for periodic survey. This record can be made more visible and accessible when it is organized in the form of a booklet the child keeps. Children can do their own collecting of their own work in alphabet books, word books, wish books, or

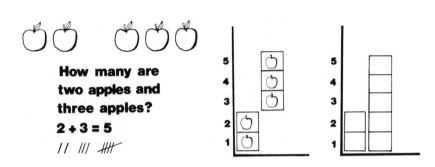

Figure 29. *Language-related records in math: From concrete to abstract displays.*

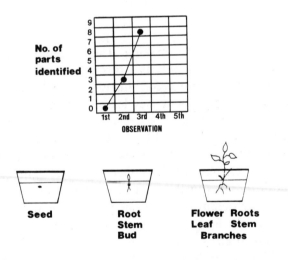

Figure 30. *Language-related records in science.*

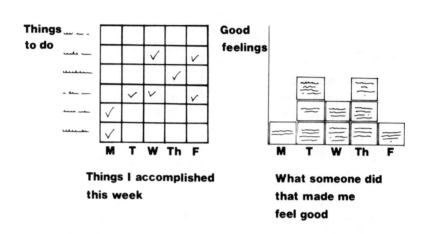

Figure 31. Language-related records in social studies for individual self-confidence and interpersonal relationships.

story books of their own making. They can also construct their own writing and reading aids as a record in itself: they can make their own picture books to illustrate sounds and their own dictionaries, adding pages as they learn. Virtually any work by the child can be collected so as to reveal a pattern of development, even scribbles or piles of blocks (by taking a photograph or drawing a resemblance of the block constructions). A summary of developmental changes in the collections over time can be made by listing differences in the quantities of features, the qualitative forms, or other details between one production and another. Even differences in the length of time a child chooses to spend on the activity can be used as an indicator.

Next, children can learn how to keep a record of actual events through the use of tokens and abstract marks, which serve as substitutes for those events. Tokens have an intrinsic appeal of their own. They do not resemble the actual event for which they

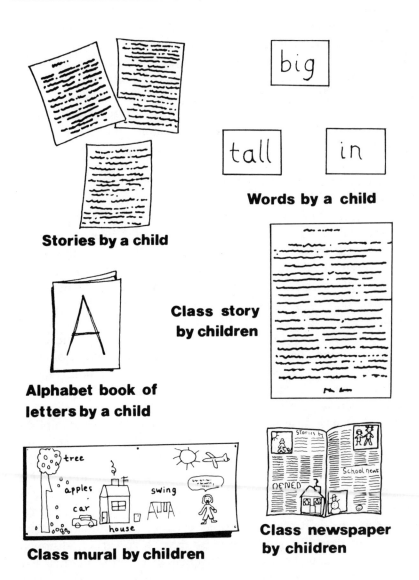

Figure 32. Individual and group collections of progress.

substitute as a record, although they often bear a resemblance to some other objects. Most of us are familiar with stars as tokens of achievement. Homemade cut-outs of smiley faces and commercial-ly-produced stickers with pictures of animals are other popular tokens. See Figures 33 and 34. Indeed, the commercial availability of tokens from "mixie" cards (5) to "scratch-and-sniff" stickers has had a remarkable growth in the last couple of decades.

Charts using tokens can be made out of whatever gives them interest and visibility. They can be a happy merger of artistic creativity and functional utility. These displays can be constructed out of the prominent features of animals, for example, adding on the body segments of caterpillars, the neck segments of a giraffe, the legs of a spider, etc., to form a graph for recording progress over time. Anything that "grows" can be used, e.g., the branches of a tree, the petals of a flower, a garden of flowers, a clown's tongue as it is pulled out. Different collections of cut-out tokens can be used to distinguish different days, weeks, months, or seasons, e.g., charts of autumn leaves, pumpkins, snowflakes, snowballs, rain drops, apples, oranges, beans, etc. These can be pasted or glued in, one after the other as in a stamp book, e.g., little flower stickers can form a flower garden, with the dates marked in, one page following the other in chronological sequence. Or, they can be simply pasted in at the point across from the scale with the reference unit or number that indicates what has been achieved.

Instead of pasting in a token sticker to indicate an accomplish-ment, the child can make a symbolic mark. Such marks are convenient to use for the ease and clarity with which they communicate information. The abstract marks may be in the form of simple tally marks like slashed lines, X's, or check marks. Even young children have learned to construct point-to-point charts that record the daily frequency of an event or the cumulative total of events to date. Bar graphs are also easy to construct, although some children may become preoccupied in coloring in their bar and not notice when to stop. In some ways, bar graphs are simpler than point-to-point charts, but they may not be any easier for the child to construct. See Figure 35.

Special	You're Nice	Think Happy	☺	Special	You're Nice
✶	Always wear a ⌣	Today I'm Okay	You're Special	✶	Always wear a ⌣
Laugh	Sharing	🐰	Have a Good Day	Laugh	Sharing
A Special Friend	You always understand	☺	Warm Fuzzy	My Special Friend	You always understand
👑	My Favorite Prinze	You're A-Okay	Love	👑	My Favorite Prinze
Thanks for Being You	You're Nice To be around!	Pretty Neat	Sunshine	Thanks for Being You	You're Nice To Be Around

Figure 33. Some examples of warm fuzzies.

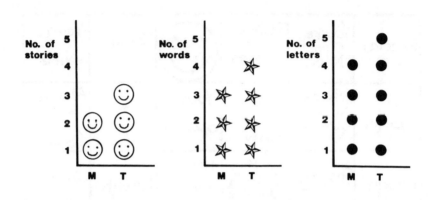

Figure 34.   "Warm fuzzy" stickers as tokens for progress.

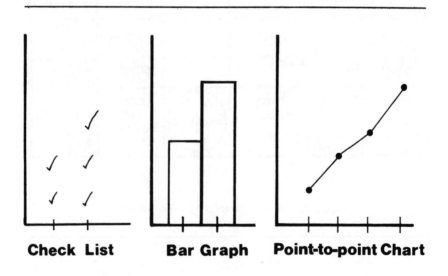

Figure 35.   Symbols of progress.

Good records clearly show what the child did, when the child did it, and indicate there was an opportunity for learning to show up. A record that does not clearly indicate what the child did is meaningless. A cumulative collection of tokens that does not reveal when the tokens were earned cannot show rate of change in the child's behavior. There is no information on whether the child's performance is accelerating or decelerating, and there is no way to determine the conditions under which the child learns best. If no pretest assessment is given and recorded about what the child can already do without further instruction, then it is impossible to separate what the child learns from what the child already knows. Similarly, once recording begins, any procedure which does not allow the child to do more than the child did on the record (if the child could or wanted to) does not provide an opportunity for learning to show up.

Different kinds of records can be used in combination for different purposes, e.g., individual charts and class charts. Good records can also be designed to conveniently summarize a child's progress in a variety of skills. Liz Rupich (6), for example, designed an early childhood record which more adequately meets many of the functions for which traditional report cards were designed. In her kindergarten, the children not only check off their progress on wall charts, but they also check off their progress on their record cards which use the same pictorial and word designations as the wall charts do. In addition, the children place samples of their actual printing and drawing on the cards. The child uses a different color of ink to indicate a different marking period on the card. See Figure 36. In combination with collections of children's actual work in dictating stories and other complex performances which can be conveniently assembled in booklets, such a wall chart and record card system provides a wealth of information on children's progress in writing and reading. None of this recording is beyond what a child can do and can enjoy doing. A good recording system is sensitive to and adapted to the level of the child. The child's performance level is not made to fit the records. The records are designed and redesigned to fit the child. Toward this end, children should

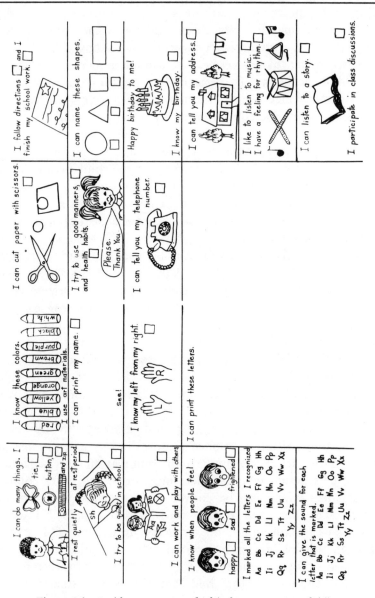

Figure 36.   Inside two pages of a kindergarten record (6).

participate in designing, as well as keeping, their own records. In the very activity of record-keeping, children can learn to increase their recording skills and their writing and reading skills at both their own pace and their own level.

There is no one best record form that is ideally suited to all purposes at all times. Sometimes a daily frequency count is useful, sometimes a cumulative record. See Figure 37. However, extensive record-keeping does lead to certain standard procedures. The vertical scale of the chart is used to indicate what is being recorded, and the horizontal scale is used to indicate when it occurred (or each trial). For recording a wide range of frequencies, a "logarithmic" scale is convenient. See Figure 38. This use of standardized charts with log cycles is a characteristic feature of "precision teaching." It does not take children long to learn how to "drop dots" on this chart, and it is easy to "read" a child's progress when the charting is standardized. This charting does not substitute for other forms of useful records, however, such as collections of the child's actual work and checklists.

Activities for providing resources. Children can participate in the arrangement of their room, its space, and the resources it contains. Children can help to design the places for learning centers, for writing and publication centers, for graphic art, block building, creative dramatics, and reading centers. They can participate in the construction of equipment, like a puppet theater, puppets, costumes, etc. They can produce their own books, dictionaries, references, stories for their own library, their own newspaper, signs, labels, lists, etc. Their products can adorn the room providing its decorations. They can do the murals and the display areas for collections under a common theme, e.g., "well-written letters."

What they cannot make themselves they can bring in. They can write for free materials. They can invite people they would like to have visit as resource people, e.g., a doctor, a writer, a carpenter, a cook, an electrician, a fireman, a policeman, a scientist, an actor, etc. They can gather their own collections of needed materials, e.g., rocks and leaves for science, newspapers and magazines for cut-outs, and toys and games for sharing. They can generate lists of things to bring in next.

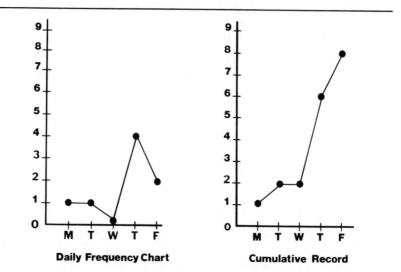

Daily Frequency Chart　　　　　　**Cumulative Record**

Figure 37.　Difference between a frequency and a cumulative count (for 1, 1, 0, 4, 2).

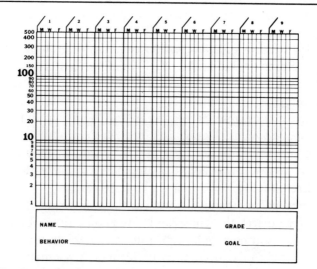

Figure 38.　Example of a standardized chart with a logarithmic scale (adapted from Behavior Development Systems).

USING CONSEQUENCES TO SELECT INSTRUCTION

The above section on writing and reading activities describes the behaviors of children that teachers should want to occur in the writing and reading curriculum. Once teachers have an idea of the present and future behaviors to look for in students, they can then develop instruction aimed at taking children from where they are to where it would be good for them to be. In organizing classroom instruction, the teacher wants to know where to begin and where to go next. It would be easy if there were simple answers to everything in advance, before the teacher even begins, but that would also mean there would be little that is new or exciting to be learned. Questions on where to begin and where to go next can be resolved over time with adequate and sensitive record-keeping. This means allowing the consequences to select and determine the instruction. The results on the records show how things are going. They show whether the present step is too easy or too difficult. They show whether the next steps are too big or too small. With sensitive feedback from the environment, adaptive changes can be made in that environment so that each child is progressing at a level of progress that is suited to his or her own unique individuality.

Teaching is a complex task. It is not a simple procedure where the teacher can start with all the answers to all the questions the teacher would want to know at the beginning. It is not a simple matter of following a recipe as in baking a cake. Nor is it a simple matter of generating verbal rules for students to follow, then seeing to it that they are followed. Nevertheless, many of the traditional approaches to formal education give that impression. Teaching is seen as dependent on past structural models, and the good teacher is one who is prepared to generate these predetermined structures for students. In effect, this leads to a trivialization of the educational process, reducing it to the imitative abilities of a photographic mind. If the goal of education is to have teachers produce children who can produce good copies, then teachers should teach children photography. Even then, a good teacher would need to know more than how to take a photograph and more than how to state the rules of photography. Ignoring the complex features of a task and focusing only on those that are easily copied only convert something valuable into something trivial.

The way to solve a complex task is to solve it in stages. Like the game of 20 Questions, it is foolish to look for the correct answer in the first guess that can be answered "yes" or "no." The experienced game player realizes he or she must progressively reduce the alternatives and patiently wait until enough alternatives are eliminated to make it easy to get the final answer. The player asks a question like "Is it bigger than a bread box?" not because the player thinks it is a bread box, but because this is a good question for reducing about half of the alternatives, whether the answer is "yes" or "no." A similar strategy must be employed in trying to guess a number from one to 1,000,000. It would be foolish to try to divine the correct number in one guess, repeating this attempt again and again until success was achieved. By asking whether the number is more than 500,000, and, depending on the answers for which way to halve the remaining alternatives, then 250,000, then 125,000, then 62,500, then 31,250, then 15,625, then 7,813, then 3,906, then 1,953, then 977, then 488, then 244, then 122, then 61, then 31, then 16, then 8, then 4, then 2, then 1, the correct answer is reached and the problem has been inexorably resolved. The teacher must take a similar approach in solving the problems of teaching.

The questions a teacher asks about instruction are in the form of what a teacher does for instruction. The answers are in the form of feedback on how well the instruction worked. However, a teacher does not depend on a simple "yes" or "no" answer to the instruction. For one thing, teachers have no one there to provide them with a "yes" or "no." For another, they need much more information much more quickly. Teaching is a much more complex task than trying to guess a number. Teachers can find their answers in the rich sources of information that consequences can provide. Teachers should, therefore, arrange for rich sources of feedback and for their increased sensitivity to that feedback so that they can progressively arrive at the resolutions for the instructional problems they confront. Learning to teach is not like learning to ride a bike. Teachers must arrange for their feedback themselves. It just won't all happen naturally.

Teachers need to arrange for consequences, and they need to arrange for an increase in their sensitivity to them. Teachers increase their sensitivity to consequences when they deliberately intervene to augment important consequences and make them more noticeable. They do this predominantly through record-keeping. The more comprehensive and adequate the record-keeping, the more comprehensive and adequate their sensitivity to consequences. Comprehensive records include not just those on the children's progress but also those on the progress made in arranging the classroom environment. See Figure 39. The teachers' sensitivity must include not only a sensitivity to specific tasks but also a sensitivity to the context for those tasks. What teachers do to make changes in these critical features more conspicuous will increase their sensitivity. When their sensitivity to the consequences of instruction is increased in this way, they are more responsive to those things that make a difference. They are brought under the control of those differences. By this means, they are given the answers to the questions they would ask.

In observing and responding to the natural and augmented consequences of their instruction, teachers learn which things to keep and which to change. If the records fail to show that the child is making progress, this is an indication that a change should be made. This may mean revising the current activity the child is engaged in or switching to a new activity. Many people have pointed out that learning is often represented by a kind of "S" curve with initially slow acceleration, then rapid acceleration, and then deceleration. When the teacher notices, for example, that the child is slowing down in his or her learning of color names (assuming that the value of learning color names has been justified), this suggests that time would be better spent in another activity. The additional effort for the child to learn another color discrimination may just not be worth it. In any activity where the child is making slow progress, the teacher needs to decide whether spending more time and effort on it justifies replacing some learning in another area. If the teacher can replace slow learning in

	ANTECEDENTS	BEHAVIORS	CONSEQUENCES
ENDURING SETTING EVENTS	*Physical Structure and Resource Materials:* How is it laid out? Randomly, in rows of seats, centers? What things are available for use? Manipulatives, books, student products?	*Social Climate:* Is the on-going interaction noisy, teacher initiated; individualistic, competitive, cooperative?	*Available Feedback:* What feedback is available on performance? Immediate natural consequences, e.g., painting; tests on matching to sample, rankings; recordings of consequences, progress charts?
ON-GOING ACTIVITY EVENTS	*Supplies and Arrangements:* What is provided to set up the activity? Paint, books, paper, and pencil; sitting on floor, sitting in circle, movement to another location?	*Student Actions:* What general activity are students engaged in? Free play, reading, small-group projects; transition between activities, individual seatwork?	*Outcomes:* What follows or results from the activity? Another activity, discussion, display of work, recording of progress?
PIN-POINTED INTER-ACTION EVENTS	*Antecedent:* What happens immediately before? Teacher leaves room, asks a question, student reads a book?	*Behavior:* What does the child (or teacher) do? Runs around, recites facts, answers questions, works on project?	*Consequence:* What happens immediately after? Attention, praise, display of work?

Figure 39. Outline of the classroom environment and its events.

one area with rapid learning in another, this suggests that a change should be considered. Children's behaviors tend to be filled in over time, and there is little evidence that the sequence in which one child learns must be the sequence in which another child learns. Since a slowing down indicates either difficulty in understanding or a lack of motivation, teachers who are sensitive to a child's rate of learning will also become sensitive to changes in the child's motivation. If it takes an inordinate amount of consequences to motivate a child in one area, this also suggests that time might be better spent in another area.

In responding to children's performances by increasing their sensitivity to the consequences of these performances in children's products and records, teachers enhance their ability to respond to these multiple events and their global feelings in ways that reliably lead to further progress. Any feeling, for example, that something important is being left out in the children's learning experiences can suggest a change. And sensitivity to consequences permits these changes to be continually modified until there is satisfactory progress.

Thus, in this functional approach to writing and reading, specific goals and objectives may be modified and changed over time. There is no need to remain with original plans simply because there is no way to change at a later date. Change can be introduced easily. Nor is there any need to rely on incidental learning for making changes. The consequences in the children's records will show how well the change is working.

Just as the children's behavior will become increasingly refined as their learning becomes differentiated and filled in, so too the teacher's management of instruction will become increasingly refined with increasing sensitivity and skill in responding to consequences. In the beginning, the teacher may do well to begin recording anything in any way. Later, the teacher will make increasingly skillful decisions on what and how the children should record their progress. The teacher will make these decisions wisely, not so much on the basis of following some rule, but on the basis of the consequences in what the children do.

Even though they see the value of good charts, some teachers procrastinate in charting because they are not sure of the best way to chart. They have a structural view that wants the answers first before they start. However, the best way to record and chart can never be determined beforehand. It can only be determined afterwards on the basis of consequences. Whether there are too many alternatives, undetermined alternatives, or limited alternatives, it is essential to begin with some indicator of progress. It is only when there is some indicator recorded that it can be modified. If there are too many alternatives to make a comfortable decision, do not worry about it. Pick one. Any one will do for a start. If you have no idea what the alternatives may be, look at an example of what the child produces. Then pick something. If your problem is that there seems to be too few alternatives to select from, again just pick one. After you choose and record with any alternative indicator, you will become aware of other alternative indicators. Over time, you will become better and better at selecting good indicators because you will be learning from the consequences of selecting an indicator. However, if you do not choose one to begin with, you cannot learn.

There is no way teachers can be guaranteed they have the right answers for instruction before they begin. And it is foolish for anyone to assume that they have. Teachers, however, can be guaranteed that their instruction in writing and reading (or any subject for that matter) will improve.

ESTABLISHING THE CLASSROOM SETTING

In developing an effective environment for learning to write and read, the teacher begins with a classroom environment as it is found. Overall changes in the classroom environment can then be considered in terms of progressive stages of development on the basis of improvements in student performance. See Figure 40 for an outline of values in the enduring classroom setting within which on-going classroom activities and specific tasks occur. The major categories of enduring setting events in the classroom include the social climate within which activities and specific behaviors occur, the available feedback in the classroom on student performance, and the physical structure and resource materials that provide the occasions for learning to write and read (7).

I. Social Climate

   A. Individualistic
      1. self-assertion (e.g., initiating or requesting to initiate an activity)
      2. "excelling" (e.g., being outstanding or the last to survive an activity)
      3. being respected (e.g., imitated, followed, listened to, submitted to)

   B. Competitive
      1. dependency (e.g., upon a "winner")
      2. independency (e.g., "winning")
      3. interdependency (e.g., team games)

   C. Cooperative reciprocity
      1. sharing (e.g., space, materials, ideas)
      2. peer tutoring (e.g., games, checking work)
      3. group projects (e.g., class plays, newspaper, store)

II. Available Feedback

   A. Subjective impression (e.g., a favorable or unfavorable attitude, an undifferentiated and confounded mixture of roles, events, images, and biases)

   B. Aggregate norms
      1. knowledge level tasks (e.g., memorization, recall, facts, names, and labels)
      2. ranking within a group (e.g., normal-curve references: norm-referenced, standardized, selective tests; grading on a curve)
      3. averages (e.g., for evaluating a group-paced activity)

   C. Individual generality
      1. concrete records of events (e.g., videotapes, student papers, and products)
      2. specific objective and behavioral indicators (e.g., criterion-referenced tests)
      3. individual progress records (e.g., collections of work, checklists, charts)

III. Physical Structure and Resource Materials

   A. Self-preservation (e.g., food, shelter, space, temperature, and contact comfort)

   B. Safety (e.g., security, protection, freedom from anxiety)

   C. Variety
      1. materials (e.g., a variety of books, paper, writing instruments)
      2. modes of instruction (e.g., stations, games, audio-visual equipment)
      3. people (e.g., students have access to other students, movable chairs, tables, carpeting)

Figure 40. Outline of values in the enduring classroom setting.

Social Climate

All children and all classrooms are likely to display varying degrees of individualistic, competitive, and cooperative behavior. The appropriate balance between these different social relationships takes time to develop. Young children have been observed to first make choices appropriate to individualistic outcomes, then to competitive ones, and then to cooperative ones (8). The likelihood of these behaviors is also dependent on the nature of the child's environment. In general, teachers will work toward developing conditions that increase cooperative interaction.

In terms of the accomplishments of a group and of individuals in a group, cooperative relationships enjoy several advantages over competitive or independent individual relationships (9). Cooperative relationships, for example, are supportive of peer-tutoring and group projects, e.g., plays, role-playing, class newspapers, video-tape newscasting, etc., where it is an advantage for everyone to help everyone else to be successful. Competitive relationships in which the success of one child necessarily comes at the expense of another child artificially suppress achievement in complex tasks and discourage some children in even simple tasks. Structuring interactions so that some must fail ensures that punishment results from the learning conditions. Some children will learn not to try. Some will learn to avoid situations of learning and evaluation. Some will learn that they can succeed by causing others to fail. Depriving a child of the resources and help of fellow peers in competitive or individualistic role relationships is a rather artificial constraint. A child who grows up without learning how to interact with others to everyone's mutual advantage is unnecessarily handicapped in society. The loss is not only to the individual but to society as well. Although competition can be motivating in game-like learning activities, it should be clearly subordinate to an overall climate of cooperation. Similarly, individualistic learning should be encouraged as a contribution to cooperative relationships.

Under a predominate climate of cooperative relationships, learning writing and reading becomes easier because the natural feedback from reciprocal interactions and exchanges of information is encouraged. In communication processes like writing and reading, it is an enormous advantage to have social relationships with a high degree of interaction in order to provide students with the consequences they need. They then know how they are doing in much more detail, and help is available to them much more easily.

The teacher can design conditions for increasing cooperative relationships in various ways. One way is to design group tasks where the task is not accomplished until each member in the group has achieved a particular level of achievement. Using group contingencies that require each child to be successful promotes peer-tutoring and peer-helping behaviors (10). Group projects and other activities that lend themselves to reciprocal peer tutoring and peer teaching will also support cooperative behavior when children see how they can benefit from the knowledge and perceptions that another shares. Promoting any sharing activity through show-and-tell, grouping at tables, and seating children at the corners of tables so that they can easily see and share what each is doing will encourage cooperative relationships.

Feedback from Assessment

In augmenting consequences for writing and reading behaviors and making them more conspicuous, the major reliance falls on the record-keeping and assessment procedures. Any classroom is likely to have a mixture of three basic kinds of information that it feeds back to the child on the child's progress: subjective, aggregate, and individual information. Subjective assessment is highly personal and guided by internal feelings and their external cues. A subjective, intuitive hunch is a good place to begin with assessment. A feeling by the teacher that the student has a writing or reading problem (or a feeling by the teacher that he or she has a problem) can lead to an investigation and an effort to remedy that problem. It is a good holistic check on whether all is well or whether something needs attending to. Students can use this information when they start to tackle their own problems in writing and reading. However, students cannot be expected to make reliable progress in solving their problems unless they get more information than subjective impressions provide.

This is where some teachers turn to standardized tests and tests resembling standardized tests. References to averages and percentages describe a property of an aggregate collection without identifying a characteristic of any individual in that collection. Such references are characteristic of standardized tests, whether they are called achievement tests, aptitude tests, or I.Q. tests, that focus on providing information about rankings. The standardization is typically in reference to a "normal curve" (or curve of error) distribution. Classroom tests that are graded "on a curve" provide a similar focus on ranking information. Test items are selected so as to produce a distribution of scores. Multiple-choice items are typically used because they are convenient to score. This results in exaggerated attention to lower-level subskills in reading (often highly questionable ones at that) and hardly any attention to the complex performances of actual writing. Moreover, the test scores do not provide explicit information on what the child can and cannot do. The teacher needs to look elsewhere for more useful information.

Information referenced to the individual tells what he or she has achieved, what he or she is working toward, and how he or she is progressing. The emphasis is on within individual changes rather than between individual comparisons. Concrete and detailed information on individual performances at a particular time can be provided by individual records (checklists and frequency counts) and collections of student work (e.g., in booklets or folders). The student can chart his or her own progress in the development of any writing and reading skills. This also leads to information on the conditions affecting individual changes, permitting frequent and extensive adaptations in the environment to individuals. Although aggregate information may seem impressively more complicated than individual information, the individual-referenced information in criterion-referenced measures is actually more powerful and more informative than the aggregate-referenced information in norm-referenced measures (11). Aggregate information is derivable from individual information but not vice versa. Individual information permits stronger *generality* for each instance than an average, more *effectiveness* in change than an aggregate probability (where "significance" can result solely from sample size), and greater *responsiveness* to consequences unobscured by intervening aggregate transformations of the data. Teachers provide more useful assessment and feedback for their children and themselves when they see to it that their classroom has conspicuous displays of individual-referenced information. Collections of children's work and charts of their progress should be readily available.

Physical Structure and Resource Materials

The occasions for writing and reading in school occur within the enduring setting of the classroom. This includes the architecture of the room, the placement of the furniture, equipment, apparatus, learning centers, stations, and the various materials and supplies within the room. All of these features are more or less present on an enduring basis, although periodic changes may be made in any one of these components. Over time, the teacher should seek to develop an appropriate relationship between the "natural" resources such as space and books that happen to be there, the "restricted" resources that must be conserved for the use of all children, e.g., when paper and pencils are limited, and the variety of "personal" resources a teacher provides to which any child will have access.

Resources for personal and self-selected access by students may include stations, learning centers, programmed materials, small-group projects, and learning machines like typewriters. Guides, aids, reference materials, and other resources (people and things) can be made available for the student to accomplish tasks easily and accurately. Later, children can learn to become independent of some of these aids when that is necessary for more efficient performance. The student's dependence on any particular resource can be gradually faded out while the student retains the ability to make the fullest use of whatever resources are available.

For writing, children need access to vast writing surfaces in large and small units of size on chalkboards, walls, and desks. They also need a variety of writing instruments from pencils, pens, and magic markers to letter tiles, stamps, and typewriters. For reading, children need a vast collection of reading materials. While some books should be the same so that small groups of children can have the same reading experience for immediate discussion, there is no need to purchase the same basal reader for everyone in the class. It would be better to spend the money for more diverse reading materials. Children also need attractive places to do their writing and reading, e.g., comfortable chairs, cubby holes, and bathtubs lined with carpeting.

SUMMARY

Managing the environment in which children learn to write and read requires attention both to the particular skills children are to acquire and the context in which they learn them. Learning activities with conspicuous, overt behavior and extended consequences should be designed for the ability level of the child and should provide for the development of a progressive differentiation of writing and reading skills. These activities should lead to increasing self-management by the children themselves in coping with the conditions under which they will learn to write and read. Specific activities should be included for teaching children how to cooperate with each other in learning communication skills, how to manage their feedback through collections and self-charting, and how to provide their own resources. In addition to designing appropriate activities, teachers must also assure that they themselves become increasingly sensitive to the consequences of what happens in the classroom. Records with a focus on a child's progress over time will make the consequences of instruction more conspicuous and increase teacher sensitivity and responsiveness. Teachers also need to develop the classroom setting for a cooperative social climate, individual assessment and feedback, and personalized resources. Teachers can accomplish this task over time in developing stages just as the child's progress in writing and reading develops in progressive stages.

Seen as an integrating process, a functional approach bridges the gap between global expressions to an immediate context and narrow responsiveness to structural rules. Learning from extended consequences helps to assure that learning from immediate experiences and learning from structural antecedents result in a harmonious integration of worthwhile learning. Meaningful, useful, and efficient ways of learning can be included in a functional approach to writing and reading.

REFERENCES

1. Sharon, A.T. What do adults read? *Reading Research Quarterly*, 1974, *9*(2), pp. 148-169.

2. Anonymous. "Warm fuzzies." *The Reading Specialist*, Summer 1973, *9*(9), pp. 21-23. Freed, A.M. *T.a. for tots* (rev. ed.). Sacramento, Calif.: Jalmar, 1974.

3. Moxley, R.A. From avoidance learning to approach learning: Stages in increasing the probability of a response. *Psychology*, November 1973, *10*(4), pp. 47-64.

4. Moxley, R.A. Social studies activities and the science of human behavior. *Social Education*, March 1980, *44*(3), pp. 250-252.

5. Sacks, A.S., Moxley, R.A., and Walls, R.T. Increasing social interaction of preschool children with "mixies." *Psychology in the Schools*, January 1975, *12*(1), pp. 74-79.

6. Taylor, T. Report card use replaced. *Wheeling Sunday News-Register*, 1 October 1978, pp. 1 and 6.

7. Meadowcroft, P., and Moxley, R.A. Naturalistic observation in the classroom: A radical behavioral view. *Educational Psychologist*, Spring 1980, *15*(1), pp. 23-34.

8. McClintock, C.G., Moskowitz, J.M., and McClintock, E. Variations in preferences for individualistic, competitive, and cooperative outcomes as a function of age, game class, and task in nursery school children. *Child Development*, September 1977, *48*(3), pp. 1080-1085.

9. Johnson, D.W., Skon, L., and Johnson, R. Effects of cooperative, competitive, and individualistic conditions on children's problem-solving performance. *American Educational Research Journal*, Spring 1980, *17*(1), pp. 83-93.

10. Litow, L., and Pumroy, D.K. A brief review of classroom

group-oriented contingencies. *Journal of Applied Behavior Analysis*, Fall 1975, *8*(3), pp. 235-246.

11. Moxley, R.A. Formative and non-formative evaluation. *Instructional Science*, October 1974, *3*(3), pp. 243-283. Moxley, R.A. Subjective, individual, and aggregate references in educational research. *Instructional Science*, April 1979, *8*(2), pp. 169-205.

Index